I0442292

Contents

INTRODUCTION

"The era of big government is over."

— Bill Clinton, 1996 State of the Union Address

When President Clinton said the era of big government is over, he wasn't just making a promise, he was reporting on his progress. The Clinton-Gore Administration has made the federal government smaller by nearly a quarter of a million jobs.[1] This is the largest, swiftest government-wide cut in the history of the United States. It's not just a post-Cold War defense reduction; every department except Justice has become smaller. (See Figure 1.)

The federal government workforce is now the smallest it has been in more than 30 years, going all the way back to the Kennedy Administration.[2] The cuts were long overdue. People had long since grown tired of new government programs initiated each year, with none ever ending. They were tired of stories about senseless sounding government jobs, like the Official Tea-Taster, tired of larger and larger bureaucracies in Washington interfering more and more with their lives. For years, presidential candidates have been promising to make government smaller. But until Bill Clinton, none delivered.

The workforce cuts are saving lots of money. For fiscal year 1996, the average government worker costs more than $44,000 a year, not including office space and supplies.[3] Cutting a quarter million jobs, therefore, can save well over $10 billion annually. But that's not the half of it. The savings from all the common sense reforms we have put in place total $118 billion.* Put that together with the benefits of our healthy economy, and you'll see that the Clinton-Gore Administration has come up with another one for the record books: four straight years of deficit cuts, for a stupendous total reduction of $476 billion.[4] (See Figure 2.)

Even though big cuts in government were long overdue, and even though they are a crucial step in getting the country out of the red, there is a right way and a wrong way to cut government. The right way is to show some consideration for the workers.

---

* This total savings figure is derived from three sources. First, $73.4 billion in savings from completed recommendations in the original 1993 NPR report have been realized. Second, another $24 billion in savings have been locked in from additional recommendations in NPR's 1995 report. And third, more than $21.5 billion in savings is attributable to agency reinvention initiatives beyond the specific recommendations made by NPR. For example, the Federal Communications Commission realized $20.3 billion by auctioning wireless spectrum licenses, and the General Services Administration's time out and review of federal construction projects saved more than $1.2 billion. Other savings from reengineering travel and other administrative processes have not been quantified, but they have saved tens of millions of dollars. In addition, another $5.2 billion in savings is contained in legislation currently pending before Congress. Appendix C provides additional details.

Figure 1: Personnel Changes by Agency
January 1993-January 1996 (in percentages)

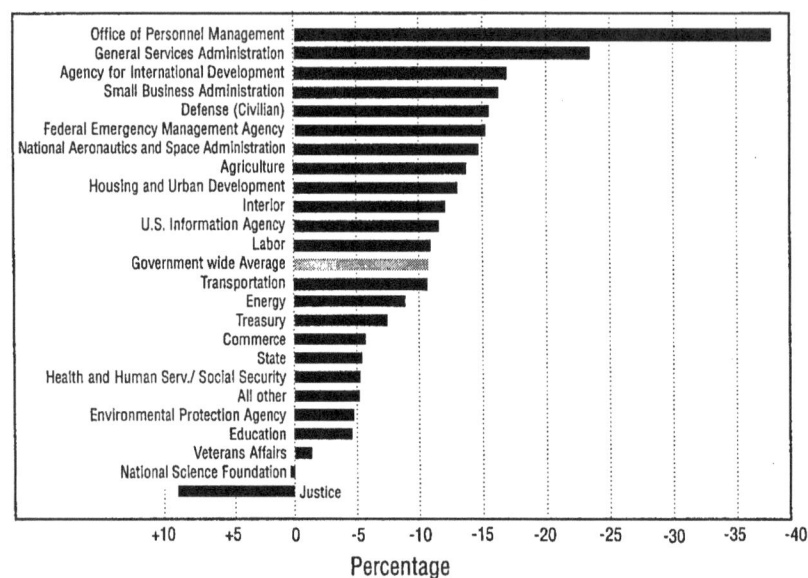

Source: Office of Personnel Management, Monthly Report of Federal Civilian Employment

It is wrong just to hand out the pink slips and let government employees fend for themselves—workers who have devoted their careers to public service and who have families to support.

We've made the cuts the right way, with layoffs as a last resort. First, we slowed down hiring. The government used to hire well over 100,000 people each year just to replace those who retired or quit. We brought hiring down to fewer than 50,000 a year.[5] We did not stop hiring altogether because many government jobs, such as air traffic controllers, simply must be filled.

Next, we encouraged our current employees to retire or quit by offering them buyout payments. The offers ranged from a few thousand dollars up to $25,000, depending on the workers' salaries and how long they had worked. It was a good deal for the employees and for the taxpayers. Even at $25,000, a buyout costs less than the paperwork and severance pay that goes with a layoff.[6] Nearly 115,000 workers took buyouts.[7]

By slowing down hiring and speeding up retirements, we've managed to limit layoffs to a small proportion of the workforce that left federal service.[8] We are helping those who have been laid off to find jobs with private companies. It's tough, but we're trying. It's all part of making cuts the right way.

Figure 2: Changes in the Federal Budget Deficit, 1980-2001

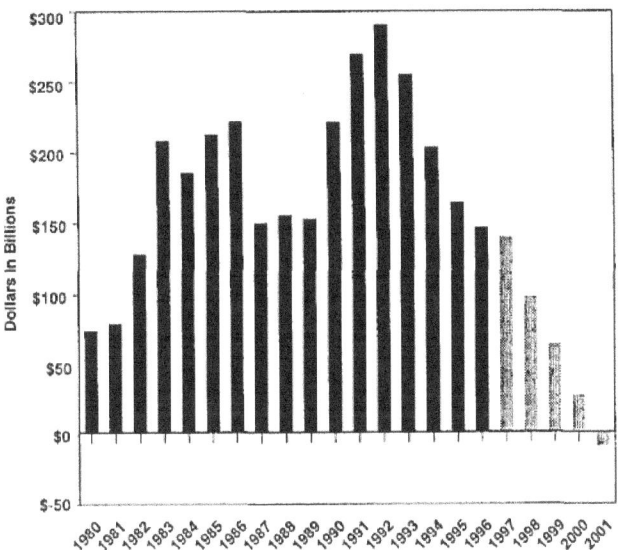

Source: Historical Tables: Budget of the United States; fiscal years 1997-2001 are estimates.

Another part of cutting government the right way is to be selective and cut out just the parts we don't need any more—not the parts we do need. It's wrong to cut activities and services that most people depend on—things like ensuring that our food and water are safe, that our neighborhoods are free from drugs and crime, that tax refunds and social security payments arrive on time. Our plan is ultimately to eliminate jobs we no longer need: jobs in bloated headquarters, excess layers of management, and offices that churn out arcane rules, like the rules that have made government procurement so costly and ridiculous. So far, the personnel reductions have occurred pretty much across the board, because we were trying to avoid lay-offs. We'll have to retrain and reassign some people to get them into the right jobs.

A lot of the credit for cutting goes to the very federal workers whose jobs were at stake. For example, it was a procurement specialist, Michellee Edwards, who suggested that we change the law to make small purchases so simple that we no longer need a procurement specialist. Those small purchases used to generate 70 percent of the work in a typical procurement office.[9] Michellee says, "I don't think any government employees would cling to senseless work just to protect their jobs. I certainly wouldn't. For me, it's more important to keep in mind the bigger picture and promote change where it makes sense. We're all taxpayers too, you know."

3

This might be surprising, but lots of government workers think like Michellee. Why else would teams of personnel specialists have worked so hard to scrap the 10,000 page Federal Personnel Manual and have then gone on to cut out much of a typical personnel office's day-to-day workload by letting employees use self-serve computer kiosks? Why else would U.S. Customs Service employees have come up with the plan that eliminated an entire layer of regional Customs headquarters that was full of high-paying jobs? Even Washington's regulation writers are tossing out 16,000 pages of their own creations and removing the bureaucratic jargon from another 31,000 pages.[10] Behind virtually every bit of our successful downsizing and streamlining are the ideas and the enthusiasm of federal workers. More than anyone, they have the know-how and the desire to make government cost less. Our hats are off to them.

A cheaper, smaller government was only half our goal. President Clinton and I were determined to make government work better, too. You probably haven't read or heard much about this part of reinvention—although we never intended it to be a secret—but we've made real progress. The government is beginning to produce more results and less red tape. I'll be the first to say that there is still plenty of room for improvement, but Americans are beginning to see the results in the form of fast, courteous service. Business owners and local government leaders are noticing the change, too, as the federal government becomes more of a partner and less of an adversary. President Clinton and I think it's time everyone knows about these changes—it's time for these secrets to get out.

No one can explain the improvements better than the people who are on the receiving end. So, in the following chapters you'll hear from a front-line federal worker, a homemaker, a business executive, and a mayor. They'll discuss their bad experiences with government in the past. And, frankly, they will tell that there are still some bad things going on. After all, putting common sense into government is a big job, it's still a work in progress, and it probably always will be. But these individuals will talk about a change the likes of which they have never seen before—a change very much for the better.

President Clinton and I are just as proud of making government work better as we are of making it smaller. It isn't good enough yet, or small enough yet, but we sure have things headed in the right direction. We are rebuilding a government that all Americans can be proud of.

Al Gore

4

Reinvention Highlights

Your government is changing dramatically so that it makes sense and serves you better. Here's what the Clinton-Gore Administration is doing to deliver on promises made three years ago:

"THE ERA OF BIG GOVERNMENT IS OVER"

- Government has reduced its workforce by nearly 240,000 as of January 1996. Thirteen of the 14 departments have reduced the size of their workforce; the Justice Department grew because of the Administration's fight against crime and drugs.
- We've cut government the right way by eliminating what you don't need—bloated headquarters, layers of managers, outdated field offices, and ridiculous red tape and rules.
- We've saved and improved the parts you want— Social Security, our National Park system, and other agencies that protect you and your family.
- We're closing nearly 2,000 obsolete field offices and have already eliminated nearly 200 programs and agencies, like the Tea-Tasters Board, the Bureau of Mines, and wool and mohair subsidies.

WE'RE RADICALLY CHANGING GOVERNMENT

Inside the federal government, radical changes are taking place to make it work better and cost nearly $118 billion less than it used to:

- Government workers can now buy $4 staplers because we've cut out the red tape that ran the cost up to $54 in the past.
- We've negotiated better deals for services that the government uses a lot and saved a lot of money in the process, like $3.62 for a three-pound FedEx delivery instead of $27. And as little as 2 cents a minute for long-distance calls instead of 16 cents a minute.
- Government workers are seeing much less of the illogical and bizarre rules and regulations:
  - One-third of the federal workforce used to write rules for and micromanage the other two-thirds. We're getting rid

5

of many of those jobs and are convincing agencies to trust their workers to use their common sense.

- We're cutting out superfluous layers of managers. We've eliminated nearly 54,000 supervisors—and a few layers.
- In some cases, the Defense Department used to spend more on getting approval for employees to travel than it did on the travel itself. Now they're testing new automated systems that make sense and will save over $100 million a year.
- With new tools like the Line Item Veto and the ability to pursue people who are seriously delinquent in their debts to the federal government, we'll be able to do a better job of safeguarding taxpayer dollars.

WE'RE SERVING PEOPLE BETTER

President Clinton told federal agencies to make customer service to the public equal to the best in business. Over 200 agencies have committed to meeting more than 3,000 standards.

- The Social Security Administration stunned the business world last year by coming in first in an independent survey on the country's best 1-800 telephone service.
- We're changing the Blue Pages in the phone book so if you want a passport, you will look up "passport," without having to know you get it from the State Department.
- Agencies are working together to provide unique services for you:
  - Veterans in New York can access Social Security and Veterans Services with one-stop service;
  - You can go to the "Trading Posts" that the Bureau of Land Management and the Forest Service have set up to get maps, fishing information, and guide permits all in one place and at times that are convenient to you.
  - In Houston, small business owners can go to the U.S. General Store to get information from federal, state, and local governments and even apply for loans.
  - Or just stay home and do government business on the Internet. You can do everything from signing on to the U.S. Business Advisor to get answers to questions, to downloading IRS forms, or filling out a Small Business Administration loan form.

WE'RE CHANGING THE WAY WE TREAT BUSINESSES

President Clinton and Vice President Gore told government regulators to cut obsolete regulations and to start acting like partners. Agencies are eliminating 16,000 pages of regulations and dramatically simplifying another 31,000.

- We're doing it the right way—rewarding companies that cooperate with us. But for those companies that don't work with us to ensure the public's safety and protect our environment, we will apply every penalty and sanction that the law allows.
- The Health Care Finance Administration eliminated the Physician Attestation Form. This ended the filing of 11 million forms each year and saved doctors 200,000 hours of time.
- The Department of Agriculture dropped three million pages of government forms.
- We're slashing the regulatory and administrative burden of government on citizens and businesses by nearly $28 billion a year.

WE'RE CHANGING THE WAY WE WORK WITH COMMUNITIES

We're letting states try new ways to reform health care and welfare so they can see what works best by focusing on results, not red tape. President Clinton and Vice President Gore have:

- Created more than 100 federal-local partnerships to focus on the needs of individual communities. These partnerships allow community residents to implement plans to solve what they—not Washington—see as their biggest problems.
- Approved welfare demonstration projects in more than 40 states in the three years before President Clinton signed the welfare reform bill.
- Approved 13 comprehensive Medicaid reform demonstrations in partnerships with states to expand coverage to 2.2 million low-income uninsured Americans.
- Signed agreements with two states—Connecticut and Oregon—to pilot new ways of doing business with less burden, and dramatically streamlined planning and other processes in a range of programs in other states.

BLANK   PAGE

SECRET ONE:
COMMON SENSE HAS COME
TO THE FEDERAL GOVERNMENT

"Whatcha got, Bootsie?"

"Coke, looks like about 10 pounds, taped to his chest."

Tommy exchanges high-fives with Bootsie, one of his undercover rovers, as she explains how she picked the unlikely looking drug mule from among the hundreds of incoming passengers on a flight from Colombia. (Don't worry, we won't give away her trade secrets.) A couple more of his rovers quickly team up to check out the smuggler's records, book him, and look for any connections to other passengers or luggage. Within minutes, the troops are back out on the floor, working the next wave of passengers.

Tommy Roland is doing something that any TV cop would envy—running one of the most successful drug-busting operations around. Tommy supervises the inspection team for the U.S. Customs Service at Miami International Airport. "I'm proud of the rovers," he says. "The stuff that they're doing now is defining where Customs is going. I'm thrilled to be a part of that. They use their intuition, their creativity, their imagination on the job. It's really beautiful to watch them. I feel like the coach of some awesome basketball team."

But Tommy says it was not always this much fun. "In the 'olden days,' the whole philosophy of what a Customs inspector was supposed to do and how he was supposed to do it was completely different. First of all, we all wore our uniforms, so we were easy for the smugglers to spot." Today, Tommy is working in jeans and sneakers, and wearing an earring. "We stood in our little enclosures waiting for passengers to come to us with their bags. We didn't know anything about them until we saw the whites of their eyes. We just stood there in our uniforms waiting. A tough way to win a drug war.

"We were looking for needles in haystacks—looking for that nervous passenger, just doing 'behavior analysis.' Everyone who walked off a plane was a suspect. Every suitcase was suspicious. We were unfocused and wasted a lot of time. And at the end of the day, we had dug through a lot of underwear and socks, but hadn't found much dope. What we were exceptionally good at was infuriating the legitimate travelers—hundreds of thousands of honest, decent American citizens and foreign tourists and business executives each year." Passengers sometimes waited in line for over three hours. Occasionally, a fist fight would break out.

Today, cocaine seizures are up by 50 percent. Heroin seizures up by 21 percent.[1] Passengers seldom wait more than a few minutes. This is reinvention.

Tommy says it all started with flowers. "We used to handle cargo the same way we handled passengers—just stabbing in the dark. We knew dope was coming into the country in boxes of flowers. So we probed flower boxes. We used these big metal flower probes and poked away from midnight 'til 8:00 a.m. This was an all night thing, night in and night out. Thirty thousand boxes of flowers came into the airport each night, and we would probe each one once or twice. That's a lot of probe holes. I totally hated Mother's Day and Valentine's Day. Finally, we realized that this was a really stupid way to look for dope—and the flower shippers didn't much like it either. So we sent our own inspectors to South America to look at every single aspect of the whole process.

"We went to the flower farms to see where the flowers were grown. We looked at how the flowers got trucked from the farm to the market, and then to the airport to see how they were staged to get on the plane—who put them on the plane, who hired the people who put them on the plane—and the same on the other end—who took them off the plane and who hired these folks. Looking at the entire process, we saw just how vulnerable a shipment of flowers is all along the way. That's when it hit home. If we were gonna make a dent in the dope, we couldn't do it alone—we had to be partners with the airlines.

"Now the airlines have their own people checking the flowers. Instead of Customs inspectors probing flower boxes here, the boxes are x-rayed before they get on the planes. The airlines have contract security people watching the x-rays. And we video the watchers as a counter-deterrent. They're not our own people so we still check them, but they are our allies, not our enemies. If we had started this earlier, I probably would have saved my shoulder. All that bending over probing flowers wrecked my shoulder."

Partnership with the airlines and shippers has turned out to be the key to success, but according to Tommy, it did not come easy. "Tell the airlines our secrets and have them work together with us to find drugs? Unimaginable. Consider the Immigration Service an ally? No way. Ask the skycaps for their suggestions? Never. Back then everything was a secret and everyone was the enemy. 'If I told you, I'd have to kill you.' That was more like it. Basically, we didn't trust anybody.

"It wasn't just that we didn't trust the folks outside the system. We didn't trust the folks inside the system that much more. A perfect example was all the stupid paper work we had to fill out. An hour or two before the end of every single shift, we would have to come into the office and fill out a shift report. It seemed like we spent more time writing these reports detailing every single thing we did during the day than we spent looking for dope. It was a real big waste of time and money. And it made me feel like I couldn't be trusted. I really hated that. But things have really changed in the last few years. We got rid of a lot of wasted motion. The guys that work for me don't fill these out anymore. They're paid to look for dope, not to fill out forms."

"I remember lots of hassles I'd have to go through just to do my job. For example, when you're looking through cargo, you might need to drill through a box to see what's inside. But if I wanted to drill, I had to go to a senior inspector who would go to a supervisor who would go to the chief's office where the one drill we had was locked up. Like I wasn't responsible enough to be given the tools to do my job or the authority to make decisions by myself. Now, when inspectors come on board, we give them their own drills. Makes sense to me.

"Even the way the agency was structured sent a loud and clear message about trust. There were just so many layers of bureaucracy to deal with. We used to have regional offices. They were like speed bumps. The guys there had been away from the field so long that you always had to slow down and explain the real world to them. Getting rid of the regions was like a miracle."

What Tommy attributes to a miracle was really the work of a team of employees that Customs Commissioner George Weise chartered to reinvent the U.S. Customs Service. They cut the size of the Washington headquarters by a third, and they eliminated all seven regions and 43 district offices. "In my book, George Weise gets an awful lot of credit," Tommy says. "Not just for cutting out some layers of management, but for really having faith in us down here—trusting us to figure out how to do the job better. It takes some leadership to turn an organization around the way Customs has. He should be proud."

Part of the turn-around came from employing modern tools and techniques. "They assigned me to start looking through the computerized cargo manifests and analyzing information from the airlines," Tommy explains. "This was the first time I had to work with computers looking for dope, and they kinda had to drag me to it kicking and screaming. But in about six weeks, I seized 3,000 pounds of coke using manifest review techniques and targeting.

"Once we realized the power of targeting freight with computer analysis, we wanted to get into pre-analysis of passengers, too. It made sense. If we could get passenger lists when the planes took off, we could start working hours before the plane arrived. We got the majority of the airlines to cooperate. They want to get the dope off their planes. They certainly don't want us seizing their multimillion-dollar 747s. Now, we screen their passenger lists and we know who we're looking for—we go right up to the plane and start working. We don't just stand there in our uniforms waiting for the drugs to come to us. We go out and find it. I hate to use a Washington term, but I guess you'd say we're proactive."

The changes at Miami International Airport are tangible. "These partnerships are changing the whole environment here. There's an energy at this airport that I've never felt in my 22 years here," says Amaury Zuriarrain, deputy director of the Metro-Dade Aviation Department, which runs the airport. "The passengers are noticing the improvements, too."

"It's kind of funny," Tommy adds. "Life is a lot easier for most passengers. They don't have to wait in lines for hours and be treated like suspected criminals. But you know what? Some passengers have written to us that we're not doing our job because the process is so easy for them now. They shouldn't be fooled by that. Just because they don't see me doesn't mean I'm not watching them."

Tommy is dead serious about keeping drugs out of South Florida. "This is where I live. This is where I'm raising my family. And I continually ask myself, 'Is it good to have dope in the schools?' Hell, my kids are in those schools. I don't want dope in my schools. I don't just go to school for Career Day. I go on field trips with these kids. They come to my home. I know every kid's name in my son's fifth grade class. This is my idea of family values.

"It may sound funny, but this experience here at work really has had an effect on my family life. Before, if one of my kids did something wrong, my wife and I would automatically decide how to handle the situation. After all, we're the parents. We're the 'managers' in our family. But we've started to look at things a little differently. We're sharing the decision-making with the boys—asking for their input. They're involved in the decision-making process."

Tommy Roland is a new style "manager" at home and on the job, and it is not just the jeans, sneakers, and earring. He works with energy, creativity, and teamwork, and he produces results. He sums it up simply: "I'm not a bureaucrat. I've got a job to do."

That's obviously the kind of attitude we want in all federal workers. We always have. And most young workers have that attitude when they first sign up. But the government's various systems—procurement, management, and personnel—can sap the energy, creativity, and enthusiasm out of the people who work for the government. Luckily for us, lots of workers all over government are like Tommy. They stick with it anyway because they want so much to do something that really matters—to do something good for the American people. Let's take a look at the systems that de-motivate people, and what the Clinton-Gore Administration has been doing to change things.

Procurement Reform

Most Americans have known for years that government procurement is a mess. But to get a full appreciation, it helps to work here. Before the reinventing government reforms launched in 1993, the typical federal worker was not trusted to buy so much as a $4 stapler for the office. Only trained procurement specialists were allowed to buy things—only a trained specialist could understand the rules—and they would make the buy only if a worker came to them with the forms properly filled out and signed by several bosses up the line—and even then, only if they thought you deserved whatever was requested.

Buying anything associated with a computer was even worse. Federal workers told us about having to get a dozen signatures, and then waiting a year or more to get a simple PC. When it arrived, it was already obsolete, and it cost more than the new, higher-powered models at Circuit City. To cap off their frustration, federal employees would read in the papers along with the rest of America, that "the procurement system," which did not trust them to buy anything, had gone out and paid $400 for a hammer.

The government's procurement system was enough of a challenge that we decided to double-team it. We got long-time critic of procurement and former Harvard professor of management, Steve Kelman, to lead some government-wide changes, and brought Colleen Preston in from a Congressional staff to lead reform at the Defense Department. Rather than try to explain all the ins and outs of the regulatory changes backed by the National Performance Review—changes that the Administration has made on its own authority, and changes we have persuaded Congress to enact into law—let's look at some results.

First, results that benefit the entire government and, of course, the taxpayers who foot the bill:

- Last May, we signed a contract with FedEx for overnight package delivery. A three-pound package, at retail—$27. For the government, and the taxpayers—$3.62.

- Long-distance telephone calls: Someone who shops around can make peak-hour long-distance calls for as low as 16¢ per minute. Starting in October, government calls to anyone anywhere in the country will cost about 5¢ per minute. Calls between government agencies are even less, about 2¢ per minute.[2]

- The government used to do over $50 worth of paperwork for every small purchase—even for something like a $4 office stapler—and there are millions of small purchases each year. Now, we have gotten rid of the paperwork and we use special Visa cards. What's special? The average American pays from 12 to 18 percent interest, and a yearly fee of up to $50. The government pays no interest, no annual fee, and we earn cash rebates for paying on time.[3]

- Earlier this year, President Clinton signed a new law and an executive order that fixes one of procurement's biggest nightmares: buying computers and other information technology.[4] Under the President's order, agencies will invest in information technology only when there is a clear payback, and they won't be locked into cumbersome contracts that can't keep up with rapidly changing technology. The idea is to buy a little, test a little, fix a little, and do it quick.

Now for the Defense Department, which accounts for about three-fourths of the federal government's purchases:

- Remember the $400 hammer? How about a $500 telephone—one especially designed for an aircraft carrier. What was so special? It worked even after the ship had sunk. Following changes in the communications system and by challenging every requirement, the Navy determined it could use commercial phones that cost 30 bucks.[5]

- Let's look at socks and underwear (it reminds us of the old days for Customs inspectors). If you were ever a soldier, your GI socks probably fell down because there was no elastic at the top, and they made everything in the washing machine with them turn olive drab. The reinvented Army now issues ordinary, color-fast socks with elastic. The sad-sack socks cost $1.99 a pair—the nice, new ones cost $1.49.

- Concerning underwear, we think this letter speaks for itself.[6]

June 7, 1996

For many years, Jockey International, Inc. declined to bid on government business. We took this position because the solicitations asked us to manufacture a T-shirt to unique government specifications. The solicitations also asked us to provide sensitive pricing data so the government could determine a fair price....

When we saw the latest solicitation for T-shirts we were excited. The government was asking for our standard product, style 9711, without all the headaches of a custom design. Moreover, our current catalog price was the basis to negotiate a fair price. It is with great pleasure that we were able to accept the T-shirt award....

The T-shirt will be made in the USA. The production is at our Belzoni, Mississippi plant, an economically depressed area. This plant was closed in 1993, but reopened in 1995 on a temporary basis. With a pick up in business and the award of this military contract we now have 175 employees at this facility....

Peter J. Hannes
President, Special Markets Division
Jockey International, Inc.

Of course, the savings are not all just from socks and undershirts—the biggest savings come from changes in buying big-ticket items. When the Pentagon and Congress agreed to a multi-year purchase and the elimination of detailed military specifications, manufacturers could use more standard commercial parts. As a result, the price tag on the contract for their new C-17 cargo plane went down by more than $2.7 billion. Similarly, they saved $2.9 billion on smart munitions, and over $100 million on the Fire Support Combat Arms Tactical Trainer.[7] NASA is doing the same kind of thing and making the same kind of savings on space gear.

In addition to some very important legislative changes, the procurement system only needed a little trust (that workers like Tommy Roland won't steal us blind), some common sense (that Jockey can make decent T-shirts without government instructions), and some shrewd bargaining (just try to find long distance rates as low as 2¢ a minute). That is the heart of the procurement reforms that the National Performance Review recommended in 1993 and that became the basis for three major legislative changes that have been signed by the President: the Federal Acquisition Streamlining Act of 1994, the Federal Acquisition Reform Act of 1996, and the Information Technology Management Reform Act of 1996. President Clinton has gone even further by issuing a variety of directives that enhance and speed the legislative reforms.[8]

Trust, common sense, and shrewd bargaining might not sound like a revolutionary formula to fix government procurement. But added all together, our procurement reforms are expected to save $12.3 billion over five years.[9] Pretty good, huh?

By the way, we are not just buying smarter, we are selling smarter, too. The government actually used to give away the incredibly valuable rights to broadcast on certain frequencies. This included radio, TV, cell phones—you get the picture. Now, the Federal Communications Commission auctions them to the highest bidder. So far, we have taken in $20.3 billion.[10]

Management Systems and Structure

Just a few years ago, the front-line federal workers had more layers of supervisors than they could shake a stick at—as much as they would like to. For example, a nurse in a government hospital would have had to communicate through a reporting chain of a dozen or more bosses before word reached the Cabinet Secretary—and, of course, the Secretary would have to do the same to get an answer back. Remember that party game called "telephone," where a half dozen players lined up and whispered a simple message from one to the next? It invariably came out garbled. Imagine what twice as many players could do. Imagine a dozen or more layers of managers, not to mention their deputies and administrative assistants, transmitting that nurse's good idea about how to save money on, say, sphygmomanometers. Every new idea needed high-level approval.

By the way, that long line of managers was not just waiting to convey the front-line workers' ideas to the top boss. They were busy producing rules and regulations spelling every detail of what front-line workers should and should not do.

Back in 1993, when we began reinventing government, we discovered that one out of every three government employees was part of a network of micromanagement and overcontrol. They were headquarters staff, personnel, budget, procurement, audit, finance, or supervisors. One-third of our employees had been assigned to keep the other two-thirds from ever doing anything wrong. They were writing and promulgating internal rules, administering internal rules, and auditing compliance with internal rules. That occupied almost 700,000 workers, who cost taxpayers around $35 billion a year, plus office space and lots of paper.[11] But at least nothing ever went wrong. Right? Wrong!

Big headquarters and big rule books never have kept the government from making big mistakes. In fact, they often kept front-line workers from doing things right. So we asked agencies to cut layers of supervisors, headquarters staff, and other management control jobs by 50 percent.[12] Figure 3 shows what they have done so far.

Because we started offering buyouts and putting the brakes on hiring, the reductions have not been concentrated in management control positions to the extent the National Performance Review recommended. But 11 of the 27 largest agencies are at least halfway to the goal on supervisors, and eight have cut headquarters staff by 25 percent or more. In addition, certain bureaus and agencies within selected departments are also making big progress that is not reflected in their departments' overall figures. Overall, it is fair progress, but we still have a long way to go.

Numbers are not everything. Many bosses are changing the way they do their jobs—encouraging innovation and customer service instead of just making workers toe the line. Many national and regional management organizations are taking on a new role whose primary job is support. Ultimately, we have to bring down the number of people in management jobs and headquarters, but the shift in attitude is every bit as important.

Figure 3: Streamlining Changes to Date: FYs 1993-1996
(in percentages)

Agency	Percentage Change in the Number of:		
	Supervisors	Headquarters Staff	Management Control Positions
Agency for International Development	-3	-14	+5
Agriculture	-21	-15	-11
Commerce	-18	-20	-16
Defense (total)	-16	-10	-8
Air Force	-13	-8	-8
Army	-14	-17	-8
Navy	-19	-7	-8
Defense Agencies	-19	-3	-8
Education	-24	-12	-11
Energy	-53	-27	-16
Environmental Protection Agency	-38	-10	+4
Federal Emergency Management Agency	-20	-22	+17
General Services Administration	-28	-21	-18
Health and Human Services	-29	-15	-11
Housing and Urban Development	-37	-36	-17
Interior	-29	-27	-32
Justice	+4	-5	+9
Labor	-19	-25	-17
National Aeronautics and Space Administration	-40	-34	-16
National Science Foundation	-24	-18	+8
Office of Personnel Management	-53	-65	-41
Small Business Administration	-28	-28	-30
Social Security Administration	-25	-23	-14
State	-8	-7	-1
Transportation	-22	-25	-17
Treasury	-10	+4	+4
United States Information Agency	-22	-15	-17
Veterans Affairs	-28	-19	-6
Average	-20	-14	-9

Note: OMB Circular No. A-11 (1995), sec. 15.4, pp. 47-48, contains the definitions of the job series included in each of these three categories. See also Appendix H.

Reinvention Labs

The first thing we did to encourage a change of attitude at headquarters and to move more authority and accountability to the front lines was to create "reinvention laboratories," where front-line workers and managers could try out their ideas for a change. Now there are about 250 reinvention labs leading the reinvention revolution. They have been called "islands of innovation in a sea of bureaucracy."[13] The place where Tommy Roland works, Miami International Airport, is a reinvention lab. Here are some other examples:

- The General Services Administration established the first electronic shopping mall for Federal customers, which cut the cost of real estate sales by 50 percent while generating revenue of $73 million.

- The Air Force medical organization prototyped an automated system for maintaining patients' records. The system will save millions of dollars and improve care as it spreads throughout the Defense Department.

- A joint effort between the Defense Contract Audit Agency and the Defense Logistics Agency cut the government's and contractors' overhead expenses by substituting international quality control standards for the government standard. Quality rose, and government costs have fallen by over $150 million so far.

- The Department of Justice's SENTRI project in southwest California uses state-of-the-art technology to reduce the average waiting time to cross the border from 45 minutes to just three minutes for registered travelers. Inspectors now can focus on non-registered, higher-risk travelers.

- A reinvention lab in Anchorage is combining seven separate libraries into a single one-stop shop for information about natural resources. The Department of the Interior is joining forces with state agencies and the University of Alaska to create a single natural resources library that will eliminate duplication, save money, require less staff, and provide better service to customers.

Personnel Reform

"Filling out the prescribed government job application used to discourage a lot of people. For many, it was their first dose of red tape. It was almost like saying to somebody who wanted to work for the federal government, 'Welcome to the fun house'."

— Vice President Al Gore, in a speech
to the Office of Personnel Management

In 1883, two years before the first gasoline-powered automobile and six years before the White House had electric lights, the U.S. Civil Service laws were written.[14] Not only is the civil service system old, our first report called it "elaborate, complex, and over-regulated, preventing agencies and their managers, employees, and unions from designing effective and mission-supporting human resource management programs." No one argued with us about that.

We have done what we could to fix it. We have done quite a bit.

Common Sense Job Applications

We scrapped the Standard Form 171, the ridiculously long job application that said, in so many words, "Welcome to the fun house." Now applicants can send in a regular resume, like regular people do for regular jobs.[15] Even better, the Office of Personnel Management has a toll-free phone service and a World Wide Web site that lets people find out what is available and even apply by phone or fax for many jobs.[16]

Less Red Tape

We junked all but a few parts of the 10,000-page Federal Personnel Manual that specified everything down to the color of personnel folders. We actually hauled it out to a dumpster in a wheel barrow. The death of the manual gave agencies more freedom to tailor things to fit their own operations.

Labor-Management Partnerships

CEOs who had reinvented big corporations told us we could not succeed without a true partnership between management and labor. The President signed an executive order in 1993 establishing the National Partnership Council.[17] Now there are more than 650 partnership councils, and labor-management relations are improving all across government. One of the most successful councils is at the U.S. Mint in Denver, led by Greg Wikberg, president of the local union, and Jack DeBroekert, the

19

manager of the Mint. Since the partnership started, disputes have nearly vanished, litigation costs have dropped by $10 million and, in 1995, they set an all-time record by producing 10.3 billion coins.[18] How's that for a money-making partnership?

Family-friendly Workplaces

Government workers should have lives, too. Moms and dads need time with the kids, with their own parents, and with each other. So, the Clinton-Gore Administration is encouraging job sharing, part-time work, alternative work schedules, telecommuting from home and from satellite locations, leave banks, and child-and-elder-care services.[19] Top business leaders agree that this approach increases productivity and morale, and reduces lost time.

Performance Appraisals

Every year, everyone who works for the government is to be formally and individually judged by his or her boss. The process can cause tension and is widely viewed as ineffective. Most government work depends on team, not individual, effort. And often, a worker's teammates and customers are better able than the boss to judge that employee's effectiveness. Several agencies are experimenting with different evaluation methods that enhance teamwork and give more influence to the customers. The Department of Education is using a 360-degree appraisal, an evaluation from all directions—the boss, subordinates, colleagues, customers, and suppliers. The other new kind of evaluation is not of the individual, but of the team. It is based on measurable results, and everybody who contributes to the results gets the same grade. Workers are being judged and rewarded in terms of how well their teams achieve measurable results. Several variations of the new systems are being tried, and all have pluses and minuses; the hope is to find better, more productive means of gauging worker performance.

New Civil Service Legislation

Right now, we cannot be as flexible or innovative as we would like to be because the personnel system applies a single set of rules to all federal employees, from patent attorneys to park rangers. No corporation would operate this way. General Electric makes light bulbs, buys and sells mortgage loans, and leases cars. GE does not try to squeeze such a diverse cadre of workers into a single set of personnel rules, and neither should the federal government.

Legislation now moving through Congress will grant agencies more flexibility in administering personnel systems that support their missions, while preserving basic common values like veterans preference and merit. It will allow each agency to set up its own method of rewarding good performance and dealing with poor performance.

Reinforcing Success: The Hammer Award

From the start, Vice President Gore has spotlighted the people and teams that were showing the way to reinvention by giving them a "Hammer Award"— a $6 hammer wrapped in ribbon and mounted with an aluminum frame. It symbolizes the dramatic change from the days when government paid a bit more for hammers. The awards are highly prized, and teams are eager to publicize initiatives that they once would have kept under wraps due to fear of criticism. Nearly 500 Hammer Awards have gone to such teams as:

- the Interior Department team that converted its rules and regulations into "Plain English";
- the Transportation team that, along with their California teammates, figured out how to get the Santa Monica Freeway back into operation in record time after the Northridge earthquake; and
- the team from the National Park Service that reduced the review time for construction of park visitor centers and other major projects by over 50 percent.

Several agencies followed the Vice President's lead of encouraging reinvention with special awards. For example, the Deputy Secretary of Veterans Affairs gives the "Scissors Award" to VA employees who have cut red tape.

Franchise Funds

Our government has long opposed private monopolies while creating public ones. A federal manager needing some administrative service—like help from personnel, legal, procurement, financial, or computer specialists—had to go to the departmental monopoly in charge of that service. This approach was thought to offer economies of scale.

Today almost everybody understands that monopolies provide poor services at high costs. So the original National Performance Review report recommended introducing competition by lifting the requirement that agencies buy supplies from the General Services Administration. GSA's Federal Supply Service gave up its monopoly on office supplies in 1994 and has been competing successfully for government business ever since. Their new motto is "Better, faster, cheaper, or not at all."

The National Performance Review also encouraged agencies to promote competition by establishing "franchise funds."[20] These funds allow selected agencies to offer their common administrative services to other agencies. Congressional approval was obtained in May 1996 for franchise funds in Interior, Treasury, Veterans Affairs, the Environmental Protection Agency, and Commerce. The funds will allow these agencies to sell to other agencies such services as mainframe computing, records storage, personnel and accounting systems, background checks, and travel management.

Our Secret Weapon

Telepathology equipment at the Veterans Hospital in Milwaukee rivals the sick bay on Star Trek's Enterprise. But, the real reason the vets get world-class care there is Dr. Bruce Dunn. Dr. Dunn thinks we owe veterans a debt that can never quite be repaid. His research to get vets the best pathology on the planet sets the scales a bit closer to balance.

Helen Wassick went to work part-time in the Morgantown office of the Forest Service in a program that employs seniors at minimum wage. Her office sends out publications all over the country on tree management. Helen prides herself on not giving up on a request until she gets an answer. She says, "I treat people the way I want to be treated." And when the Forest Service started giving comment cards to customers, Helen wrote her own name on the cards. Hundreds of customers told the Forest Service that Helen is the greatest. So now Helen's on the payroll full-time serving customers.

George Hawkins works for EPA in Boston. He used to practice law at Ropes and Gray for more money, and he had a lot less fun. George is the champion in EPA's Boston office for EPA efforts to build partnerships with companies and communities that want to protect the environment. George thinks that this is the future of environmental protection and that building that future is worth doing. He'll tell anyone who will listen. In fact, he wrote 1,000 letters to businesses and towns offering to come and explain the partnership programs. He got a lot of takers. True to his pledge he has made 150 visits so far this year.

Bruce, Helen, and George all have something in common. A big part of why these people work for government is that they want to make a contribution, to add value, to serve. They brag about it too, over a back fence or at a soccer game. Federal employees haven't done much of that for years. But, in offices where reinvention has begun, the employee teams are inspired by the idea of finding ways to change the system so it serves Americans again.

This motivation is a potent force, a kind of pure energy source for change that has been bottled up. Reinvention turns it loose. The government is filled with good people like Bruce, Helen, and George—and don't forget Tommy Roland. The problem is that for years we have kept these good people trapped in bad systems. We are changing the systems so all our people can devote more of their time, intelligence, and energy to what they signed up for in the first place—serving the people of America.

SECRET TWO:
GOVERNMENT IS SERVING PEOPLE BETTER

"I stumbled from the office dazed and confused,
completely disoriented by what had just happened."

— Elizabeth Childs, describing her feelings after having
contact with the federal government

Beth Childs lives in the shadow of the government—literally. Her neat, cozy, second-story apartment opens onto a porch overlooking a federal office building in Sacramento. They are separated only by a hedge of white flowering oleander, the kind found in the median strips of the California freeways. Beth has lived there for eight years with her husband Bill, a drug and alcohol counselor in a nearby high school, and Sydney, her junior high-aged daughter. Sydney has recently taken up playing the flute, following in the footsteps of her self-taught mother.

"The government is a rude neighbor," Beth complains mildly. "They get out here sometimes on Sunday mornings around 7:00 making all kinds of noise with leaf blowers and garbage trucks. But I guess they might feel the same way about us, considering Fred." Fred is their gray cat—they also have a calico. "Fred's learned how to open the federal building's electronic doors, and he goes into the cafeteria kitchen. The health inspector caught him in there once. Caused quite a stir." Beth's smile shows that Fred is making up for the Sunday morning noise. Being the government's neighbor is not what made her feel "dazed and confused, completely disoriented" as she wrote in a recent letter. That came from one of the times she visited a government office, when she needed something only the government could supply.

"My twin sister, Tami, just adopted a Russian baby while she and her husband were living in Belgium. The baby's named Amy, and she's absolutely beautiful. Tami had to fill out lots of forms in Russian, Flemish, and French. At the last minute, Tami realized she needed a form in English from INS—the U.S. Immigration and Naturalization Service. It's just a one-page form—a single piece of green paper. I offered to pick the form up at the INS office."

The INS office is in a nondescript concrete and smoked glass building on J Street, one of the main drags in Sacramento. Its address is the only thing printed on the facade of the building, 7-Eleven. But it is no convenience store.

"There was a sign on the wall that said the capacity was 250, but there had to be 500 people in there. I finally figured out I was supposed to take a number. But there were different windows, and there were different numbers and a different number dispenser for each window. One was for forms, but I wasn't sure which one I needed so I took a number for the 'information' window. There was a sign on the window that said, 'Now Serving 143.' My ticket was number 327 and it said right on the ticket there would be a 72-minute wait. So I went out and had some lunch and bought a book. When I got back almost an hour later, the 'Now Serving' sign said 145—I had only advanced by two.

"I decided to skip the 'information' window and took a numbered ticket from the 'forms' window dispenser. It was number 79 and the ticket said I would only have a two-minute wait. Three and a half hours later, I was getting near the window. The reason it was so slow was that clerk kept getting interrupted with questions from people who were dropping appointment forms in a box right by his window. I was impressed by the number of different languages he spoke, and he seemed rude in every one of them. Finally, the clerk had called number 75, so a couple others and I moved up close to the window. Then the lighted sign over the window changed from number 75 to 320! They had switched from 'forms' to 'information.' When we protested, the clerk snapped that he had to do what his supervisor told him, and that he would switch back to forms in 40 minutes.

"With that, he called out number 320, but no one showed. After a second call and no answer, he went to 321 and a young woman stepped up to the window. Well, an elderly woman with 320 had been struggling through the crowd and finally made it. In broken English, she tried to explain that she couldn't get to the window in time. The clerk reprimanded the old woman and refused to help her until she had turned around and apologized to woman number 321. He was really on a power trip.

"I was so mad that I went to a pay-phone in the back of the waiting room to call someone in charge. I got put on hold. I was on hold long enough that the window switched back to dispensing forms. So I hung up and got back in line. When I got to the counter, the clerk said 'Well now, that wasn't so bad, was it?' I had waited a total of five hours. All that time, I could see the forms on the shelf behind the clerk. Why did I have to go through that? He wouldn't even give me two copies of the form in case Tami made a mistake. To get another copy, I would have had to come back another day and wait in line again."

Beth's bad experience at the INS office happened less than a year ago, but even then INS recognized they had problems and was doing something about it. Throughout the country, the agency is beginning to put customers first. For example, they have a new easy way to get forms. Customers can dial 1-800-870-3676 and ask for what they need. In a week or so, the forms come in the mail.

But that's not all. INS has designated two offices—one in Detroit and one in El Paso—as "reinvention labs," where the workers can try out their own new ideas to improve customer service in ways that all INS offices will be using soon. And elsewhere throughout the country, INS's new attitude is catching on. Seven districts are undergoing intensive customer relations training and are running a series of customer focus groups. Incidentally, that same El Paso office recently processed more than 14,000 applications for citizenship within a two-month period; over 10,000 aspirants became new citizens in the El Paso District alone between July 3 and August 30, 1996!

Beth Childs' experience with INS wasn't what left her "dazed and confused, completely disoriented by what had just happened." It was a more recent and more unusual encounter with government that dazed Beth—this one on February 22, 1996. Beth Childs gave her daughter an extra hug as she left for school that day. This time Beth was ready for the long, unpleasant journey ahead. She had made all the plans others make when they go out of town on business for an indefinite stay. Her best friend had agreed to pick up Sydney after school. Not knowing when she would return, Beth wore comfortable, casual clothes and packed her cross-stitching.

To prepare herself psychologically, she closed her eyes and tried to concentrate. She lowered her expectations. She did not expect things to run smoothly or efficiently. Prepared for the humiliation and frustration she had experienced before, Beth drove away to face the government again—this time, the Social Security Administration.

When Beth entered the Social Security office on Fulton Avenue in Sacramento that day, she was shocked. She expected an office filled with long lines of people with screaming children. She wondered if she had gone to the wrong building. The place was quiet. The clerks were smiling. As Beth remembers it, "A strange vortex opened up at the Social Security office and bureaucracy was suspended. I was in shock. I was totally blown away by the service I received. Everybody was just so nice. They almost offered to carry my bags. I felt like they were fanning me with feathers while I filled out this form." Beth was so moved by her experience that she wrote the following letter:

Sir/Madam:

I had cause to visit your office on February 22, 1996.... I was greeted by an efficient, friendly, helpful staff in a timely manner and was able to complete my business in one visit. I then stumbled from the office dazed and confused, completely disoriented by what had just happened. I wandered the parking lot for a while before regaining my composure and returning home to relay my experience to family and friends. They were spellbound. Thank you for giving us all a new perspective of government agencies and their employees.

Beth is not the only one who has a new perspective on government. Something similar happened when Beth's twin sister, Tami, brought newly adopted Amy home to the United States this past July. "We got into Logan Airport in Boston at 5:30 in the evening," Tami explains. "Amy was still on European time—almost midnight— so she was a bit cranky. When we got to the Immigration counter, we showed the

25

man Amy's Russian passport and her application for citizenship—you know, to get her green card. He told us that the photo on her application was too small. I thought, 'oh boy, here we go.' But he was so upbeat and friendly. He had a camera in his office, he took Amy's picture, and gave us the right size. Then he noticed that our address on the application was a post office box—we'd been living overseas. He said we'd need a street address to get Amy's green card in the mail. I couldn't remember my parents' ZIP code in Maine, so he asked me their phone number, picked up his phone, and called them. He let me chat a minute to let them know we were safe and sound, got the ZIP code, and sent us merrily on our way. As we left, he called out: 'Your tax dollars at work.'"

They certainly are your dollars, and that certainly is how government should work. Thanks to strong leadership from President Clinton and the hard work of federal employees who have been wanting a chance to do this all along, government is beginning to serve the people better.

President Clinton's Marching Orders

In 1993, President Clinton gave the executive order, and he gave it loud and clear: Every agency that deals with the public should deliver service equal to the best in business. That goal is easy to understand. Government telephone representatives should be as fast and courteous as those at leading mail-order companies. Front-line federal employees should be as eager, able, and happy to serve as the folks at Wal-Mart. The government should serve the people the way America's best companies serve their customers.

America's best companies did not get that good overnight, and neither will the government. But we are making progress, and we are measuring our progress the same way top companies do. Their #1 rule in customer service is that you're not making the grade unless the customers say you are. According to letters from some of our customers, we are headed in the right direction:

This is from a recently retired businessman in Mesquite, Texas.— *"Years of less than ideal contact with a host of government agencies had made a 'civil service basher' of me—not particularly kind on my part, but based on experience. And so, on April 8, 1996, I visited the Dallas-Lake June Social Security Office with some trepidation. The waiting room was crowded but I waited only 12 minutes. It's hard to describe what a pleasure that encounter was. Throw out the stereotype of the Civil Service employee. These people were so friendly and helpful that you would have expected that they would be asking favors of us, not the other way around. I can only say that I would hate to be going head to head against you in business. You would win in a walk."* [1]

And this is from a lawyer whose client had some unpaid taxes and a delinquent return.— *"With a few telephone calls (no unending busy signals or being put on indefinite hold) to the Baltimore IRS office, I was able to have an installment agreement put*

26

PRESIDENT CLINTON'S EXECUTIVE ORDER 12862
"Setting Customer Service Standards"

Embark upon a revolution within the Federal Government.

- Identify customers who are, or should be, served by the agency.

- Survey customers to determine the kind and quality of services they want and their level of satisfaction with existing services.

- Post service standards and measure results against them.

- Benchmark customer service standards against the best in business.

- Survey front-line employees on barriers to, and ideas for, matching the best in business.

- Provide customers with choices in both the sources of service and the means of delivery.

- Make information, services, and complaint systems easily accessible.

- Provide means to address customer complaints.

The standard of quality shall be equal to the best in business.

Bill Clinton

in place, the levy released by telecopier, and my client's life able to go on. In 24 years of private practice, I can't recall an easier resolution of what I had anticipated to be a procedural nightmare."

From a San Diego resident who works in Mexico and used to spend hours waiting in line to come home.—*"What a relief it has been, not to worry about long border lines.... I'm not sure how to quantify anxiety, stress, and frustration levels, but the dedicated commuter lanes have minimized these levels significantly. Who knows, maybe I will live longer."* [2] Another frequent border crosser notes, *"I don't get the stomach aches that I used to."* [3]

From an energy analyst who uses Department of Energy technical information. *"I would like to thank you especially for the world-class customer service you have given me over the last few years. Employees at Federal Express, Nordstrom's, and Land's End have nothing on you in terms of helpfulness, thoroughness, and responsiveness. As far as I'm concerned, you set the highest standard for excellence."* [4]

From a Montana sheriff who had to deal with a derailed train with tank cars leaking deadly chlorine gas; he had to know which way and when the wind would blow.—*"Brenda and [the National Weather Service] staff were there for us, in the field, at all hours, and under all conditions. [Their involvement] goes a long way toward dispelling the stereotype of bespectacled scientists in a windowless room grouped around gauges and radar screens (or a crystal ball)."* [5]

From an inventor in Massachusetts.—*"Joe Cheng [an examiner at the U.S. Patent and Trademark Office] went out of his way to clarify the specifics of patent law. It is people like Mr. Cheng who make it possible for small, independent inventors like myself to survive...."*

From a Detroit police officer who worked security along with the U.S. Secret Service when some international bigwigs visited Motown (movies and TV shows often portray how pleased the local cops are to see the feds show up).—*"In the past, when local and federal agents came together, it would seem like the clash of the titans, but not in this case. It's really hard to put into words, how wonderful and refreshing it was, everyone working together with one common goal ... [and] no finger pointing. Your people are the world's greatest."* [6]

This is part of a letter from a World War II veteran who had gone to a Veterans Affairs clinic four years ago and *"was extremely disappointed by the lack of courtesy and coordination within the clinic."* Recently, he went again. *"What a pleasant surprise! I was impressed by the cleanliness and organization. The clerks were very polite and helpful. Congratulations on a job well done. As my daughter says, we deserve it."* [7]

We agree, you do deserve it—all Americans deserve much better service from government agencies. But it does not come easy. Just listen to what has been going on behind the scenes to make the customers notice a difference.

Who Is the Customer?

We had to start with the basics. Some agencies had never thought in terms of customers before, so the National Performance Review conducted workshops for agencies to figure out who their customers were. In private business it's easy—the customer is the person with the money, the person who might go to your competitor. But most agencies have no competition, and they saw Congress as their source of money. We even had complaints from taxpayers saying they were the government's owners, not its customers. They are right about being the owners, but they are customers, too, like a Ford Motor Company stockholder who buys a Ford.

For some agencies, it was easy to find the customer. The Social Security Administration serves beneficiaries. Veterans Affairs serves vets and their families. But what about agencies that don't usually serve the public directly?

The Department of Education exists to help those trying to learn, their ultimate customer. Yet the Department doesn't directly operate schools or other learning programs. To get its job done, the Department has to work well with educating organizations, getting them what they need to do their jobs. It's a three party deal—feds, educators, learners—and thinking about that may produce new answers. For example, the Department wants to reach kids with a literacy program. Libraries are looking for new services to attract the public. Kids like pizza. The result is Read*Write*Now, which reached a million kids this past summer.

In the first weeks of summer, Read*Write*Now kits went from the Department to 16,500 libraries. The libraries signed up kids and learning partners—family, teens, seniors, or neighbors. Kids agree to read and write for 30 minutes each day, learn a vocabulary word a day, and meet with the learning partner for help once or twice per week. When the kids finish the challenge, they get a coupon for a personal pan pizza from Pizza Hut, who is a partner in the whole thing.

A different kind of customer relationship exists for regulators—if someone wants to comply with the regulations, treat them right, find out what they want, and give them all the help you can because that will increase the compliance. That's why Richard Hansen, who chairs a transportation committee of Illinois school officials wrote to the Wage and Hour Division of the Department of Labor about Zorka Martinovich and her investigation of an employee complaint. He described her as someone to "work with" rather than someone they have to "deal with." That's why OSHA compliance officers work with S.D. Warren employees who are looking for safety hazards. It's why EPA sits down with Intel to tailor an air permit. And it's why, in public reports, FDA, in an ongoing pilot program, includes company fixes for problems found in FDA inspections. Throughout government, regulators are adding customer-friendly ideas because they get better results than they got with badges and fines. It's a key tool in building partnerships to reach regulatory goals.

When we thought it through, we found that the idea of customers actually worked for all agencies, at least for part of what they do. It's even true for the law-enforcement agencies. The Justice Department is not planning to put mints on pillows in prisons, but they are thinking "customers" when answering requests from other law-enforcement organizations for criminal histories and fingerprints checks. And customer approaches certainly apply to treatment of victims and witnesses.

Ask Customers What They Want

The next step was for agencies to ask the customers what they wanted. Just asking turned out to be harder than one might imagine. In 1980, Congress passed the Paperwork Reduction Act to protect people from having to fill out too many forms.[8] Diligently, the Office of Management and Budget then wrote detailed regulations with stringent requirements that agencies had to satisfy before mailing out any new forms—for example, surveys to find out what their customers wanted. But when the President ordered a new customer service focus, OMB responded and reengineered their system, and now agencies can survey their customers more quickly and easily.

Once agencies began surveying customers, they got some surprises. For example, the Internal Revenue Service had assumed that what people wanted most was to get their tax booklet in the mail as soon as possible after New Year's Eve. But what the customers said they wanted most was little or no contact with the IRS. The Department of Veterans Affairs assumed that vets welcomed long delays in the waiting room so they could swap war stories; their customers told them, "Wrong." (The VA Regional Benefits Office in New York now serves customers so fast that they do not need a waiting room anymore. In fact, they are turning it into a museum of VA memorabilia.) The Federal Emergency Management Agency assumed that disaster victims wanted help to arrive much faster. They were partly right, but the victims FEMA surveyed also said that they wanted someone to take a little time, listen to their worries, and reassure them.

Most people had never even heard of the Pension Benefit Guaranty Corporation or what it does. So PBGC went back to the basics and ran focus groups with customers. When PBGC took over the pension plan from the defunct Cooperweld Steel Company, Rosemary Thomas of PBGC held a town-hall-style meeting. She started by telling 200 worried steelworkers that the agency insured their under-funded pension plan, and that their checks were safe, and how soon the checks would start. That calmed things down right away.

If we've learned anything from reinventing government, it is that the way to get things right is to start by asking customers. By the way, customers like being asked. It was a new experience coming from the government.

Setting Standards

Once customers have said what they want, it is good business to tell them what to expect, the way FedEx promises they will deliver a package by 10:30 the next morning, or Disney World has signs posted along the line for Space Mountain saying how much longer visitors have to wait. Setting customer standards is powerful. They focus on the things that are most important to customers. They also—and this is critical—tell federal employees where to focus. Federal employees need to know what their goal is too. For so long the goal has been not to make mistakes, mistakes as defined by rulebooks too thick to lift. Now the goal is built on the golden rule of customer service, treating people the way you want to be treated.

STANDARDS THAT TOUCH MILLIONS

- **Internal Revenue Service:** tax refunds on complete and accurate paper returns are due in 40 days; 21 days for electronic returns.

- **Social Security Administration:** new and replacement cards mailed within five days; they'll tell customers the Social Security number in one day if it's urgent.

- **Coast Guard:** search and rescue on demand, 24 hours a day, seven days a week.

- **Environmental Protection Agency:** in voluntary programs, publicly recognize the achievements of business partners.

- **Occupational Safety and Health Administration:** inspectors will be respectful and helpful, and focus on the most serious hazards.

- **U.S. Mint:** orders taken 24 hours a day, seven days per week.

- **National Park Service:** Great Smoky Mountains visitor center open every day but Christmas.

- **Bureau of Labor Statistics:** data any way customers want it: from a live person, or by recorded message, fax, microfiche, diskette, tape, Internet, or TDD.

Making firm promises was new territory for government agencies that were used to hedging. At first, only three agencies—the U.S. Postal Service, the IRS, and the Social Security Administration—were willing to stick their necks out and say how fast or courteous they would be. The next year, after the President's order and more workshops, 150 agencies took the plunge. Now, 214 agencies have published more than 3,000 specific customer service promises. President Clinton and Vice President Gore compiled a book of them, organized it according to type of customer—not agency—and put it on the World Wide Web for all to see.[9]

31

Making promises is risky, but it does force improvement. The U.S. Postal Service promised that local first-class mail would be delivered overnight.[10] They did not make it in key cities. Only 50 percent of the mail was being delivered overnight in New York and Washington; in Chicago, mail burned under bridges. The news media covered it all. But since 1993, on-time delivery in Washington, New York, and Chicago has improved steadily to better than 85 percent by last spring. The national average was up to 90 percent last spring for the first time.[11]

The Convenience of the Customer

After they asked customers what they wanted and set standards, many agencies had to do things differently so they could deliver what they promised. The customer service program is huge. It's customer service teams and customer service representatives and front-line employees in all federal agencies knowing they can truly make a difference and pounding away at the old ways of doing things. It's agency heads sitting down with their customers all over the country to find out what they think. It's federal employees and private sector partners benchmarking best practices in 1-800 service, complaint systems, and more, looking for ideas to improve government's service. It's the President's Management Council aligning planning, budgeting, and operating systems to make sure customer service is mainstream.[12] And we're starting to see results. Enough so that we know that in time we can turn the whole government around.

Here's an example: The Federal Emergency Management Agency had been a national disaster all by itself. Congress was seriously considering scuttling the agency because, when emergencies struck, FEMA was not much help to anyone. Part of the problem was the way FEMA was organized—it had divisions for man-made disasters like riots or nuclear war, and divisions for natural disasters like floods or earthquakes. Each division had people and equipment that could not be used for another division's disaster. FEMA Director James Lee Witt stopped that, reorganizing FEMA into an "all-hazards" team. Other agencies also had to change the way they were organized once they started to concentrate on their customers' needs instead of their own.

In some cases, agencies have organized for the convenience of the customer by banding together. They developed one-stop shops, where the idea is for the government to get together so the customers no longer have to wander around. For example, Houston, Boston, Kansas City, and Atlanta now have a "U.S. General Store" offering almost any service from the federal government in one place, with state and local governments there, too. SBA is there for loans and advice. The IRS is there for help with tax questions. The agencies that don't have people in the stores have set up hot-lines to answer questions right away. This way, for example, EPA advice is easy to get. One-stop.

"Trading Post" meant one-stop for everything on the American frontier. Now the Bureau of Land Management and the Forest Service, who often manage adjoining lands, are teaming up in new Trading Posts. Customers told the agencies it didn't make much sense for people to make two stops for maps, fishing information, woodcutting fees, and guide permits. So the agencies are moving in together. In Canon City, Colorado, they got the Colorado Division of Wildlife to join them, giving outdoor enthusiasts a better deal still.

And to gather firewood in Oregon, citizens can stop by the local convenience store, where they buy milk and bread, to buy a permit for federal wood, whether it grows in an Agriculture Department National Forest or a Bureau of Land Management area. We figured it out so the taxpayer doesn't have to.

There is no doubt that one-stop works for customers. Maybe that is how government services should have been put together in the first place.

Phones

Workers need good equipment to give good service. Let's stick with FEMA as the example: FEMA's main equipment used to be tents and tons of paper. After a flood, FEMA would set up a tent on dry ground and all the victims would have to go there to fill out forms. FEMA inspectors would stop by the tent, pick up a batch of forms, slog out to the damaged houses to check them out, then slog back to the tent to exchange those forms for the next batch. To give better service, they needed better tools, and they got them. Now, flood victims can call a toll-free number to apply for aid, and inspectors have hand-held computers with modems that receive claims and transmit their evaluations without any slogging. Many other agencies needed and got modern equipment to give better service, too.

Telephones are a top priority in customer service all across the government because more Americans contact the government by phone than any other way. The attention is producing better service.

Last year the people at the Social Security Administration were judged the best in the business at handling calls. An independent survey by Dalbar, Inc. picked SSA as the best toll-free telephone service, compared to several top private sector firms. SSA beat Xerox, Southwest Airlines, L.L. Bean, and Disney.[13] But SSA wasn't satisfied— it took too long to reach an operator. The service was world-class, but the access was not. This year, Social Security transferred staff to the call centers, converted data centers to handle calls, put in technology so that all claims representatives could handle overflow calls on the busiest days, and installed a 24-hour automated system for frequently asked questions. Now, less than half as many callers get busy signals, and 90 percent of all calls go through in less than five minutes.

FEMA and Social Security are not the only ones who see phones as the key to better service:

- The Food Safety and Inspection Service has a 24-hour, seven-day-a-week, toll-free number with safety tips and information on recalls of meat and poultry.
- The Food and Drug Administration has a 24-hour phone line and a World Wide Web site with information on food, drugs, and cosmetics.
- Starting in November, travelers worried that a new passport will not arrive before their flight leaves can dial the Passport Services' new 1-900 number and find out the status of their application.
- The Consumer Product Safety Commission's toll-free hotline runs around the clock. Callers can report hazards or hear about recent product recalls. For auto safety information, the Commission will transfer callers to the National Highway Traffic Safety Administration's hotline.
- The Immigration and Naturalization Service now has a toll-free number for forms (so no one has to suffer what Beth Childs did). They also have a gizmo that employers can attach to their phones to call the INS computer and verify the legal status of job hunters.
- IRS is always on the phone. The TeleTax system is available to provide recorded information to all taxpayers. And this year, three million taxpayers called in and filed their returns by touch-tone phone using a pilot program called TeleFile. TeleFile checked their math and sent their refunds to them within three weeks.

That Number, Please

Auto Safety Information 1-800-424-9393

Consumer Product Recall Notices 1-800-638-CPSC

Export Assistance For Business 1-800-USA-TRADE

Immigration and Naturalization Forms 1-800-755-0777

Meat and Poultry Safety Tips 1-800-535-4555

Social Security Information 1-800-772-1213

Taxes, Recorded Information 1-800-TAX-4477

Number, Please

With the government providing more and more services over the phone, what is the phone number? Try 411—information. Ask the operator about a government service, like getting a passport. The information operators hate calls like these because, like the rest of us, all they have to work with are the government listings in the phone book. The low-tech puzzle that must be solved before reaching the high-tech government is the "blue pages."

The blue pages are not like the yellow pages. Yellow pages list things and services. Blue pages list names of organizations. The information operator would have to know that the question about passports would be answered by the State Department (listed under "S").

We are fixing the blue pages. The General Services Administration handles phone services for the government, but each agency creates its own listings in each phone book around the country, so changing the blue pages is a big coordination job. Nonetheless, as a start, GSA and the agencies have promised to have new blue pages in at least five cities reaching 11 million people this fall.[14] Soon, callers wanting a passport will look under "P" for passport.

Computers

Some technologies have just been waiting to be discovered by the government. The corner ATM machines and supermarket checkout stands used by most Americans already hold the technology needed for a national Electronic Benefits Transfer system. This grand reinvention plan, announced in 1994, will deliver food stamps, social security, veteran, and local assistance payments using a single debit card for each beneficiary. By 1999, about 25 million Americans will be using the card to get benefits totaling $110 billion per year, instead of getting checks or food stamps.

All states are planning Electronic Benefit Transfer systems. Thirteen are already delivering some benefits this way, with about 3.5 million citizens using the card. Checks are no longer mailed or carried around so there is less chance of theft. Electronic records make it easier to spot fraud. When the program is completely up and running, it will save about $230 million per year in administrative costs.[15]

Since April of 1996, a service to order your personal benefits estimate from the Social Security Administration, called PEBES, has been available via the information superhighway to the World Wide Web site.[16] The statement of expected retirement and other benefits has been around for years, but you had to get the paper form, fill it out, and mail it in. This all happens now from your computer screen in about five minutes.

The Web site provides a place for people to offer comments. Reactions are overwhelmingly positive, about how it is easy to use and convenient. For example,

Ralph Sabelhaus said he meant to get the form for months and never got around to it. But the best compliment comes from Reggie Lewis, who visited the Web site and left this message, "This is too easy—is this a trick or something?"

The World Wide Web and technology are not for everyone—not yet. However, for more and more Americans technology plays a central role in their lives. It brings them new options, like how to pay for groceries. It brings convenience, like making a call from the car. It gives them control over their own lives, like booking travel reservations from their computer on their desk at midnight. In a world where so much is out of our personal control, anything that lets us drive is welcome. In addition, many visitors to the government's new Web pages talk about the feeling of once again being in touch with their government.

Inside government, the technology lets us get and share information more quickly. We can push it out to the front lines, where change is encountered first and customers want decisions now. We can collect information overnight from everywhere and get it to managers so they can react to changing needs. Technology lets us think of brand new ways to do things, one-stop ways, paperless ways, in flatter organizations, with lots of people working on the same thing at the same time, what computer techno-weenies call massive parallel processing. In short, technology is the great enabler for reinventing government.

But, but, but our idea is not to force people to use technology. Our customers are being given choices. They can come in, call up, fax an order, or go by Internet. They can get a tax check by mail or direct deposit. Often the technology will be invisible, behind the wizard's curtain helping the government employee who serves them.

When government's customers choose technology options, the burden on other services that depend directly on face-to-face, or voice-to-voice contact goes down. That means better service for those still choosing the old routes. For those choosing new routes service should be better too. The technology solutions are going to be faster, with fewer steps in front of and behind the curtain, and they are going to be cheaper. And cheaper is the critical word if we are to improve customer service in a balanced budget world.

Social Security's PEBES project is not a lone government success on the Internet. At the Department of Agriculture, they put the first ever standardized data base for plant species on-line. A niche product? Not exactly. There are 200,000 requests per month at the Web site, which was built by the Natural Resources Conservation Service for users that include scientists, teachers, and other state and federal government agencies.

The most used home page in government, and maybe anywhere, belongs to the IRS. It looks and reads more like small town newspaper than a part of government. It answers frequently asked questions, goes over 148 tax topics, and explains recent regulations, trying to be as easy to understand as possible. It also provides access to IRS forms, publications, and instructions. From January to June 1996, there have been 60 million electronic accesses on the home page. Just on April 15, taxpayers downloaded 104,000 files. The next day there was a run on the forms for late filing.

Students and teachers have been enjoying "Ask-a-Geologist," the U.S. Geological Survey's new Internet service.[17] Sorry, kids, they'll answer questions but they won't write your reports.

Existing technologies are getting new uses all over government. John Conroy is a realtor in Naples, Florida, and back in May he had a little problem. He needed 75 years worth of Consumer Price Index data to calculate the value of a property he was working on. It was late in the afternoon, but being an optimist, John called the fax-on-demand hotline at the Bureau of Labor Statistics.[18] Zap, he got a catalogue, called in an order, was surprised to find that he didn't seem to be bothering the people at the Bureau, and got his data by 10:37 the next morning. "Refreshing change," says John.

Some agencies are writing neat software packages and giving them to customers. HUD has an amazing little package that draws a city map and, block by block, shows where in the city all the HUD grant moneys are being spent.[19] Among other things, cities and interest groups use the software to play "what if" with alternative plans to use the money.

The Bond Wizard responds to requests from holders of U.S. Savings Bonds for a simple way to calculate the redemption value of their bonds. The Wizard is from the Bureau of the Public Debt and is available as a diskette or on-line to Internet users.[20]

For over a decade VA has been taking shots for using outdated technology in medical care for vets. But in Milwaukee, VA is setting medical standards for a remote diagnosis technique that is a breakthrough in the field of telemedicine. With this technique, expert pathologists in Milwaukee use a high-speed data link and microscope robotics to assist doctors diagnosing patients 218 miles away in Iron Mountain, Michigan. The technology gives results as good as those the pathologists get in Milwaukee. The obvious payoff is better care for vets through wider access to experts. At the same time, VA keeps the lid on physician costs by making better use of specialists.

Just A Little Common Sense

So much of what is happening to improve customer service comes from simply giving federal employees the goal of serving customers and the freedom to do it. Often their ideas are low-cost or money-saving testimonials to the return of common sense.

One morning, Hugh Doran, Director of the VA Medical Center in Kansas City, walked to his office from his reserved parking space just outside the clinic entrance. His parking space was in a lot also used by physicians and other health care providers. That morning, Director Doran decided to charge a diverse group of employees, patients, and service officers with evaluating the overall parking situation. The group recommended converting the existing reserved lot to patient parking. Now, Doran parks with all his employees and walks through the new patient parking lot next to the building.

A few months later, Doran and his team were discussing the need for space to accommodate primary care patients. They realized that the most convenient place for primary care was on the first floor, and Doran decided to move the director's and administrative offices out of their prime first-floor space. Very soon, they were relocated to the fifth floor, and the first floor was converted to primary care facilities. Today that area is dedicated to serving over 3,500 veterans.

Moving administration around to make life better for veterans is a trend at VA. They did it in Lebanon, Pennsylvania, and Wichita, Kansas. In Boston, Pittsburgh, Philadelphia, and Biloxi, they moved to make first-floor space available for easy-to-reach facilities devoted to women's needs.

Common sense changes save some money, too. Gail Mirsky works with victims and witnesses at the Justice Department. She noticed that witnesses and victims who needed to travel for the Justice Department had to book their own travel. After their trips, they sent in travel vouchers and waited to be paid. Gail figured that, instead, the government could set up an account with a travel agent, where travel could be booked at the government's volume discount and paid directly, so witnesses could avoid being out of pocket for expenses. This works like a charm and also saved the government about $150,000 in the first 15 months.

Forest Service employees are also putting their money-making, common-sense ideas to work. Did you ever wonder what happens to all those big trees cut each year from city streets and parks? Most end up in landfills or, at best, in a compost pile or firewood stack. In New Jersey, the Forest Service showed a couple of towns how to cut the trees for sawmill use, resulting in new wood products, jobs, and income for the cities.

Training

Finally, there is training for all the front-line workers who actually see and talk to customers. All the clerks waiting at the counters. All the operators poised for your call. And training for the managers, too. They have to learn what the best companies in business know—that employee satisfaction is the key to customer satisfaction. Some of the nation's top experts in customer service have volunteered their time to teach at a couple dozen customer service workshops for federal workers.

A new organization, formed by cutting and combining three old agencies in the U.S. Department of Agriculture, hadn't settled on a name for their new operation, but they had figured out that they existed to serve customers, the farmers, and rural communities. So their first goal was to train everyone—all 12,000 employees—on customer service. This, they said, was the only sensible thing to do. For them, the National Performance Review's customer service program was not just another program. For them, it is *the* program.

They have a name now. It's "USDA Rural Development." The first round of training is done, and if you talk to the employees, they'll tell you it made a big difference. They learned things that let them understand what customers are going through, and they know they are doing a better job. The nice fan mail they are getting says they are right.

The trick was to pull together all the new awareness of who the customer is and what the customer wants, all the capability of the new organization and the new equipment, and all the common sense and caring that federal workers bring to their jobs. The reorganized FEMA, for example, has done exactly that. With the new toll-free phone service and their inspectors using hand-held computers, FEMA's "all-hazards" teams can move a lot faster, get plenty of resources on the job quickly, and cover more territory in less time. But they had to be trained to spend some of that extra time just listening to people's troubles and reassuring them, like the customers said they wanted.

It's a big job to get an entire government turned around from focusing on red tape to focusing on results that customers want. The Clinton-Gore Administration is leading the way, and we think we're getting there. But the only opinion that really counts is the customer's:

Dear FEMA,

The morning of August 9th [1995] completely changed our lives. Vermilion, Ohio, had five inches of rain in under one hour. Our basement began to fill with water and when the pumps failed we knew we were in for some problems. The basement windows burst in with incredible force and within an hour and a half we had eight feet of water in the basement and five feet on our first floor. We were completely helpless, and had just enough time to rush our two small children to safety. We lost nearly everything we owned. I cannot begin to explain the feeling of watching the water come up in the doors and windows. Frantically we tried to move things but the water just came in too fast. It was truly terrifying and so incredibly sad that everything we worked so hard for was now five feet under water. It is a feeling that will never ever leave me. We were at that moment without a place to live, no clothes other that what we had on, and a realization that we had no flood insurance (we were not in a flood plain area). It was very devastating.

Then the Red Cross and FEMA arrived. I must tell you that the people working for you are some of the nicest, most caring individuals we have ever met. They were so willing to do anything in their power to help. They were so wonderful, each and every one of them. They treated each person that walked through the door as if they were their own family.... They were so unbelievably organized, whatever they said they would do—it was done. They had answers and got right back with us. They were always right on time and were so helpful.

Thanks to you, and only you, we were able to get back on our feet. Our children were truly traumatized by the flood and you enabled us to get things back to normal, and get into a home again. We owe you and the President more thanks than we can ever express. If I had the chance to tell the President one thing it would be that FEMA is the answer to prayers.

In closing there is nothing I could say as to how FEMA could work better to help its customers...

Sincerely,

David and Kelly Bodde, Jordan and David[21]

BLANK PAGE

SECRET THREE:
GOVERNMENT IS IN PARTNERSHIP
WITH BUSINESS

All Regulators Will:

☑ Cut obsolete regulations

☑ Reward results, not red tape

☑ Get out of Washington—create grass
roots partnerships

☑ Negotiate, don't dictate

Bill Clinton   Al Gore

February 22, 1995

The relationship goes way back. In the early 1800s, the U.S. government drew on the resources of Saint Simons Island off the southern coast of Georgia—its tough live oaks made the sides of the frigate USS Constitution withstand cannonballs like iron. Almost a hundred and fifty years after Saint Simons made "Old Ironsides" famous, a group of island entrepreneurs turned the tables and drew on the resources of the U.S. military—they leased large freezers from the local Navy base that was closing and became SeaPak, the nation's first commercial producer of breaded shrimp. Today, half the nation's retail frozen breaded shrimp, millions of pounds of breaded fish filets, onion rings, French toast sticks and cheese sticks come from Rich-SeaPak, whose corporate offices are still on Saint Simons Island.[1] The long relationship with the government has had its ups and downs.

"The seafood industry traditionally had very adversarial dealings with the FDA" (Food and Drug Administration), says Ray Jones, SeaPak's corporate director of quality assurance and regulatory affairs. "In the early days, it was all small, independent producers—basically fishermen—who didn't want anything to do with the government. It was a matter of getting away with whatever you could. So when bigger companies like SeaPak started to be formed, the residue of that adversarial relationship was still around.

"When I came here nine years ago, our lawyers were telling us, 'Don't talk to them, don't give them anything.' We could do that legally. The law says that we have to let FDA come into the plant and go anywhere they want. But, we don't have to give them our production records or consumer complaints or let them take pictures. So we didn't.

"One of the things the food industry has always feared is giving FDA access to customer complaints. Most customers give us good, legitimate feedback on what they think about our product, but there are some complaints that we get that may not be legitimate—such as where a customer alleges they found something in a package of shrimp or fish. We were afraid that FDA might misinterpret or overre-act to the complaints, so we chose not to let FDA see them. They would come in, ask for the customer complaint file or some other records, we'd refuse, and things would go downhill from there.

"The thing FDA did that hurt us the most was taking samples of our product. They would take the samples and send them off for analysis. Sometimes it could take weeks to get the results back. We were not required to hold the product off the market until the testing was finished, but we almost always did. So sometimes we might have to hold two or three days production until we got the results back. Even if we were sure the product was in compliance, we did not want to risk the possibility that FDA might find a problem and then we would have to recall the product if we had already shipped it. So we would hold the product and wait.

"Keep in mind that, all this time, SeaPak was running a clean operation. We're very careful about the wholesomeness of our product. Not just when the FDA shows up, but all the time. The only thing that was coming between us and them was a bad attitude. Ours, at least as much as theirs.

"In 1992, I sat down with our CEO, Frank Holas, and looked at our latest inspec-tion report. We agreed it was ridiculous. We had set high standards of quality for ourselves—that's what our customers demanded. We exceeded the regulatory requirements as we understood them. So why were we always at odds with the FDA? We were as ethical or more ethical than anybody else we knew in the business. FDA should have had us up on a pedestal as an example. But it was the pits.

"At any rate, we got tired of the old adversarial relationship at just about the same time Clinton and Gore started pushing the agencies to try partnership. It all worked together in parallel. We called the FDA and said we'd like to talk. So we went up to Atlanta (FDA's regional office) and all the players were there—including our local inspector from Savannah. We asked them what we had to do to change things. They said, 'How about knocking off all these refusals when we ask for files and records.' We said we would if they would work with us to solve any minor violations they might find. We wouldn't expect them to ignore real safety issues—we didn't think we had any of those anyway—but we didn't want them to punish us for minor paperwork problems we could quickly fix, or force us to recall a product due to an obviously phony customer complaint."

42

"Well, no more than 30 days after we got back from Atlanta, they came to inspect us. I guess they wondered if we were for real. We let them see everything they asked to see. Our lawyer almost had a heart attack. The key to this whole approach is one-to-one relationships. I told their inspector 'Look, my job is on the line here. We got to have trust on both sides.' We came out of that with the best inspection report we ever had. And they've been back three times to inspect us since and it keeps getting better."

All the time SeaPak was changing its combative attitude, FDA was changing, too. FDA's field investigators traditionally have been rewarded for detecting violations and levying fines. But FDA has begun to emphasize public safety over disciplinary action. This reorientation encourages more open communication between FDA and industry. For example, FDA recently inspected a food-canning operation and found a malfunction in the sealing equipment, a serious problem that could have led to a botulism outbreak. Instead of launching a lengthy, formal enforcement action, FDA inspectors quickly recommended to the cannery owners that they destroy all cans in the lot and repair the sealing equipment. They agreed and the problem was resolved immediately. This on-the-spot teamwork saved the agency and the company thousands of dollars and immediately protected consumers from dangerous products. That's the way of the future for FDA.

What does Ray Jones at SeaPak see in the future? One word: "HACCP." Ray's not clearing a fish bone. He's talking about the Administration's new scientific way to insure the safety of our food.

"It means 'Hazard Analysis Critical Control Point,' and basically, it's the same method the Japanese used to beat the pants off our auto industry in the seventies and eighties. You build in quality all along the line—don't wait 'til the end and just spot check the product. It's a much better way to ensure food safety. In simple terms for the seafood industry, it means making sure cooked fish stays hot enough long enough that no germs could possibly still be alive—and for raw fish, that it stays cold enough until you're ready to cook it, so that no germs can grow. The FDA will be looking at our production control records to make sure we get things hot enough, or keep things cold enough. They'll check the product randomly to verify the other checks. But the quality's built in. We think it's great. In fact, I'm training to become a certified HACCP instructor so I can teach our suppliers and even our competitors the new techniques."

Ray explains why SeaPak welcomes a new regulation that gives FDA access to production records. "We think it will improve the consumer's confidence in seafood. Seafood's taken a bad rap because of things like raw oysters. But shrimp and breaded fish filets are the safest foods you'll ever eat. This new scientific inspection will boost confidence. Five years ago, we would have been worried about letting more government in the door. But we're not afraid of that anymore. We trust each other. We have the same goal—top quality food for our customers. We're partners."

Forming Partnerships

Can federal regulators really be partners with industry? We are not naive. We know that not everyone is going to play by the rules. There will still be bad actors who will not comply. For them, we reserve every penalty and sanction that the law allows. And because regulatory time and effort is no longer being wasted on the good guys, agencies can better focus their attention on the few cheaters.

But experience shows that the vast majority do play by the rules—if they can figure them out, that is. In dealing with that majority who want to do the right thing, partnership can achieve very good results. If we agree on the goals, allow room for innovation, and help each other all we can, that will increase compliance.

With that in mind, we called together all of the top regulators in Washington for repeated meetings to reach consensus on a new approach—a way to make the rules make sense, a way that works better and costs less.

The Environment

The Environmental Protection Agency (EPA) used to focus on cleaning up pollution. Now the idea is to prevent pollution, and to use partnership as a mainstream approach. EPA has found that when they let companies volunteer to cut pollution without the government dictating how they had to do it, thousands of companies jumped at the chance.

Since 1992, EPA has more than tripled membership in its "Partners for the Environment" program, with over 7,100 companies now participating.[2] One of these partnerships was forged by EPA's Regional Administrator in Boston, John DeVillars, with The Gillette Company, which has a good track record of compliance. Under a program DeVillars calls "Star Track," an independent firm audits Gillette's compliance with environmental regulations, and makes the audit reports public. Gillette pays the cost of the audit and gets amnesty to fix non-criminal violations without being fined. EPA makes no other inspections, and Gillette makes no other reports.

In March 1995, President Clinton offered this additional challenge to companies: "If you can meet even higher environmental performance standards, we will provide flexibility and cut red tape so you can find the cheapest, most efficient way to do it." Today, EPA's Project XL—for excellence and leadership—has more than a dozen projects with industries, states, and cities getting underway around the country.

Altogether, EPA's partners removed from circulation an estimated 4 billion pounds of planetary poisons just in the last year.[3] Since the companies did it their way, instead of Washington's way, they saved $360 million in the process. It is such a clear winner that EPA expects to sign up 10,000 new partners in the next four years.[4] (See Figure 4.)

Figure 4: Number of Participants in
EPA Partnership Programs

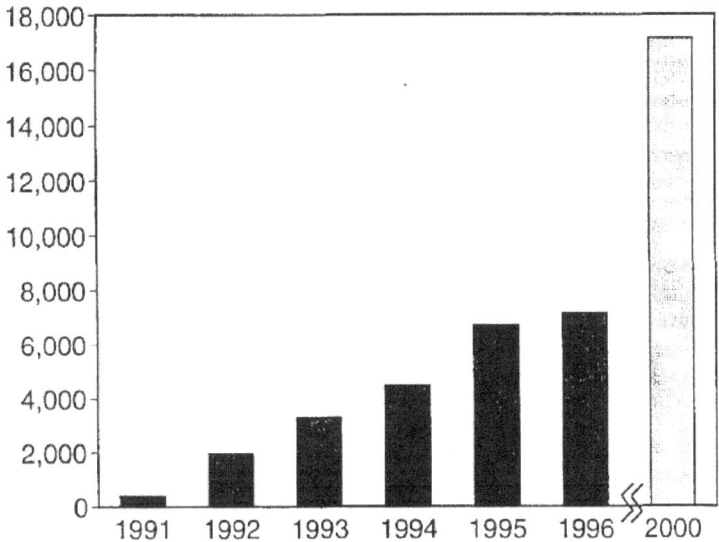

Source: Unpublished data from the Environmental Protection Agency; data for
year 2000 is an estimate.

Medicine

FDA has been cultivating partners in the drug industry, too. Their new goal is to "make safe and effective drugs available" to Americans, whether from the most conventional processes or from the newest biotechnology. FDA will never compromise on safety, but that is not stopping them from cutting out bureaucracy. Scios, Inc., a northern California pharmaceutical manufacturer, recently wrote the agency thanking it for its new approach, in which inspectors work with companies to identify and correct problems, rather than just issue reports of deviations.[5] Citing a recent visit to its facility by an FDA inspector, a company vice president remarked on the frustrating history of industry relations with the agency, noting that, "... since the late 1980s, relations between FDA and its regulated industries have been on a steady and disheartening decline." However, the new approach taken by the FDA inspection team was a refreshing change: "Our goal is to get safe and effective therapies on the market as soon as possible; you've contributed to this effort," the executive states in commenting on the new and welcome change in the FDA.

FDA has been working in partnership with industry researchers to create safe, effective new drugs against cancer and other killers, and to market them fast. For example, they worked with Merck & Co., Inc., to make an important new tool in the fight against HIV/AIDS available faster. Knowing that scientists at Merck were nearing a breakthrough on a new drug to treat HIV/AIDS, the FDA set up advance teams for regulatory review and manufacturing inspection to reduce delays in the approval process. In particular, the Baltimore district office of FDA worked with Merck's Elkton, Virginia, facility to integrate the review process with the construction of the new manufacturing plant and validation of the manufacturing process. As a result, Crixivan, one of a new class of protease inhibitors offering significant new treatment in the fight against HIV/AIDS, was cleared for the market in 42 days, the fastest ever approval of a new drug by the FDA.

Worker Safety

When workers contact the Occupational Safety and Health Administration, they are usually worried about life and limb in the place where they go to make a living every day. The "old" OSHA would send off letters to the employers, some of whom didn't have a clue they had a problem. In the meantime, the worker waited up to a month for action. Not anymore. Now OSHA calls the employer—usually within 24 hours—and works out a plan to fix the hazard. The fax speeds documents back and forth. It's common now for hazards to be resolved in a week rather than a month.

Industry leaders like this "new" OSHA. The new OSHA emphasizes increased partnership with companies, and it's paying off. Joe Dear, Assistant Secretary of Labor for Occupational Safety and Health, set up a team of experts from OSHA's compliance officers, managers, union representatives, and support staff all over the country. He asked them to design a new way to protect American workers. This "design team" created an approach that puts more stock in results than in rulebooks, and they're using it in field offices nationwide. The new way includes not only rapid response to worker complaints but also partnership with companies to work on long-range prevention of health and safety hazards.

One partnership is with Horizon Steel Erectors Company. Horizon teamed up with OSHA's Atlanta office, Argonaut Insurance Company, and the Department of Defense. Horizon, building a Defense facility in Florida, said that each worker would use fall protection and that supervisors would enforce this commitment. In the first 90 days, Horizon had a 96-percent reduction in accident costs per work-hour—from $4.26 to 18 cents. In six months, the total cost of workers compensation claims fell from more than $1 million to $13,200.

There's more. Horizon President Ken Sanders told OSHA that three lives were saved in three separate falls because the workers were wearing fall protection gear.

Now Horizon Safety Director John Paulk travels at company expense to tell others about the new OSHA.

Even though we believe the partnership approach has a big payoff, we will never lose sight of the government's basic responsibilities and will never give up the ability to enforce the rules. In the Maine 200 program, OSHA told the 200 most hazardous companies in Maine that, if they would run good safety programs, traditional inspections would be a low priority. Worker safety soared, and OSHA is establishing similar programs nationwide. When one of the Maine 200 companies reneged on its commitment and subjected its employees to extremely unsafe and unsanitary conditions. OSHA stepped in quickly, cited them for dozens of violations, and fined the company $3.6 million.

Pensions

The departments of Labor and Treasury are simplifying the rules and regulations that ensure company pension plans are financially secure. Under the new rules, companies file less paper and do less mind-numbing math. More small businesses will be able to start pension plans covering more workers. And the workers can feel more secure than ever that their money will be there when they reach retirement age.

In August, President Clinton signed legislation to provide better pension coverage and security for workers. The new law expands opportunities to save for retirement. It improves the protection of pensions and removes obstacles facing many workers who want to bring their retirement savings with them when they change jobs. It also simplifies the pension rules to make it easier for small businesses to set up and run pension plans. Ten million workers in small businesses could benefit from the new, simplified 401(k)-type plan—no red tape, just a simple form.

Health Care

The Health Care Financing Administration is shifting from red tape to results so doctors and hospitals can focus more time and attention on their patients. For example, doctors will no longer have to sign an additional form for each patient attesting to the fact that all of the medications and treatments they ordered were proper. That alone eliminates 11 million forms and frees up 200,000 hours of doctor time each year. And instead of holding frequent inspections to make sure procedures are being followed and all the paperwork is in order, HCFA will check to see how the patients are doing. And they will publish the results to help consumers make informed choices. They will inspect laboratories more selectively, focusing on those with past problems, and they will stop wasting money regulating lab tests that are done by machines that rarely make mistakes.

Meat and Poultry

Every year, Americans consume over 43 billion pounds of beef, pork, and poultry—more than 160 pounds per person.[6] Ensuring that meat is safe for American families is an important governmental mission. For most of the last century, federal inspectors have carried out that mission by using the old "poke and sniff" system, in which an overworked cadre of U.S. Department of Agriculture inspectors physically checked 95 percent of all that meat, using their eyes, noses, and hands to try to detect any problems.

In July 1996, President Clinton announced the overhaul of USDA's meat and poultry inspection process. The new system is HACCP, the same scientific methods that are making seafood safe. The government sets the goals, but gives each company the flexibility to design a plan to meet them. It replaces a reliance on outdated procedures with new scientific testing that will keep diseases out of the food supply far better than the old inspections ever could. The new food safety system balances government regulation and industry responsibility. Industry will assume some costs for new equipment and technology, including its own scientific testing to ensure food safety, while USDA will conduct other testing and oversight to ensure that industry is meeting its food safety responsibility. These changes will add an estimated one-tenth of one cent to the cost of a pound of meat—and will save an estimated $1 billion to $4 billion a year in the cost of food-borne illnesses. That's not much of a price to pay for a system that will far better ensure the safety of our food supply.[7]

Consumer Products

The Consumer Product Safety Commission is a government agency that touches virtually every American. It ensures that nearly 15,000 consumer goods under its jurisdiction do not pose undue risks to their users. Under Chairperson Ann Brown, the CPSC is a model of partnership with industry to achieve goals. Working with industry, the agency has developed over 300 voluntary standards, while promulgating only 50 mandatory, traditional rules—a six-to-one ratio. This approach yields results faster, and at less cost. For example, in April 1994, the CPSC presented information to manufacturers of children's clothing that drawstrings on jackets, coats, and sweatshirts posed a significant risk and were, in fact, killing children. Working with industry, the CPSC crafted a voluntary agreement to remove the dangerous drawstrings from most of the 20 million children's garments manufactured annually in the United States, without having to issue any new regulations. The problem was addressed in the span of four months—less time than it would have taken even to draft typical government regulations.

Similarly, the CPSC worked with manufacturers to address the hazard that window blind and drapery cords posed to small children. Since 1981, over 140 children between the ages of eight months and four years had died after being caught on such cords. When she took over the CPSC, Chairperson Brown saw the need to deal with this tragic situation. Working together, the agency and industry devised a program to eliminate the hazard. This was accomplished in six months and, again, without going through the expensive and time-consuming regulatory process. Most importantly, it will save children's lives.

Drug Interdiction

One of the latest alliances between business and government is the Business Anti-Smuggling Coalition, which started last August in San Diego and is spreading to other ports. Led by Mattel, Inc., in cooperation with the Customs Service, the Coalition is stopping drug smugglers from using shipments of toys and other goods from overseas. It is purely voluntary, but Mattel executives are having no problem recruiting dozens of other patriotic business leaders to join the alliance.

Helping our Partners

The U.S. Business Advisor gives business one electronic stop to all the agencies that deal with business.[8] The Advisor was designed the way a commercial software product would be. Originally shown as an "alpha product" by President Clinton at the White House Conference on Small Business in 1995, with the President's direction it was designed and redesigned based on user groups of business customers.

These users from big and small businesses around the country worked with the product and told us what to change. They loved the idea of one electronic stop, but wanted to change just about everything else. So we did. A central theme in their thinking was that government is drowning them in information—they said "make it easy to find what we need and then let us do business." They wanted the ability to make transactions, such as applying for permits, or to find out how to solve problems, like getting rid of a health hazard.

The new Advisor, released this past spring, lets business search 106,000 federal World Wide Web addresses for information by typing in simple English queries, like "show me the regulations for cutting Christmas trees on federal lands." The President typed that in, and the Advisor answered. Results are returned in seconds, with a key passage highlighted.

The Advisor provides several ways to quickly reach agency home pages that are critical to business. The SBA's home page is often mentioned as one of the Web's most popular and is always adding new, "cool" stuff. Responding to business's requests for on-line transactions, SBA just put their fast-track loan applications on-line to be filled out and submitted without paper. Another Advisor link takes business to the OSHA home page. Employers can get "how to" advice there. Do you think you need to get rid of asbestos in your building? OSHA has an expert system that helps you decide if you have a problem and what to do about it. Similar electronic tools address cadmium, lead, and the hazards of work in confined spaces.

The Advisor is a modern, state-of-the-art, electronic one-stop shop. There are some shops made out of good old bricks and mortar, too. Houston's U.S. General Store for Small Business dispenses nearly any service or information that a small business owner needs from the federal government in one place—with local government there, too. So far, the General Store has had about 4,000 customers. An independent survey says they love it. One customer, Roy Owens, got help with a loan, tax advice, and even contract leads with the Post Office. Roy says he has more work than he can handle, and he'll "go anywhere, any time to tell anybody that the store is the best thing he's ever seen from government." Business owners can get the same kind of one-stop service at the U.S. General Stores and SBA's "one-stop capital shops" in Atlanta, Kansas City, Philadelphia, and Boston.

EPA is making it easier for businesses to comply with environmental regulations. EPA has funded Small Business Compliance Assistance Centers for the metal finishing, printing, automotive repair, and farming industries to help these small businesses identify—in plain English—low-cost compliance and pollution prevention strategies. EPA also waives or reduces penalties for first-time violators if the business corrects the problem or comes into compliance with the law. And to top it all off, EPA is simplifying more than 70 percent of its regulations on business and eliminating 1,400 pages of obsolete rules.

There are also 88 U.S. Export Assistance Centers where companies that want to sell goods overseas can receive the collective assistance of staff from Commerce, the Small Business Administration, the Export-Import Bank, and state and local agencies. These centers and the 1-800-USA-TRADE number place all government export assistance resources at anybody's fingertips.

The Treasury, Labor Department, and Social Security Administration have teamed up with state and local governments and private organizations to reduce the paperwork burden of reporting and depositing payroll taxes by the nation's 6.2 million employers. Reports will only have to be filed with one agency, which will distribute the information to all federal, state, and local agencies that need it. This goes for withholding and reporting income tax, social security, unemployment insurance, and Medicare information. There is even an electronic version in the works that will be on the Internet. Federal tax deposits are now being made electronically too. The law says 1,500 big businesses must deposit payroll taxes electronically, but IRS made it so easy that 64,000 more companies do it voluntarily.

The biggest assistance that many small businesses need in order to get off the ground, or to expand, is a loan. The SBA has cut way, way back on the amount of paperwork and time it takes small entrepreneurs to obtain the backing they need. SBA has also boosted the amount of private capital available. The results speak for themselves: SBA arranged 55,000 small business loans last year, more than twice the number for 1992, for a total of $7.8 billion—a real shot in the arm for small business and the economy.

Who's the Enemy?

Some of the new partnerships are going so well that, frankly, it is a little embarrassing. 3M just nominated EPA for an award, for goodness sake.[9] The international trade community in Miami named Customs Commissioner George Weise their "Man of the Year." As Tommy Roland said, some people might think we're not doing our job because we're not hassling everybody anymore. Well, hassling never was our job, and corporate America never was the enemy. The enemy is pollution, contaminated food, workplace and product hazards, and the small percentage of people who smuggle drugs, cheat on taxes, and deliberately pollute our environment. Our job is to stop all of them, and we are doing it better than ever—along with new partners eager to help get the job done.

BLANK   PAGE

SECRET FOUR:
GOVERNMENT IS PARTNERING
WITH COMMUNITIES

"And there's something else we can do together.
We can reinvent government. We can switch from
red tape to results. We can put the days of
almighty, holier-than-thou, mister-know-it-all
Washington behind us. We can become partners."

— Vice President Al Gore,
Remarks to U.S. Conference of Mayors,
Austin, Texas, July 23, 1995

"Clinton and Gore are trying to change this huge bureaucracy. It's like climbing a three-mile-high mountain, and they've made it to mile post one. Nobody's ever gotten to the one-mile post before. But there's still a long way to go." So says a big city leader with a national reputation for straight talk—a successful city government reinventor, Philadelphia's mayor, Ed Rendell.

"Most of our dealings with the federal government are with HUD" (Housing and Urban Development), Rendell explains. "HUD would get an A+ from me, across the board. Henry Cisneros is a *great* Secretary of HUD—he's the embodiment of the Administration's policy to cut regulations and red tape, and to give local government the maximum amount of flexibility to use money most effectively."[1]

"Empowerment Zones are an example," says Rendell. Philadelphia and neighboring Camden, New Jersey, share one of 105 new flexible federal grants to revitalize both urban and rural communities. These communities were chosen from over 500 applicants, based on the strength of their strategic plans and community partnerships.

Grants of up to $100 million, along with tax breaks to attract new businesses, go to "Empowerment Zones" in six big cities and three rural areas; two more cities received grants of over $100 million without tax incentives. There are smaller grants and tax breaks for 94 other areas (64 urban, 30 rural) called "Enterprise Communities." All told, Washington is providing more than $1.5 billion in flexible grants and more than $2.5 billion in tax incentives. The communities also receive special assistance in removing red tape and regulatory barriers that prevent the innovative uses of federal funds.[2]

53

Deciding how to revitalize the community and get the most for their money was a grass-roots effort. To qualify, the community residents themselves, with help from city and county governments and local businesses, drew up plans to solve what they, not Washington, saw as their biggest problems. Most communities that got grants need more businesses, more jobs, and better low-cost housing, and they plan to stimulate all of that not with handouts, but with low-cost loans so the money will be replenished.

Rendell continues: "The Empowerment Zone really lets the people in the communities take control and be responsible for the outcome. But that was kind of easy for HUD to implement without lots of red tape, because the law itself had the right spirit. I'm more impressed with things like HUD's housing regulations. They've gotten rid of some of the most onerous, inflexible requirements on cities, like the 'one-for-one' rule on public housing. That rule said that if we tore down an abandoned high rise that had 580 units, we had to construct 580 new units, even though there hadn't been anybody living in there for five years. It was the same thing with single units. You can go to some blocks in Philadelphia where everybody's done a great job with their houses—put money into rehabilitating their houses—and right in the middle of the block there are two HUD scattered housing units that are *terrible*—places for drug dealing, places where kids got into trouble, a big negative on the neighborhood. But in the past, we couldn't demolish them without plans to build two new ones. So they'd sit there without ever being demolished or rehabilitated, doing nobody any good. HUD's shown the common sense to eliminate that rule. So we've brought down a number of high-rises and scattered units." Philadelphia is not the only city that has been able to get rid of those high-rise nightmares. In the past few years, 30,000 units have been razed, more than in the previous 12 years. And President Clinton recently set a goal to tear down another 70,000 in the next four years—a total of 100,000 urban eyesores gone.

Tearing down houses is not the ultimate goal. HUD has also created National Partners in Homeownership, comprising 58 national organizations representing lenders, real estate professionals, home builders, nonprofit housing providers, and federal, state, and local governments. The goal is to achieve an all-time high rate of homeownership—67 percent of all American households by the end of the year 2000, creating up to eight million additional homeowners. The partners are making headway. By the spring of 1996, the national homeownership rate was 65.1 percent, up from 64.2 percent at the end of 1994 (an increase of more than 1.5 million households). This is the highest rate since 1981, and the sharpest year-to-year increase in over three decades.

"HUD's made a wonderful change," according to Mayor Rendell. "And it's the same story on money for economic development. They've given us all kinds of flexibility to use that money most effectively. It's a night and day difference from the old way. They've done an excellent job. They haven't gotten rid of *all* the regs and *all* the burdens, but they've gotten rid of a tremendous share of them."

What about getting rid of all of them? Would the mayor welcome the kind of complete freedom some in Congress advocate in the form of block grants? "It's not freedom, it's baloney," says Rendell. "First of all, freedom from federal rules would have to be passed along to us by the state. And the state government is, if anything, less sympathetic to the cities than the feds are. So we'd never see all that freedom.

"But the main thing is that even if we got freedom from rules and red tape, we could only operate maybe 10 or 15 percent cheaper. They're talking about 25 percent cuts. You might be able to be just as effective if you had freedom and 10 percent less money. But no way are you going to be effective with 25 percent less. No way."

Rendell moved on to discuss the Environmental Protection Agency. "Under prior administrations, EPA was the single worst bureaucracy, promulgating regulations that avoided risks of one-in-a-trillion and had huge price tags to local governments. They've gone from that absurd starting point to . . . fair. For example, there's a scrap dealer here who handles old refrigerators. An EPA regulation says that you have to put a red tag on them certifying the safe disposal of freon. He employs a ton of people in jobs that pay $20 an hour, and they were about to fine him more than a million dollars, which would put him completely out of business, because he didn't have the tags right.[3] We argued it with them at the local level, the regional level, even the Washington level. I think we got it worked out, but they were going to put our guy out of business."

"But on the plus side, EPA's Brownfields effort makes a lot of sense," Rendell says. The Brownfields program is EPA's new way of getting abandoned industrial sites cleaned up and put back into the economy. The first success was in Cleveland, Ohio, at a 20-acre eyesore owned by Sunarhauserman, Inc. It had been sitting in Superfund limbo land for years, with prospective buyers and developers afraid to touch it, not so much because of the actual pollution but because the clean-up liability was unlimited. Now it is being cleaned up and houses four new businesses that contribute 180 new jobs and $1 million to the local tax base.[4] One of the latest Brownfields projects is right inside Philadelphia's American Street Empowerment Zone. EPA has agreed that the site of a small, abandoned gasoline tank farm can be sealed, paved over, and developed by businesses that are attracted by the Empowerment Zone's tax incentives and low-cost loans.

Here is a recent example from the West coast: The creosote-soaked site of the Wyckoff Company's wood treatment plant on Seattle's waterfront is about to become a world-class port facility for American President Lines. If EPA had not become a partner, the 1,000 jobs that are coming would have gone south—literally—and the land would have lain there oozing poison into the harbor while the lawyers wrangled in court for years. But EPA and the Port of Seattle worked out a common-sense deal that is good for everybody.

"Look, there's clearly plenty of work to do yet—two more miles of mountain to climb," says Rendell, going back to his original metaphor. "But things are sure headed in the right direction."

Cities, Counties, States—Partners

Each year, the federal government attaches strings to nearly a quarter of a trillion dollars and gives it to state and local governments[5]. The strings that are attached make the state and local governments go through strange motions that frustrate citizens and state and local governments alike.

Tillamook County, Oregon, is on the end of some of those strings. The head of their health department, Sue Cameron, gives some good examples of the motions they go through. "We get federal money to immunize kids. That's a great idea, but it's not that simple. There are six different kinds of federal immunization money. One kind is for diphtheria. Another is for hepatitis-B, but only for teenagers. There's a different one for hepatitis-B for infants. Not a different shot—just different money. But that's not all. For the best protection, babies should get their first shots within two weeks of the day they're born, and most babies are born in hospitals. So, common sense tells you to have the hospital nurses give the shot while the babies are there. But before President Clinton launched the 'Vaccine for Children' program, the shots had to be given in public or private health clinics. That rule had kept some babies from ever getting their shots.

"And the bookkeeping! With each different kind of money for each different kind of thing—not just the different kinds of immunization, but nutrition programs, mental health, teen pregnancy, and so on—we have to keep separate records. That means that everybody who works here—from the receptionist to the doctor—is keeping track of which federal program they work on each minute to fill out time sheets for Washington."

Ask around Washington about all that red tape and it becomes clear that all the programs and all the rules are based on good intentions. All the strings were attached for good reasons. This is true; everybody in Washington is trying to achieve good government. But, as Gandhi said, "Good government is no substitute for self government." Somehow, we have to give government back to the people.

So how about having the feds cut all the strings and just hand money over in block grants? Mayor Rendell said the result would be too little freedom and way too little money. Here is what another potential recipient of block grants says. He is Jono Hildner, and he is the essence of Oregon—tall, fit, and outdoorsy, he runs wild rivers for fun. He also runs everything from public housing to the dog pound in Clackamas County, Oregon. Never heard of Clackamas County? In the 1800s it was the end of the Oregon Trail. Today, it is the beginning of Christmas—the nation's most prolific producer of Christmas trees. "Block grants are tempting," Jono says, "but I don't think the feds should just leave the money on a stump for us. I've seen that tried before. The money disappears and you're never sure what you got for it."

The Oregon Option

So where is the happy medium? We do not want all these Washington rules anymore. But we do want to make sure we get good results for all that money. Well, Sue Cameron and Jono Hildner are up to their necks in the happy medium right now in something called a "performance partnership."

In Oregon, the partnership is known as the "Oregon Option," and it is the wave of the future.[6] In December 1994, Oregon's Governor and numerous mayors and county commissioners signed an agreement with Vice President Gore and seven Cabinet Secretaries. They agreed to pilot a redesigned system that is:

- structured, managed, and evaluated on the basis of results;
- oriented to customer needs and satisfaction;
- biased towards preventing problems, not just fixing them afterward; and
- simplified and integrated as much as possible, delegating responsibilities for service design, delivery, and results to front-line, local-level providers.

Government reinventors believe in the adage, "Lead, follow, or get out of the way." In the Oregon Option, we are following. Through surveys in the early nineties, the people of Oregon sorted out which issues were most important to them—like cleaning up rivers, increasing adult literacy, and reducing teen pregnancy. They also set some performance goals—like going in three years from 18 pregnant teens in a thousand to only 10. They called the goals "Oregon Benchmarks."[7] And they started tearing down the old-fashioned state and local bureaucracy that stood in their way. In 1994, they invited the feds to join them—to follow their lead. We followed proudly.

"The feds don't make us fill out those stupid time sheets anymore," says Sue Cameron. "And the seven different immunization funds have been consolidated." Jono Hildner adds, "The biggest improvement is communication. I've got somebody in Washington who knows me now, who I can talk to, who understands our problems and helps us get them fixed. I think the feds should be doing a lot more of this."

Performance Partnerships

We agree, Jono. Based on the success of the Oregon Option, President Clinton has asked Congress to combine 271 separate grants and programs, which now have lots of strings attached, into 27 performance partnerships that are focused on results, just like Oregon's benchmarks. Each of the President's performance partnership grants would consolidate funding streams, eliminate overlapping authorities, create financial incentives to reward results, and reduce micromanagement and wasteful paperwork. So far, Congress has approved performance partnerships for rural development and the environment. The recently enacted Farm Bill created three new rural development performance partnerships in which a large number programs—for rural utilities, economic development, and housing—will be administered together flexibly, with input on local needs from state and local officials, and focused on results.[8]

We are eager for Congress to complete its work in other areas where the President has proposed performance partnerships, and we and the states are ready to move as soon as Congress does. The Department of Health and Human Services, for example, has met with over 1,000 folks around the country—from states, localities, and consumer groups—to identify the public health results we all want and how best to measure progress. We also have partnerships with states and cities everywhere we could think of, in every way the current laws allow.

President Clinton has established a Community Empowerment Board of the major federal domestic agencies to support community-driven economic revitalization. The board helps break down the bureaucratic walls that sometimes keep agencies from responding effectively to state and local partners. The President has directed agencies to eliminate unnecessary regulatory and legal impediments. We are moving control and responsibility back to the people—providing top-down support for bottom-up reform.

The Environment

"These partnerships are based on a shared vision of environmental protection that is based on trust, respect, and a commitment to changing the way we do business. These grants are one of the top 25 [environmental] initiatives for reinventing government that President Clinton announced last March 17 [1995]"

— EPA Administrator Carol Browner[9]

Last May, EPA signed the first performance partnership grant agreements with Colorado and Utah. Through negotiation, EPA and states agree upon broad goals and priorities to achieve better environmental outcomes. The new, one-step grants replace up to 16 separate agreements the states used to have to negotiate and allow the states to shift money as priorities change, without time-consuming appeals to EPA. Gone are the 16 separate reports; there is just one report under the partnership grant. It is just the kind of change in government that we envisioned in the title of the first National Performance Review report: "From Red Tape to Results."

EPA is creating partnerships at the local level, too. When EPA became involved at a potential Superfund cleanup site in north Boulder, Colorado, several parties were entrenched in litigation about groundwater contamination. First, EPA informed the parties as to the potential risks involved in the status quo and then gave the community a chance to develop a solution before EPA put it on the Superfund list. Next, EPA invited all parties—including citizens—to accept some responsibility for resolving the disputes and cleaning up the water. Within six months, they had come up with a solution and a way to pay for it locally. This approach saved millions in federal dollars—and saved the community from being immersed in the Superfund program for the next decade.

EPA, Energy, and other federal agencies, along with 22 state environmental agencies, have pioneered a successful partnering effort to improve the cleanup process for contaminated toxic sites. Together, these groups break down the barriers to using innovative environmental technologies for remediation and treatment of hazardous and radioactive wastes. Partnering has streamlined the regulatory process for environmental technologies and moved states and federal agencies toward results-oriented cleanup.

The Bureau of Land Management has created 24 resource advisory councils in the Western states to advise the Bureau on issues concerning management of the public's lands and resources. These councils, developed under the Federal Advisory Committee Act, are made up of 12 to 15 members appointed by the Secretary of the Interior from among individuals nominated by the public and state governors. Three groups are represented on these councils: business; conservationists; and local citizens, including representatives of local government and Indian tribes. The councils have been very successful at bringing diverse—and often competing—interests to the table to deal with each other on issues of mutual concern. The approach shows great promise in successfully solving long-standing problems of public land management. Many individuals who were initially skeptical of the councils are now quite supportive of their work and are optimistic that they will be a strong force in resolving disputes about the uses of public land in the West.

Connecticut Neighborhood Revitalization Partnership

In 1995, Connecticut passed an innovative law, the Neighborhood Revitalization Act, which requires the state and its municipalities to break down barriers in response to neighborhoods' comprehensive plans and measurable goals to revitalize their economies and neighborhoods. In 1996, the federal government joined the party. This partnership allows federal barriers to be overcome along with state barriers and allows federal, state, and local partners to work together to improve Connecticut's poorest communities through economic development and neighborhood revitalization. The Neighborhood Revitalization Zone process invites residents, businesses, and municipal officials to develop a strategic plan to revitalize their neighborhood. Grassroots planning and community organizing are the key components of this concept, just as in the Oregon Option, Empowerment Zones, and Enterprise Communities.

Addressing Unfunded Mandates

The Clinton-Gore Administration fully understands the burdens states and localities face when the federal government imposes mandates without providing adequate funding. In October 1993, President Clinton signed the first executive order requiring all federal agencies to consult with state and local organizations before promulgating any rules or regulations that impose new unfunded mandates.[10]

In March 1995, President Clinton signed the Unfunded Mandates Reform Act, which restricts the ability of Congress to impose costly mandates on states, localities, and tribal governments.[11] Based on analyses required by the Congressional Budget Office, mandates costing states and localities $50 million or more in any of the first five years after becoming effective are not permitted—unless waived by majority votes in both the House and Senate. The Act also requires greater intergovernmental consultations in the administrative rulemaking process and allowance for the least expensive means of complying with federal regulations.

Welfare and Health Care Reform

One of the best pieces of evidence that Washington is changing its ways—becoming a partner with communities instead of a know-it-all—is its willingness to clear the way for welfare reform. We all have the same goal, to make welfare a hand-up to a decent life, instead of a hand-out for life. But there are different ways to get there. While Congress was debating the different ways over the past few years, the President let states try them to see what worked best. The Clinton Administration has approved welfare demonstration projects in more than 40 states—twice as many as the previous two administrations combined.[12]

The new, national welfare reform legislation incorporates many of the good ideas being tried by the states. The Indiana welfare reform plan, which is typical of the scores of demonstration projects approved by the Clinton Administration, puts 12,000 able-bodied welfare recipients on a "placement track" where they get special help finding a job—including subsidies for employers. Parents have to keep their kids in school and get them immunized. Adults receive up to two years of special help finding a job, then their welfare benefits run out. Children's benefits continue, but there are no new benefits for additional children conceived on welfare. The President approved Indiana's plan in late 1994, and between March of 1995 and March of 1996, Indiana's welfare rolls dropped by 22 percent.[13]

President Clinton has done the same thing for states wanting to try health care reforms. Tennessee, for example, can now expand health care coverage to over 400,000 people who were previously uninsured. To date, the President has approved 13 comprehensive health care reform demonstrations similar to Tennessee's—working in partnership with states to increase the use of managed care, improve the quality of care, and expand coverage to 2.2 million low-income uninsured Americans.

These are not Washington's latest bright ideas being imposed on communities. They are ideas from the communities themselves—from the people who understand the problems best and who will live with the results. To be fair, Washington does have some experts with a wealth of experience to share and, of course, the financial resources that communities need. But now, communities don't have to follow Washington's rules to get Washington's money. It is the people's money and Washington is becoming the people's partner.

Fighting Crime

Some of our partnerships are making America's streets safer. Legislation that President Clinton fought for is putting 100,000 community police on the streets, and crime in our cities is now at its lowest rate in years. But fighting crime is more than just a matter of brute force. The Justice Department has teamed up with state and local police on some innovation that really works.[14] It is called, appropriately enough, COPS, for Community Oriented Policing Services. Just look what it did for Tampa, Florida: A few years ago, Tampa had a tough crime problem.[15] Then, with a $3.8 million partnership grant from the Department of Justice, a 15-officer COPS squad joined forces with the local police and made a 23 percent dent in every crime category, with drug busts up by 51 percent.[16]

How? First, COPS got out of the patrol cars and mixed in with the community. The Tampa COPS immediately investigate crimes themselves, instead of relaying the information and responsibility to detectives. COPS keep kids in school and off the streets, a tactic that has drastically reduced crime during school hours. COPS hold auctions where kids bid community service hours in exchange for impounded, unclaimed bicycles. COPS organized the area's first Girl Scout troop, and they are starting a Boy Scout troop. COPS organized crime-watch groups made up of volunteers who canvass their communities and help eliminate crimes such as vandalism, street-drinking, curfew violations, and prostitution. For every COPS officer in the community, there are dozens of watchful citizens who take pride in the cleanliness and safety of their community. This is government in partnership with the people.

Another crime-fighting partnership, Operation Safe Home, teams local and state law enforcement with the resources of HUD, Justice, Treasury, and the Office of National Drug Control Policy. This innovative partnership has not only combated gangs, drugs, and violence, but has also brought together a range of crime prevention initiatives to ensure long-term safety. Since 1994, Operation Safe Home has made a nationwide improvement in the safety of public housing with results like 8,000 arrests and the confiscation of 1,000 weapons as well as $5 million in drugs and drug money.[17]

61

Education

"Over the last two years, the Congress and the U.S. Department of Education have made tremendous progress in transforming the federal relationship with the states on education. It has changed from one based on regulatory compliance to one based on accountability and performance."

— Robert V. Antonucci,
Massachusetts Commissioner of Education[18]

Some of the most impressive examples of the way government is changing to partnership are in the Department of Education. In Goals 2000, the Education Department led states to set challenging academic standards for their students, and then the reinvented Department of Education let them get to work.[19] States no longer have to submit their plans to the experts in Washington for approval; they just need to have a plan, a schedule for progress, and a way to measure progress. And they don't have to report their progress to Washington, either; they report it to the people. If selected federal laws or regulations stand in the way of progress, the Secretary of Education has the authority to waive them—he has waived more than 100 already.

States that really want to get on board—those willing to waive their own rules and let local school districts be accountable—can waive federal rules without even asking Washington for permission. The program is called Ed-Flex. The measure of success is simple: improved academic performance of the students. Eight states have signed up and there is room for four more; the legal limit is 12, for now.[20]

Since the goal of all this academic freedom is better academic performance, let's look at some results. Maryland, one of the Ed-Flex states, reports a 52 percent leap in the number of schools whose students are doing well at the third grade level. They are up by 13 percent at the fifth grade level and by 32 percent at the eighth grade. Forty percent of all students statewide met the state standards—that's a 25 percent gain over 1993.[21]

It is no surprise that flexibility, local control, and measured accountability produce good results. Kentucky has been doing it since 1990 with great success, and we copied the idea from them. Kentucky schools manage themselves through councils that include teachers, parents, and community members. They set goals and measure success by looking at things like student test scores, dropout rates, success at getting jobs, and how many students go on to college. Schools that make their goals get bonuses that school staffs decide how to spend. Schools that do not make the grade get special help from the state.

The National Education Goals

BY THE YEAR 2000:

- All children in America will start school ready to learn.

- The high school graduation rate will increase to at least 90 percent.

- All students will leave grades 4, 8, and 12 having demonstrated competency over challenging subject matter in the core academic subjects.

- U.S. students will be first in the world in mathematics and science achievement.

- Every adult American will be literate and will possess the knowledge and skills necessary to compete in a global economy and exercise the rights and responsibilities of citizenship.

- Every school in the U.S. will be free of drugs, violence, and the unauthorized presence of firearms and alcohol and will offer a disciplined environment conducive to learning.

- The nation's teaching force will have access to programs for the continued improvement of their professional skills and the opportunity to acquire the knowledge and skills needed to instruct and prepare all American students for the next century.

- Every school will promote partnerships that will increase parental involvement and participation in promoting the social, emotional, and academic growth of children.

Results? Grades have been going up steadily the last two years, especially for fourth, eighth, and twelfth graders. The fourth graders were best of all—their grades went up about 10 percentage points overall, and a whopping 16 percentage points in reading.[22] Way to go fourth graders! Way to go Kentucky!

From teaching kids how to read to fighting crime in the streets, from big cities like Philadelphia to rural counties like Tillamook, from both coasts and places in between, people in governments closest to the people are seeing the change for the better. The National Performance Review is leading the shift away from Washington's well-intentioned efforts at good government toward the grass-roots power of self-government. Ed Rendell is right—we are at the one-mile post of a three-mile mountain. Let's get a good grip and keep climbing.

BLANK   PAGE

Conclusion

I haven't tried to compile an exhaustive list of all the problems the President and I have faced trying to reinvent government, or of all the successes we've scored—there just aren't enough pages in an easy-to-read book to be fair to all the hard-working government reinventors that are helping us. I have invited the Cabinet Secretaries and heads of some of the larger government agencies to tell you what they are proudest of having accomplished—their stories fill the following pages. But if you'd like an even more complete story about how the federal government is getting its act together, turn on a computer and call up our World Wide Web site.[1] There are hundreds of success stories there.

The point of this short book is just to show you that we "get it"—President Clinton and I understand what's wrong with how the government has been doing things—and we are turning things around. The battle against the old forces of big government, central control, and mistrust isn't won yet, but everything is moving in the right direction. And, we have a plan to continue the changes.

First, we are turning some of today's agencies into smaller, sleeker organizations that won't look like government at all. They will be like private companies, with a real CEO on contract to cut costs, and a free hand when it comes to the remaining government rules about procurement, personnel, and the like. The British government did this a few years ago, and costs have been dropping steadily. We'll borrow their good idea.

On customer service, we'll stick our necks out even further. The top boss of every agency that touches millions of Americans—like the IRS and VA and Customs—is on the line to make dramatic improvements in service this year. There's even a Web page where you can read their specific goals and let them know what you think.[2]

Regulatory agencies are on orders to make partnership with businesses their standard way of operating. We have tested it long enough to know it increases compliance with the laws of the land. After all, compliance is what we're after—not meaningless hassles. Now we can move beyond pilot programs for partnership into the mainstream.

The same goes for federal grants to state and local governments. No more having to follow the federal rule books to receive federal funds. We will focus on results and consider replacing many grant programs with performance-based partnerships. And to dispel the last vestiges of nameless, faceless bureaucracy, we will give each of our community partners a single, live federal employee, complete with name and face, who will help them with any and all business in Washington, regardless of which agency's turf it is.

Finally, we are going to do better by our workforce. Any *Fortune* 500 company would be lucky to have a workforce like the federal government's. We need to invest in it: better tools and training, closer partnership between labor and management, more opportunities and challenges for our senior executives.

All of the progress we have made, and all of our plans for the future are focused on one goal—restoring the American people's faith in their own system of self-government—the people's belief that we can solve our national problems by working together through the institutions of self-government. Faith in government is at a low point, and that lack of faith threatens the nation's future. Government can't do everything, and it certainly shouldn't try. But some national problems like drugs, violence, poverty, and pollution can be solved only by Americans working together through our system of self-government. If we lose faith in that, we abandon the future to chaos.

Reinvention restores our faith. Americans find government service improving over the counter and over the phone. Business leaders find federal regulators ready to use common sense and to look for common ground. Communities find the walls coming down between agencies and levels of government, and beyond the old walls they find partners ready to do whatever it takes to solve problems. Reinvention is securing the future of self-government in America.

So, if you see government changing, don't keep it a secret. Tell your friends, your business associates, your neighbors. Tell them government can do things right. I'm the first to admit that government isn't the answer to all our problems. But when government has to be part of the solution, more and more, we Americans can count on getting results.

Al Gore

NOTES

Introduction

1. The Postal Service is not included. It has grown because it has more mail to deliver, but it is financed primarily from the sale of stamps, not from taxes.

2. For historical trend data on federal employment, 1965-1995, see Appendix F, Table F-1.

3. Unpublished calculation prepared by the Office of Management and Budget, based on civilian pay and benefits budgeted for fiscal year 1996.

4. Office of Management and Budget, *Budget for Fiscal Year 1997, Historical Tables*, "Table 1.1 - Summary of Receipts, Outlays, and Surpluses or Deficits: 1789-2002" (Washington, D.C.: Government Printing Office, 1996), p. 20.

5. Office of Personnel Management, Office of Workforce Information, Central Personnel Data File (unpublished data).

6. General Accounting Office, *Federal Downsizing: The Costs and Savings of Buyouts versus Reductions-In-Force* (Washington, D.C.: Government Printing Office), GAO/GGD-96-63, May 14, 1996.

7. Office of Personnel Management, Office of Workforce Information, Central Personnel Data File (unpublished data). This figure (114,856 buyouts) includes all civilian defense and non-defense personnel who took buyouts between January 1993 and January 1996.

8. Office of Personnel Management, Office of Workforce Information, Central Personnel Data File (unpublished data). Between January 1993 and January 1996, 239,286 personnel left federal employment. Of these, 21,125 were separated involuntarily.

9. Stephen Barr, "A Simple Suggestion Worth Millions: Civil Servant's Idea Expected to Mean Big Savings in Procurements," *Washington Post*, October 13, 1994.

10. Vice President Al Gore, *Common Sense Government: Works Better and Costs Less* (New York: Random House, 1995), p. 26.

Secret One:
Common Sense Has Come to the Federal Government

1. Unpublished data on drug seizure activity in passenger processing provided by U.S. Customs Service, Miami. The data include seizures as of July 31, 1996.

2. Unpublished data on FTS2000, the Federal Telecommunications System, from the General Services Administration.

3. General Accounting Office, *Acquisition: Purchase Card Use Cuts Procurement Costs, Improves Efficiency* (Washington, D.C.: Government Printing Office), GAO/NSIAD-96-138, August 6, 1996.

4. Public Law 104-106, *National Defense Authorization Act for FY 1996*, February 10, 1996; Executive Order 13011, *Federal Information Technology*, July 17, 1996.

5. Unpublished data from the Office of Management and Budget.

6. Letter from Peter J. Hannes, President, Special Markets Division, Jockey International, Inc. to Mr. Dennis Dudek, Department of Defense, June 7, 1996.

7. Department of Defense, Office of Assistant Secretary (Public Affairs), "Defense Acquisition Pilot Programs Forecast Cost/Schedule Savings of Up To 50 Percent From Acquisition Reform," News Release No. 138-96, March 14, 1996; and unpublished data provided by the Department of Defense.

8. See Presidential Memorandum, *Streamlining Procurement Through Electronic Commerce*, October 26, 1993; Executive Order 12931, *Federal Procurement Reform*, October 13, 1994; Executive Order 12979, *Agency Procurement Protests*, October 25, 1995; and Executive Order 13011, *Federal Information Technology*, July 17, 1996.

9. See Appendix C.

10. Unpublished data from the Federal Communications Commission.

11. Al Gore, *Creating a Government That Works Better & Costs Less*, (Washington, D.C.: Government Printing Office, September 7, 1993), pp. 13-14.

12. For more information on streamlining management, see Appendix H.

13. James Thompson, "The Reinvention Revolution," *Government Executive*, Vol. 28, No. 5, May 1996, pp. 39-41. See also, General Accounting Office, *"Management Reform: Status of Agency Reinvention Lab Efforts"* (Washington, D.C.: Government Printing Office), GAO-GGD-96-69, March 20, 1996.

14. President and Mrs. Harrison were afraid to touch the light switches, so a civil servant was assigned to switch the lights on in the evening, let them burn all night, and return in the morning to switch them off. James Trager,

The People's Chronology (New York: Henry Holt and Company, Inc., 1996), pp. 561, 572, 587.

15. Congressional Testimony by James King, Director, Office of Personnel Management, before the House Committee on Government Reform and Oversight, October 12, 1995.

16. Each agency now has the authority to do its own hiring (Public Law 104-52), but many agencies choose to hire through the Office of Personnel Management's phone-in center.

17. Executive Order 12871, *Labor-Management Partnerships*, October 1, 1993.

18. U.S. Mint, "Denver Mint Receives National Partnership Award for Improved Labor-Management Relations," Press Release, February 14, 1996.

19. Presidential Memorandum, *Expanding Family-Friendly Work Arrangements in the Executive Branch*, July 11, 1994; Presidential Memorandum, *Supporting the Role of Fathers in Families*, June 16, 1995; and Presidential Memorandum, *Implementing Family Friendly Work Arrangements*, June 21, 1996.

20. Michael Serlin, "The Competitors," *Government Executive*, Vol. 28, No. 6, June 1996, pp. 29-33.

Secret Two: Government Is Serving People Better

1. Undated letter from Robert J. Lacombe to Shirley Chater, Commissioner, Social Security Administration.

2. Letter from Lloyd Hartford regarding the Dedicated Commuter Lane Project, April 12, 1996.

3. Anonymous comment sheet from the Dedicated Commuter Lane.

4. Letter from Chris Petersen to the Department of Energy, Energy Information Administration.

5. Letter from Michael R. McMeekin to D. James Baker, Undersecretary for Oceans and Atmosphere, National Oceanic and Atmosphere Administration, May 6, 1996.

6. Undated letter from an unidentified police officer to Eljay B. Bowron, Director, United States Secret Service.

7. Undated letter from Alexander Schuster, veteran, to Director and Chief of Staff of a Veterans Affairs hospital.

8. Public Law 96-511, *Paperwork Reduction Act of 1980*, December 11, 1980, 94 Stat. 2813.

9. Bill Clinton and Al Gore, *Putting Customers First '95* (Washington, D.C.: Government Printing Office), October 1995, The electronic version is located at "http://www.npr.gov".

10. Ibid., p. 123.

11. Postal Service, "It's A Record—90 Percent On Time Delivery!" Press Release No. 49, Washington, D.C., June 4, 1996. The U.S. Postal Service's Internet address is "http://www.usps.gov".

12. President Clinton directed agencies in 1993 to appoint chief operating officers—normally the deputy secretary of the department or the head of the agency. He then convened two dozen of the chief operating officers of the departments and largest agencies as the President's Management Council to share their best practices and advise him on ways to implement reinvention.

13. Dalbar Financial Services, Inc., "Social Security Administration Tops in Customer Service," Press Release, Boston, Massachusetts, May 3, 1995.

14. Although the General Services Administration promised to have blue pages in five cities, seven cities have already signed up. They are: Baltimore, Chicago, Denver, Indianapolis, Los Angeles, New York, and San Francisco.

15. Unpublished calculation from the Office of Management and Budget.

16. PEBES stands for "Personal Earnings and Benefit Statement," and it is located at "http://www.ssa.gov".

17. Send your geology questions by e-mail to "ask-a-geologist@usgs.gov".

18. The fax number for the Bureau of Labor Statistics' Fax on Demand is 202-606-6325.

19. The World Wide Web address for HUD's city maps is "http://www.hud.gov/communit.html".

20. The World Wide Web address for the Bond Wizard is "http://www.ustreas.gov/treasury/bureaus/pubdebt/savwizar/html".

21. Undated letter from the Bodde Family to the Federal Emergency Management Agency.

Secret Three:
Government Is In Partnership With Business

1. Bob Bauer, "A Swimming Time for Shrimp; Frozen Sales Up in 1994," *Supermarket News*, Vol. 44, No. 52, December 26, 1994.

2. Unpublished data provided by the Environmental Protection Agency.

3. Calculation based on unpublished data from the Environmental Protection Agency.

4. Unpublished data provided by the Environmental Protection Agency, Environmental Assistance Division.

5. Letter from Jack Cohen, Ph.D., Vice President for Quality & Compliance, Scios, Inc., to Gregory Bobrowicz, District Director, Food and Drug Administration, Alameda, CA, May 29, 1996.

6. U.S. Department of Agriculture, National Agricultural Statistics Service, "Livestock Slaughter 1995," March 1996.

7. Jerry Knight, "Meat Inspection Changes Produce an Unusual Unanimity," *Washington Post*, July 9, 1996, p. D1, citing Administrator Michael R. Taylor of the Food Safety and Inspection Service, U.S. Department of Agriculture.

8. The U.S. Business Advisor is located at "http://www.business.gov".

9. The EPA 33/50 team was nominated by 3M for Vice President Gore's Hammer Award and received the award in June 1996.

Secret Four:
Government Is Partnering With Communities

1. To learn more about HUD partnerships with Philadelphia and other cities, visit the HUD homepage at "http://www.hud.gov".

2. Department of Housing and Urban Development, "Empowerment Zones and Enterprise Communities," *Community Connections*. To learn more about the Empowerment Zone/Enterprise Community initiative, visit the homepage at "http://www.ezec.gov".

3. EPA believed that some of the scrap refrigerators still contained freon, which could have escaped into the atmosphere. Freon is harmful to the environment because it destroys ozone.

4. Environmental Protection Agency, "Removing Liability Barriers and Encouraging Development," unpublished information, June 20, 1996.

5. Office of Management and Budget, *FY 1997 President's Budget, Analytical Perspectives*, "Aid to State and Local Governments," March 1996, p. 167.

6. Memorandum of Understanding, "The Oregon Option" (unpublished), December 1994, p. 1.

7. Oregon Progress Board, "Oregon Benchmarks: Standards for Measuring Statewide Progress And Institutional Performance," Report to the 1995 Legislature, December 1994.

8. Public Law 104-127, *Federal Agricultural Improvement and Reform Act of 1996*, April 4, 1996.

9. Environmental Protection Agency, "Environmental News," Press Release, Washington, D.C., May 16, 1996.

10. Executive Order 12871, *Enhancing the Intergovernmental Partnership*, October 1, 1993.

11. Public Law 104-4, *Unfunded Mandates Reform Act of 1995*, March 22, 1995.

12. See Appendix A, "Department of Health and Human Services," for more details on the welfare demonstration projects.

13. Unpublished data from the Administration for Children and Families, Department of Health and Human Services.

14. Justice cut all the red tape associated with COPS. Communities need only fill out a one-page application.

15. Pam Noles, "No Tax Increases in New Budget," *The Tampa Tribune*, July 31, 1996, p. 1.

16. Unpublished information from the Department of Justice, June 21, 1996.

17. Nicole Marshall, "65 Arrested in Sweep of Public Housing," *Tulsa World*, May 31, 1996, p. A8.

18. Robert V. Antonucci, Massachusetts Commissioner of Education, The Federal Role in Education Reform, Testimony before House Subcommittee on Early Childhood, Youth and Families, House Committee on Economic and Education Opportunities, June 21, 1995.

19. Department of Education, *Goals 2000: Increasing Student Achievement Through State and Local Initiatives* (Washington, D.C.: Government Printing Office) April 30, 1996.

20. The Ed-Flex states are: Kansas, Oregon, Massachusetts, Texas, Ohio, Vermont, Maryland, and Colorado.

21. Maryland State Department of Education, "High Expectations Producing Better Schools, State School Superintendent Grasmick Says," Baltimore, MD, Press Release, December 12, 1995.

22. "Kentucky Accountability Results," *The Cincinnati Enquirer*, February 8, 1995, p. B2.

Conclusion

1. The National Performance Review homepage address is "http://www.npr.gov".

2. Customer service standards can be found at "http://www.info.gov/Info/html/customer_service.htm".

APPENDIX A:
STATUS OF REINVENTION EFFORTS IN
DEPARTMENTS AND MAJOR AGENCIES

The National Performance Review's (NPR's) September 1993 report contains 245 major recommendations affecting principal government agencies. Separate accompanying reports break these recommendations into 833 specific action items. Governmentwide, agencies report that 43 percent of these action items are complete, 42 percent are in progress, and the remainder are on hold or not proceeding as expected.

NPR's September 1995 report contains an additional 187 recommendations affecting these same departments and agencies. To date, 19 percent have been completed, 62 percent are in progress, and the remainder are on hold or not making expected progress. Additional information on the progress of specific recommendations is available on NPR's World Wide Web home page (http://www.npr.gov).

In addition to these recommendations, departments and agencies have undertaken a wide range of related reinvention activities to make their operations work better and cost less. Following are highlights of their reinvention efforts over the past three years.

Department of Agriculture
Dan Glickman, Secretary

Mission Statement

The mission of the U.S. Department of Agriculture (USDA) is to ensure the well-being of Americans—with special emphasis on people engaged in commercial agriculture and sensible management of natural resources; families needing nutritional services; consumers dependent on a safe, affordable food supply; and residents of depressed rural areas.

Within its new structure, the Department continues to operate over 200 programs organized into seven mission areas:

- farm and foreign agricultural services;
- rural development;
- food, nutrition, and consumer services;
- natural resources and environment;
- food safety;
- research, education, and economics; and
- marketing and regulatory programs.

Summary Budget Information

FY 1993 (Actual)		FY 1996 (Budgeted)	
Budget	Staff	Budget	Staff
$67.857 billion	114,420	$54.064 billion	105,452

Reinvention Highlights

USDA, a leader in streamlining the federal government, has undertaken the most massive restructuring in its 134-year history. USDA's dramatic reinvention is helping to make government work better but cost less.

At headquarters and at field locations throughout the country, we are providing better service to our customers—to the farmers who depend on us for program information; to the families who visit our national forests; to the rural Americans who look to us for help with their housing, their water systems, and even for links to advanced technologies such as the Internet.

As part of this Administration's commitment to providing better customer service, we have reorganized USDA around the seven mission areas listed above. The number of USDA agencies has been reduced from 43 to 30. And we have consolidated our field operations into multi-agency service centers.

These service centers house several USDA agencies under one roof, providing one-stop shopping. Instead of having to travel to many different sites for help, farmers can now go to one centrally located office, making it more convenient for people to participate in USDA farm, rural development, and conservation programs. And if people have a question about farm programs, or rural development, or soil conservation, they call one number, not three different numbers. They talk to one USDA employee, not three or more. We've even changed the way we answer the phone. For example, Susan Stevick of the USDA Service Center in Lyndon, Kansas, answers the phone, "Hello. This is the Osage County Department of Agriculture," and not "the Farm Service Agency," or "the Natural Resources Conservation Agency." She knows that most callers don't care which agency they reach, but they do want USDA to answer their questions and provide the services they need.

In the field and in Washington, that's what we're doing—and we're doing it better and at a lower cost to taxpayers. Already, in our creation of one-stop service centers, we have closed or collocated 538 offices in 224 counties.

We have reduced our staff by nearly 10,000 people in the last three years—ahead of schedule. And the savings resulting from these reductions are ahead of schedule, too—already more than $900 million. We expect to save about $4.1 billion between 1993 and 1999 as a result of streamlining the Department.

Our field office employees serve America on the front lines. Their positive attitudes about their jobs, about the federal government, and about serving America are contagious. Here are a few examples of USDA individuals and offices that are making government work better and cost less:

- A group of employees from the National Finance Center has been nominated for a government computer award for excellence. Their new system replaces voluminous paper and microfiche reports and greatly improves productivity. Instead of spending 400 hours to prepare a report, employees now spend 11 hours. First year savings are expected to exceed $500,000.
- The School Meals Initiative for Healthy Children is improving the health of our nation's 50 million school children. Requiring the nation's 94,000 schools to serve meals meeting the *Dietary Guidelines for Americans* will improve long-term health and life expectancy.
- The Economic Research Service (ERS) is 25 percent smaller now than in 1993 and is already working better. The service is using the Internet to make it easier for the public to get information. ERS employees set up an information center to help customers get ERS products and services. And they have a new phone line to respond to questions.
- Over 3.5 million Americans in 13 states now receive food stamp benefits through electronic benefits transfer (EBT) cards, which enable them to access their benefits directly at the supermarket cash register, in the same way many Americans already use automated teller machine cards. EBT technology reduces administrative costs to states and eases the administrative burden on retailers who redeem food stamps.
- USDA's Food Safety Inspection Service has dramatically overhauled and reinvented the entire meat and poultry inspection system. Three years of Administration efforts recently culminated in a sweeping reform of federal food safety rules that will use hard science to prevent and reduce contamination of meat and poultry. This is part of a comprehensive effort to protect consumers from food-borne illnesses, which cost $1 billion to $4 billion each year in lost prodictivity and medical costs.
- The USDA AmeriCorps national service program has enabled about 2,000 Americans to help pay for their postsecondary educations by performing vital services fighting hunger, protecting the environment, and rebuilding rural communities. In its first year of operation, the services provided by the program helped 828,000 citizens and improved 234,000 acres of land. Because this program empowered local communities to help solve their own problems, less than 2 percent of its entire budget went to Washington-based administrative overhead.
- The Department is pioneering new uses of technology to boost the economy and aid communities. USDA has improved access to information and education to help producers and

others involved in the agricultural economy make sound choices and decisions in an increasingly risky business. Through use of the Internet and other information technology, USDA provides quick access to important economic information. Also, since 1993, USDA has provided grants totaling $27.5 million to rural projects in 39 states to help rural schools, libraries, and medical facilities acquire advanced telecommunications systems.

- Major changes have been initiated in administrative processes and systems. USDA has been a leader in initiating Electronic Commerce (a procurement system) and Employee Express (a personnel system). One business process reengineering project on credit card reform is expected to improve service and has the potential to realize up to $45 million in administrative efficiencies and cost avoidances by the year 2000.

- The Agricultural Marketing Service completed a review of all its regulations. As a result, 2,000 pages will be removed from the *Code of Federal Regulations* during the next two years. Net annual savings will amount to $200,000.

Reinventing government is not easy. It involves people. It takes time. But the end result is worthwhile—a more responsive, more flexible, and less bureaucratic USDA that better serves the American people. Our top priority is, and will continue to be, customer service. USDA employees are on the front lines where they can deliver information, answer questions, and provide needed services to the American people.

Dan Glickman

Department of Commerce
Mickey Kantor, Secretary

Mission Statement

The Department of Commerce promotes job creation, economic growth, sustainable development, and improved living standards for all Americans by working in partnership with businesses, universities, communities, and workers. The Department's mission is to:

- build for the future and promote U.S. competitiveness in the global marketplace by strengthening and safeguarding the nation's economic infrastructure;
- keep America competitive with cutting-edge science and technology and an unrivaled, forward-looking information base; and
- provide effective management of our nation's resources and strengths to ensure sustainable economic opportunities.

Summary Budget Information

FY 1993 (Actual)		FY 1996 (Budgeted)	
Budget	Staff	Budget	Staff
$3.216 billion	38,343	$3.632 billion	35,842

Reinvention Highlights

When the late Secretary of Commerce Ron Brown joined the Department, he knew it was time for a new customer service contract with the American people—and time for a new guarantee of effective, efficient, and responsive government. His goal was to make the Department of Commerce more streamlined and results-oriented—to create incentives and tools that allow managers to manage and deliver services more effectively. In addition, he wanted the Department to strive to identify opportunities to reduce costs while maintaining the same or better levels of service to customers.

As Secretary of Commerce, I plan to continue to strive towards the goal of creating an organization that encourages innovation and focuses on bottom-line, pragmatic results. Techniques such as strategic planning, business process reengineering, selective rightsizing, and organizational streamlining have been vital to that goal. Immediately upon taking office, I moved to institute certain specific, measurable management and administrative reforms with the following goals:

- Reduce the Department's workforce this year by an additional 5 percent beyond what has been called for by both the Congress and this Administration.
- Eliminate two existing regulations for every single new one imposed. Dramatic results have already been attained. For example, the Economic Development Administration deleted 62 percent of its regulations.

- Cut unneeded layers of management. Here, too, there has been progress, as evidenced by the example of the Import Administration's reduction of its management structure from five layers to three.

With the smallest budget of any Cabinet Department, Commerce provides the biggest bang for the buck by helping businesses, workers, and communities build a stronger U.S. economy. We are successful not by accident, but because we have learned serious lessons from the business community. We have improved functions that support Commerce's core mission — to enhance and ensure economic opportunity for all Americans — and eliminated activities and jobs that do not. In fact, the Commerce Department has a major role in the President's plan to balance the budget by cutting government. With major new initiatives, some of which are highlighted below, we are achieving significant savings.

Census Bureau Reengineering and Entrepreneurship Laboratory. We are reengineering the year 2000 decennial census by using a simple new machine-readable questionnaire, coupled with sampling techniques to complete the enumeration. The reengineered decennial census will save nearly $900 million from 1995 to 2002 and deliver the most far-reaching, accurate census ever.

Together with the private sector, the Census Bureau will market custom tabulations of census data. We anticipate that this venture will yield a revenue of $50 million ($10 million for fiscal year 1996 and an additional $40 million expected from 1997 through 2000).

Export Assistance "One Stop" Centers. Meeting customer needs has been a top priority for both former Secretary Brown and me. In the past, businesspeople looking for help in exporting had to contact several federal agencies separately. Secretary Brown's solution was the U.S. Export Assistance Center—a single office that brings together in one location information and often staff, from Commerce, The Small Business Administration, the Export-Import Bank, and state agencies. We have expanded the original four pilot Centers to 88 located throughout the country.

National Oceanic and Atmospheric Administration (NOAA). Initiatives under way at NOAA include the following:

- **Reinvention of the NOAA Corps.** An estimated $27 million will be saved from streamlining that reduced the NOAA Corps by 130 employees from the 1994 level. In addition, the administration is finalizing a legislative proposal to terminate the corps as a uniformed service which may generate additonal savings.
- **Streamlining of the National Weather Service (NWS).** By restructuring and modernizing the technology for predicting the weather, we can close about 200 unneeded NWS field stations, resulting in a savings of $273 million over five years. We will continue to privatize certain specialized weather services, allowing a bigger role for commercial weather services that provide information to marine and agriculture users. This will save $44 million.
- **Establishment of Polar Satellite Program.** In cooperation with the Defense Department and the National Aeronautics and Space Administration, we are establishing a civilian operational environmental polar satellite program and exploring new ways to share technology and environmental data. This satellite convergence initiative is expected to yield significant cost savings—over $1 billion over the lifetime of the program.

Commerce Performance-Based Organizations (PBOs). This initiative is designed to reinvent operations at three bureaus into more flexible and autonomous operational units and make managers directly accountable for measurable results. The program is based on the British "next steps" agency approach to reinvention, in which business-like agencies with separable policy and operational functions are given operating flexibility in exchange for strict management accountability for improved performance. We are proposing four pilots under this initiative. For example, the National Technical Information Service is currently self-funded from sales of government-created information products to the public. As a PBO pilot program, this service will be able to use flexible business practices to serve its customers better.

Streamlining Operations and Workforce. As a result of our reinvention initiatives, we have cut 2,501 jobs from the Commerce payroll since 1993. In addition to reducing the workforce, we have streamlined our operations and cut regulations to ease the burden on the business community. For example, Commerce has accomplished the following:

- We changed export controls on computers and telecommunications equipment, eliminating requirements for prior approval on over $32 billion worth of exports. The Department has also completed the first comprehensive rewrite of Bureau of Export Administration regulations in 45 years.
- We have drastically cut regulations. For example, NOAA consolidated, eliminated, and repealed obsolete or redundant regulations, reducing its regulatory burden by 45 percent.
- We have reduced grants processing time across the Department by 25 percent. We have simplified forms, encouraged electronic filing, and coordinated data sharing with other statistical agencies to reduce respondent burdens, thereby saving the private sector hundreds of thousands of dollars in time and money.
- We have simplified forms, encouraged electronic filing, and coordinated data sharing with other statistical agencies to reduce respondent burdens, thereby saving the private sector hundreds of thousands of dollars in time and money.

Finally, we have focused our efforts on being a customer-driven organization. Twenty-seven separate customer service plans are now in place, including advisory and assistance services, business facilitation, export licensing, weather services, patent and trademark information, and a variety of other activities. These plans contain nearly 200 specific standards by which our customers may judge our performance and let us know if we are meeting our promises and their expectations. Aided by these plans, we will continue to work in partnership with businesses, workers, and communities to improve U.S. competitiveness and enhance economic opportunity for all Americans.

Mickey Kantor

Department of Defense
William J. Perry, Secretary

Mission Statement

In the uncertainty that has followed the Cold War, the United States has not only the opportunity, but also the responsibility, to help ensure a safer world for generations of Americans. President Clinton has said, "As the world's greatest power, we have an obligation to lead and, at times when our interests and our values are sufficiently at stake, to act."

In this new era, the Department of Defense (DOD) mission is to:

- prevent threats to our security from emerging;
- maintain well-trained, ready forces able to deter or respond quickly to a range of potential threats and prepared to seize opportunities;
- defend the national interest through military force as a last resort and after balancing the risks and costs associated with such intervention; and
- use military forces in certain specific situations to address humanitarian crises when other approaches have failed.

Summary Budget Information
*Total obligational authority in current dollars.
**Includes only direct hires.

FY 1993 (Actual)			FY 1996 (Budgeted)		
Budget*	Civilian**	Military	Budget	Civilian**	Military
$270.300 billion	931,300	1,705,100	$254.500 billion	800,300	1,481,700

Reinvention Highlights

Contrary to the hopes of many and the predictions of some, the end of the Cold War did not bring an end to international conflict. The threats to our national security have been replaced with new dangers in regions such as Central and Eastern Europe. These new dangers make the task of protecting the nation's security in some ways more complex than during the Cold War. The new security environment has required a significant evolution in our strategy for managing conflict and has required new innovative defense programs and management philosophies to implement that strategy successfully.

No security strategy is better than the forces that carry it out. Today, the United States has forces that are the best trained and best equipped. Their performance over the last several years in the Persian Gulf, Haiti, and Bosnia demonstrates their superior capability. The Department has maintained unprecedented levels of readiness through a drawdown of historic proportions. From fiscal year (FY) 1993 through FY 1996, the Department's military forces will decrease from 1,705,100 to 1,481,700, while civilian employment (direct hires) will decline from 931,300 to 800,300 in the same period.

The Department will also undertake a new round of modernization through increases in expenditures, while achieving significant savings from infrastructure reductions of base closings, defense acquisition reform, and outsourcing of additional support activities. These efforts, which support the initiatives of the President and Vice President to make government work better and cost less, are described below.

Downsizing Goals and Accomplishments. The DOD Streamlining Plan charges Pentagon leadership with identifying high-payoff areas, establishing realistic goals that link authority with responsibility, eliminating unnecessary controls, and creating opportunities for innovators.

The focus of the civilian reductions called for in the National Performance Review (NPR) is limited to the direct hire portion of DOD's workforce. Because current DOD plans call for continued downsizing through FY 2001, and NPR reductions cover the period FYs 1994-99, DOD expects to exceed the reduction target set by NPR.

During the FYs 1994-95 period, civilian reductions have amounted to 110,000, or 12 percent of the workforce. The reduction plan for FYs 1996-99 should produce a reduction of another 100,000 civilians. Thus, by FY 1999, DOD expects to have cut its civilian workforce by 210,000, or 23 percent.

Management Innovations and Infrastructure Reductions. The Department has launched major efforts to restructure, reorganize, and reduce overhead in a wide variety of support activities ranging from logistics to transportation; from finance and accounting to printing, map-making, and commissary operations. A newly compiled list of dozens of success stories involving major initiatives at all levels within the Department shows that DOD employees have seized the opportunity to propose changes of an innovative kind that will make the Department more efficient and less costly to operate.

For example, the Defense Mapping Agency has reorganized its operations, consolidated its locations, modernized its operations, and reduced its costs to customers, while putting in place a greatly improved customer service operation. The Defense Commissary Agency has introduced new methods for improving the efficiency of delivery of goods to its stores. A new payment method is in place that uses the delivery ticket accompanying each shipment as the invoice. This new method of payment has reduced the labor associated with bill-paying by 40 percent, or by 140 staff jobs.

The Defense Logistics Agency (DLA) received a Hammer Award from NPR for an ongoing program to improve, streamline, and redesign its civilian personnel program. DLA focused on simplified, cost-effective work processes and relied on employee ownership of programs and methods to evaluate the effectiveness of its programs in order to meet the key goal of putting customer needs first. DLA also reengineered parts of its distribution process at Columbus, Ohio, cutting average time to fill a customer order at the depot from 11.8 days in 1993 to 2.0 days in 1994. DLA has initiated dozens of other efficiencies in its large supply and contract management businesses.

The Defense Printing Service has, since its establishment in 1992, reduced its staff by 43 percent, reduced the number of facilities by 30 percent and square footage by 700,000 square feet, disposed of over 4,000 items of obsolete or traditional printing equipment, and saved $70 million annually. In the past year, the Service has won five Hammer Awards for its innovative approaches to management.

Two Army organizations won the two top quality awards in the federal government this year. The Army Armament Research, Development and Engineering Center's Picatinny Arsenal in New Jersey is this year's winner of the Presidential Award for Quality. This is the public sector equivalent of the Malcolm Baldrige National Quality Award to private sector companies. This organization reduced internal overhead costs by $70 million annually while maintaining quality operations. The Army's Communication-Electronic Command Logistics and Readiness Center at Fort Monmouth, New Jersey, is the winner of the Quality Improvement Prototype Award.

The Department has made major use of NPR's reinvention laboratories, designed to allow and encourage organizations to reinvent themselves and seek waivers of regulations to help them do so. The Department has more than 80 such labs.

Financial Management Reform. Since its inception in January 1991, the Defense Finance and Accounting Service (DFAS) has been the Department's pivotal agent for financial management reform and consolidation. Through FY 1995, DFAS achieved budget savings of $314 million and has reduced its staffing from approximately 30,000 to 23,800.

The consolidation of DOD finance systems is well under way:

- By 1997, the Defense Civilian Payroll System will be fully implemented, replacing 27 separate payroll systems.
- By 1999, the Defense Joint Military Pay System will be fully implemented, consolidating the original 22 military pay systems down to two.
- The Defense Debt Management System became operational in 1993. It standardizes the collection of debts from military and civilian personnel not on active payroll, as well as delinquent contractor payments.

Another important financial management reengineering effort is simplifying the process for travel by DOD civilian and military personnel. The goal is to eliminate many of the steps now required to initiate travel, process a voucher, and receive payment. A new paperless system will meet the needs of travelers, support mission requirements, and save as much as $100 million annually.

Base Closure and Realignment. A change that makes good sense and saves money is closing and realigning military bases. Since 1988, 20 percent of the major military installations in the United States and over 200 smaller installations have been approved for closure. We project that when these closures are fully implemented, we will save $6 billion in FY 2000 and each year thereafter. We have also reduced overseas installations by 58 percent, for annual savings of over $1 billion. Our efforts to manage this process have been aimed at saving money while ensuring that troops have the training and equipment they need to be ready in the future.

Acquisition Reform. We continue the efforts to fulfill the Defense acquisition reform vision—that DOD will become the world's smartest (use of best practices), most responsive buyer (timely and flexible) of the best value goods and services that meet our warfighters' needs. The Department will continue its efforts across the entire acquisition spectrum from statutory reform to cultural change, from the beginning of the process—when a requirement is generated—to the end of the process—when the contract is closed.

The following two initiatives reflect continuing progress toward reinventing and reengineering the DOD acquisition system.

- **Acquisition System Reengineering.** In FY 1994, the Department implemented the Electronic Commerce/Electronic Data Interchange system for the procurement of items within the simplified acquisition threshold. The system will allow vendors to connect with commercial value-added networks that access the entire DOD system at one primary and one backup site and receive data on all planned purchases.

- Policy Limiting Government-Unique Procurements. In FY 1994, the Pentagon established a policy that relies upon nongovernmental performance standards and specifications for most procurements, in place of the old "milspecs" system.

Outsourcing. The purpose of the Department's outsourcing initiative is to sustain or improve readiness, generate savings for modernization, and improve the quality and efficiency of support to our men and women in uniform. It involves the transfer of a function previously performed in a government facility to an outside, private sector provider. Doing so offers us significant opportunities to generate savings and perform tasks more efficiently. For instance, a system in which medical suppliers deliver products directly to their DOD customers, rather than to a warehouse for storage and subsequent distribution, has cut delivery time by 75-to-90 percent and cut costs to taxpayers by 25-to-35 percent. There are, of course, limits. The Department will not pursue outsourcing activities that compromise our core warfighting missions.

As the Department of Defense completes the transition to a post-Cold War military force, it has undertaken policies and programs to prevent threats to our security from emerging; and to maintain well-trained, ready forces able to deter or respond quickly to a range of potential threats. The Department is moving rapidly to change the way it manages its resources so that it can use them efficiently, reducing overhead costs and ensuring a strong military force into the future.

William J. Perry

Department of Education
Richard W. Riley, Secretary

Mission Statement

The mission of the Department of Education is to ensure equal access to education and to promote educational excellence throughout the nation. To accomplish this, the Department of Education will:

- help children achieve higher academic standards,
- help states and communities create systems for comprehensive school-to-work opportunities,
- ensure access to high-quality postsecondary education and lifelong learning, and
- transform the Department of Education into a high-performance organization.

Summary Budget Information

FY 1993 (Actual)		FY 1996 (Budgeted)	
Budget	Staff	Budget	Staff
$31.471 billion	4,876	$30.385 billion	4,750

Reinvention Highlights

The Fort Worth Independent School District launched top-to-bottom reforms at four inner-city elementary schools marked by a very high percentage of financially and academically disadvantaged students. When school officials needed financial assistance for this effort and flexibility in how the money was spent, they turned to the U.S. Department of Education.

Fort Worth received from the reinvented Department of Education a waiver of federal regulations, providing extra money for disadvantaged students in exchange for higher expectations in student performance. To enhance student achievement, Fort Worth is now trying an array of reforms: lengthening the school year, intensifying instruction in reading and math, providing extensive training for teachers, and strengthening the schools' links to their communities.

The waiving of federal regulations as a means of encouraging school improvement efforts is just one example of how the Department of Education is simplifying federal programs without sacrificing accountability and results.

The direct loan program, a streamlined alternative to the current guaranteed loan program, typifies our focus on the customer. In direct lending, federal funds are electronically transferred to students via their campus financial aid office, eliminating the complicated involvement of federally subsidized banks and other financial institutions. The direct loan program simplified loan application procedures, resulting in less paperwork for colleges and quicker and more accurate payments to students. Students also benefit from the broadest array of repayment options available anywhere.

The Department provides colleges that participate in direct lending with computer software and an on-line connection to the Department to expedite the delivery of funds to students. For the first time in the history of student lending, on-line, real-time information is available to help us serve customers better and ensure accountability in the loan program. Response among colleges enlisted in the program has been very positive, as shown by surveys conducted by the Department and the media. On a related front, an increasingly vigilant focus and the availability of new legal options enabled the Department to drive up collections on defaulted student loans from $879 million in 1990 to $1.9 billion in 1995.

To an unprecedented degree, the Department's employees are united in pursuit of a shared goal: reinventing the Department under a "less is more" approach. With fewer regulations, the Department's customers gain greater flexibility. With fewer supervisory employees, front-line employees have greater decisionmaking powers in serving customers. With fewer levels in the Department's organizational chart, more employees are at the reinvention table, increasing the chance for continuity in the educational improvement efforts now being implemented.

One effort that cultivated input from every level of the Department is the Low-Hanging Apples Team, a squad of career employees named for the apples on the lowest branches of the tree — the ones that are the ripest and easiest to pick. In reinvention terms, this means identifying unnecessary and burdensome red tape that impedes work progress but can easily be eliminated or changed. The fruits of this team's labor include more than 100 streamlining recommendations, including the abolition of excessive reviews, the elimination of unnecessary personnel paperwork, and better use of technology.

Less Paperwork for Everyone. The Department is meeting its commitment to the President, under his regulatory reform initiative, by eliminating or reinventing our regulations. To date, 1,699 pages have been eliminated or reinvented, with an additional 285 pages planned for elimination or reinvention by September 1996.

Future regulatory efforts will be guided by my commitment as Secretary to "regulate only when necessary and then with as much sensitivity and as little burden as possible." Clinton Administration initiatives reflect this approach — the Goals 2000: Educate America Act and the School to Work Opportunities Act have no new regulations at all.

The Department's streamlined approach to regulation, combined with advancements in technology, is easing the paperwork burden for America's schools and colleges. The Goals 2000 school reform grant application is just four pages long, a feat of simplicity that was honored with a National Performance Review Hammer Award. States are encouraged to submit a single consolidated application for all of their elementary and secondary programs in the Improving America's Schools Act.

Recognizing that information is one of the most valued products that the Department offers, we are making the Department a world-class clearinghouse for education information. Our toll-free phone numbers offer easy access for people to order Department publications, receive a referral to the correct office within the Department, or obtain student financial aid information. The Department's World Wide Web site — recognized by Internet World magazine as one of the most useful education resources on the Internet — and on-line bulletin board systems provide information.

The Department also restructured its grants process to eliminate unnecessary requirements and improve the timeliness of grantee notification. We cut the number of steps taken to make a discretionary grant by 50 percent, the processing time by 25 percent, and the notification time by as much as three months. We also eliminated annual submission of continuation applications and the annual negotiation of 6,000 continuation grants.

Union of Labor and Management. Among the most vivid displays of stronger collaboration within the Department is the formation of its first-ever Labor-Management Partnership Council. When the Clinton Administration took office, labor-management relations at the Department were at an all-time low. Today, labor and management have an ongoing dialogue about all issues affecting both policy and personnel.

The 12-member council draws its roster equally from management and labor representatives. The council is playing a major role in reinvention by helping shape changes in areas such as employee performance appraisal, reward, and incentive programs; and employee training and development. More significantly, the council has provided a permanent framework to tackle head-on problems that once festered because of historically poor labor-management relations. The involvement of our most senior-level officials in the council's creation and operations is an important symbol of the Department's commitment to the partnership.

Richard W. Riley

Department of Energy
Hazel R. O'Leary, Secretary

Mission Statement

The Department of Energy (DOE), in partnership with our customers, provides effective leadership—for this country and internationally—in promoting efficient energy use, diversity in energy sources, a more productive and competitive economy, improved environmental quality, and national security.

The Department has established four clear business lines to accomplish this mission:

- **Energy Resources.** We encourage energy efficiency; advance alternative and renewable energy technologies; increase energy choices for all customers; ensure adequate supplies of clean, conventional energy; and reduce U.S. vulnerability to external events that could disrupt energy supplies and services.
- **Science and Technology.** We use the unique resources of the Department's laboratories and the country's universities to maintain leadership in basic research that is focused on national defense and, increasingly, on applied research in support of the Department's other business lines, including energy efficiency and environmental cleanup. We maintain international technical leadership through long-term, systemic reform of science and mathematics education.
- **National Security.** We effectively support and maintain a safe, secure, and reliable weapons stockpile without nuclear testing; we safely dismantle and dispose of excess weapons; and we provide the technical leadership for national and global nuclear nonproliferation activities.
- **Environmental Quality.** We have identified and controlled the environmental, safety, and health risks and threats from DOE facilities and decisions; are actively cleaning up contaminated sites; and are developing new, more cost-effective technologies required for solving domestic and global environmental problems.

Summary Budget Information

FY 1993 (Actual)		FY 1996 (Budgeted)	
Budget	Staff	Budget	Staff
$19.341 billion	20,410	$16.189 billion	19,762

Reinvention Highlights

I became Secretary in 1993, more than three years after the fall of the Berlin Wall and the end of the Cold War. The Department that I inherited was struggling to define its new role in the post-Cold War world.

The past three-and-a-half years have been a time of aggressive internal reform, organizational change, and fundamental rethinking at the Department of Energy. More than ever before, the entire DOE family—which includes both federal and contractor employees—has accepted the premise of change and continuous improvement as the only course to a successful future. We are taking the risks that change requires.

Defining Purpose. In 1993, we found an agency beset with uncertainty about its fundamental purpose, responsibilities, and missions. By early 1994, with the input of hundreds of our own employees, we developed and released the first strategic plan for the Department of Energy. This document clarified our core missions and set our priorities. By defining who we were, our outlook, and strategies and measures by which to evaluate our accomplishments, we put into place a new cornerstone of support—a prerequisite for the success of any business.

Reforming Contract Management. We found a contracting system plagued with problems, including inadequate oversight and management controls. In February 1994, after months of intensive effort, our contract reform team issued a report that set the stage for enhanced competition for contracts and a shift to performance-based contracting, which ties payment to performance and specific accomplishments rather than to a contractor's level of effort. During the past two years, we incorporated provisions into 11 of our largest contracts related to greater financial accountability, cost reductions, and performance-based incentives. We are continuing to incorporate these reforms into other contracts as they come up for extension or competition. These fundamental changes will result in significant savings in the coming years.

Reassessing the Role of Laboratories. In February 1995, the Task Force on Alternative Futures for the Department of Energy Laboratories, acting under the leadership of Robert Galvin, Chairman of the Executive Committee of Motorola, Inc., produced the first post-Cold War assessment of our defense laboratories. We are now well under way in implementing most of the report's recommendations to reduce the cost of doing business, redefine the mission of the laboratories, and further advance the impressive record of the laboratories' scientific achievements. Our newly established Laboratory Operations Board will ensure dedicated management attention on a continuing basis.

Reassessing Applied Energy Programs. We committed ourselves to substantial savings for the taxpayers by assessing our $1.8 billion portfolio of applied energy programs. In June of 1995, a task force led by Daniel Yergin, the Pulitzer Prize-winning author and President of Cambridge Energy Research Associates, Inc., completed this review. We are implementing the recommendations of the report and will save $1.2 billion over the next five years.

Reinventing Internal Management Practices. After reviewing the Department's management and administrative practices, we realized that we needed to take a hard look at ourselves and how we were operating. In the fall of 1994, we launched the Strategic Alignment Initiative, an intense four-month, no-holds-barred self-examination by 37 of our most seasoned and enthusiastic career employees. Collectively, this group knew more about who we were and how we could improve than any other group that could be assembled.

The issue papers prepared by the alignment team reflected interviews, reviews of work documentation, and collaboration with the political leadership of the agency, stakeholders, customers, contractors and others. Every idea that had ever been advanced for the Department to work smarter or better was filtered through this group for analysis. During the course of this review, every process was touched, every office was scrutinized, and virtually every departmental product and service was tested for value.

We announced the results of the Strategic Alignment initiative in May 1995. The plan represented a major package of organizational, legislative, and cost-cutting actions to drive down costs and at the same time enhance the performance of our missions—$1.7 billion will be saved over five years.

This employee-driven initiative will result in downsizing the workforce of the Department by 27 percent over the next five years—almost 5,000 employees. We also promised that more than 65 percent of the reductions would occur in the first two years, and we are right on track. We project to exceed the fiscal year 1996 target by 22 percent, saving $10 million more of the taxpayers' dollars this year than was projected.

After reviewing the management of the Department's national defense complex, comprising dozens of industrial facilities and laboratories across the country, we promised to cut our travel costs by $35 million annually and sell $75 million of precious metals and other assets in our inventory. We also committed to save $450 million through reductions in our use of support service contractors, and $245 million by restructuring information management systems over a five-year period.

We are now delivering on those commitments. We expect to exceed the 1996 projected savings in travel costs by $5 million because of particular diligence by our contractors. We have already sold more than $4 million from our inventory of precious metals and other assets. We expect to save $30 million more than promised this year in expenses for support service contractors because our managers have agreed to ceilings that are lower than the original targets. We also project to save $11 million more this year than targeted in restructuring information systems because of aggressive efforts by our Information Resource Management team.

Our first year savings of $221 million have already been confirmed by a General Accounting Office review.

What is the bottom line on all these initiatives and efforts? The Department of Energy is really improving and changing for the better. During the past three-and-one-half years, we have redefined a critical national and international mission, streamlined and downsized, and reengineered many of our key processes—which will culminate in savings to the taxpayer of more than $10.5 billion over a five-year period. This is what reinventing government is all about.

Hazel R. O'Leary

Environmental Protection Agency
Carol M. Browner, Administrator

Mission Statement

The mission of the United States Environmental Protection Agency is to protect public health and to safeguard and improve the natural environment—air, water, and land—upon which human life depends. EPA's purpose is to ensure that:

- federal environmental laws are implemented and enforced fairly effectively, and cost effectively;
- environmental protection is an integral consideration in U.S. policies concerning economic growth, energy, transportation, agriculture, industry, international trade, and natural resources;
- national efforts to reduce environmental risk are based on the best available scientific information; and
- all parts of society—business, state and local governments, communities, citizens—have full access to information so that they can become full participants in preventing pollution and protecting human health and the environment.

Summary Budget Information

FY 1993 (Actual)		FY 1996 (Budgeted)	
Budget	Staff	Budget	Staff
$6.928 billion	17,479	$6.523 billion	17,416

Reinvention Highlights

Three and a half years ago, when President Clinton, Vice President Gore, and I came to Washington, we were determined to build on the environmental successes of the past 25 years. We committed to take a series of common-sense, high-priority actions to change our system of environmental regulation—to move beyond mere regulation to true protection and to streamline the means by which we guarantee these protections.

As President Clinton has said, our philosophy of reinvention is simple: Protect people, not bureaucracy; promote results, not rules; get action, not rhetoric.

Today, the changes we have made are reaping benefits for business, strengthening environmental protection, and achieving real results for communities across the country.

Paperwork and Red Tape Reduction. Fifteen-million hours of paperwork burden required of business and communities at the beginning of 1995 are no longer required of them. This includes 12-million hours from requirements changed or deleted, and three-million hours from requirements completed or expired. By the end of 1996, we expect to eliminate another eight million hours of paperwork, including 4.5-million hours from requirements changed or deleted,

90

and 3.5-million hours from requirements completed or expired — time that will no longer be spent filling out needless forms.

Good Faith Efforts by Business. We lowered penalties for small business owners who come forward with a commitment to fix environmental problems. To meet the needs of small businesses for precise, easy-to-use information on how best to comply with environmental laws, we are establishing Small Business Compliance Assistance Centers.

But for those intransigent polluters—those who carelessly disregard their responsibility to protect our air and water—the public has every right to demand that their government take swift, aggressive enforcement action. And we have taken that action. We have collected the largest penalties ever from those who violate the law, those who pollute the air, the water, the land.

Innovation and Flexibility. Through our cutting-edge program called Project XL—for excellence and leadership—businesses work with their communities not just to meet environmental requirements, but to exceed the minimum and get better environmental results than ever. Our Common Sense Initiative and Environmental Leadership Program also challenge companies to take innovative approaches to controlling pollution.

Our Performance Partnerships give states and tribes the flexibility they need to target federal environmental funds to meet the particular environmental needs of their communities.

Community Participation in Public Health and Environmental Protection. We strengthened the public's right to know about toxic pollution in their communities, expanding both the number of companies that must report about pollution and the number of toxic chemicals on which they must report.

We launched the Brownfields Action Agenda to provide seed money and tax incentives to clean up the idle, abandoned industrial properties that dot the cities of this country and once again turn them into centers of economic activity. We removed 27,000 sites from the database of potential Superfund sites, clearing the way for redevelopment.

Strengthened Public Health Standards. This Administration, in accordance with the Clean Air Act, adopted new air toxic standards that should result in a reduction of 2.5 million tons of toxic air pollution per year. We set tough standards for dioxin emissions that will achieve a 99 percent reduction in dioxin emissions from municipal incinerators. We banned the use of dangerous pesticides.

The Clinton Administration set the first-ever toxic water quality standards for all of the Great Lakes—lakes that provide drinking water for 23 million people. We negotiated a consensus plan to protect the San Francisco Bay Delta and announced a bold new plan to protect the Everglades. Through the voluntary Partnership for Safe Drinking Water, EPA worked with water suppliers to protect the public from drinking water contamination.

This Administration accelerated the pace of cleanup of toxic waste dump sites by 20 percent and significantly reduced the cost. In just three years, we completed cleanup of more toxic waste sites than in the previous 12 years of the Superfund cleanup program.

A Healthy Economy Begets a Healthier Environment. By changing the system, by strengthening the standards, by enforcing the law, we can enjoy the benefits of a healthy environment and a healthy economy. President Clinton has always believed that environmental protection and a growing economy can and must go hand in hand—that we do not have to choose between our jobs and our health.

Today, unemployment is at its lowest in six years. Inflation is in check. Under the Clinton Administration, the economy has delivered over 10-million new jobs, two-million new businesses, and 4.4-million new homeowners. At the same time, toxic pollution from industry declined by more than 19 percent between 1992 and 1994 alone—the latest years for which we have figures. A healthy economy begets a healthier environment; a healthy environment, in turn, a stronger economy.

Carol M. Browner

Carol M. Browner

Federal Emergency Management Agency

James Lee Witt, Director

Mission Statement

The mission of the Federal Emergency Management Agency (FEMA) is to reduce the loss of life and property and protect our institutions from all hazards by leading and supporting the nation in a comprehensive, risk-based emergency management program of mitigation, preparedness, response, and recovery.

FEMA has adopted five mission-associated goals and one organizational goal to guide its management and program decisions. These are to accomplish the following:

- create an emergency management partnership with other federal agencies, state and local governments, volunteer organizations, and the private sector to serve our customers better;
- establish, in concert with FEMA's partners, a national emergency management system that is comprehensive, risk-based, and all-hazards in approach;
- make hazard mitigation the foundation of the national emergency management system;
- provide a rapid and effective response to, and recovery from, disaster;
- strengthen state and local emergency management; and
- revitalize the agency and develop a more diverse and effective cadre of FEMA managers and employees.

Summary Budget Information

FY 1993 (Actual)		FY 1996 (Budgeted)	
Budget*	Staff**	Budget*	Staff**
$3.106 billion	4,476	$4.328 billion	3,930

*Actual obligations and estimated obligation for discretionary funds, including the Disaster Relief Fund and disaster supplemental appropriations. It excludes fee-supported insurance funds.
**Also reflects temporary staff used for disaster operations.

Reinvention Highlights

When I became director in 1993, the agency was under intense fire from Congress and the media. There was a widespread lack of confidence in the abilities of the agency to respond to and help communities recover from disasters.

We are proud that through a total reorganization and a basic cultural change internally we have regained the trust of the citizens that this is an agency that responds quickly, efficiently, effectively, and with compassion. When we announce that we are from the federal government and we're here to help, it's not a joke—people really believe us.

My first day at FEMA, I taped a permanent sign on my desk for all to see. It says, "Please don't say we've never done it that way before."

Reorganizing Operations. The agency overhaul aligned its programs and activities along functional lines. We created an all-hazards agency, making personnel and material assets once reserved strictly for national security available for deployment during any major disaster regardless of the cause. One of the assets, our Mobile Emergency Response System—which includes transportable telephone, water purification, heating and air conditioning systems, and satellite communications—has been used to support field offices at many disasters. These include the Midwest floods, the Northridge earthquake, Hurricane Marilyn, and the Oklahoma City bombing.

Using Technology. FEMA's Disaster Assistance Program was reorganized to employ new technologies to register disaster applicants, conduct property inspections, process information, and distribute checks for disaster-related housing needs. This new streamlined program has cut in half the time it takes for assistance to reach disaster victims and has reduced the program's annual administrative costs by an estimated $35 million. The overall program won an award for excellence in public service. The changes in this program include the following:

- **Teleregistration.** Previously, disaster victims had to register for aid at disaster application centers in the field, which took four to five days to set up. Now, we use a toll-free number to gather applications by phone, allowing victims to begin applying for aid within hours of a presidential declaration. This has also eliminated the costs of setting up and staffing these centers.
- **Computerized Application Forms.** These forms have eliminated steps in the process, increased accuracy, and reduced time to process applications.
- Computerized Inspection. The Automated Construction Estimating system is a palm-pad computer that allows inspectors to download addresses to be inspected and upload damage data to central processing. This used to be done by hand and sent by mail. Accuracy of awards has been improved by 30 percent with this system. The system won the Federal Technology Leadership Award for 1995.
- **Central Processing.** The old paper-driven process that was deployed at each disaster site has been replaced by a completed computerized system, consolidated at two central locations for the nation.

Under the newly created Response and Recovery Directorate, several programs have been developed to speed disaster assistance. They include three Emergency Response Teams, each team on call for 30 days on a rotating basis. Team members train together, are fully equipped with specialized "go" kits, are deployable within hours, and are ready to hit the ground running. The Field Assessment Teams (FasT) are now pre-positioned when we can forecast an impending disaster such as a hurricane, and provide better and faster assessments after a disaster.

We've improved communications with the public through the Recovery Channel, a satellite-delivered television production set up in major catastrophic events; this also won a Federal Technology Leadership award. *The Recovery Times* is a newspaper we've created for disaster victims; it has won top honors from the Public Relations Society of America. FEMA's very popular World Wide Web site carries real-time situation reports on disasters.

We found that there was no inventory of federal-owned and contractor-supported disaster resources such as plastic sheeting, cots, tents, and generators. We set up a computer data base of these supplies and are in the process of establishing warehouses where they would be stored and returned for reuse. We also found that there was little oversight on supply purchases using the Presidential Disaster Fund. We established the Disaster Review Board to ensure need and accountability of these expenditures.

Response Teams and Training. Two initiatives significantly helped in the emergency response to the tragic Oklahoma City bombing. FEMA provided federal leadership and support for the formation of 25 Urban Search and Rescue teams. We deployed 12 of these during the response to the bombing. The Oklahoma City Fire Department was one of 75,000 fire departments to undergo specialized training at FEMA's National Emergency Training Center. The instruction coincidentally had taken place just a few weeks before the bombing and provided valuable training that helped department members do an outstanding job after the terrible incident.

Reducing the Effects of Disasters. Improving response and recovery is critical, but so too is working to reduce the effects of disasters. That's why we established a Mitigation Directorate. We've ensured broad participation in the development of a National Mitigation Strategy through the first ever National Mitigation conference. We worked with Congress to gain passage of the Hazard Mitigation and Relocation Assistance Act of 1993. The Volkmer Bill led to an interagency "buyout" program to relocate flood-damaged structures. To date, more than 12,000 properties in over a dozen states have taken part and will never be damaged by flood again. In Missouri alone, the governor notes that the buyout program will save over $200 million over 10 years.

Accomplishments Reflected in Performance. We've accomplished a lot in a short time. The people of FEMA are proud of the turn-around in their agency. The proof of our effectiveness is in our performance. We know that when we perform well, people are safer, recover faster, and keep the faith that someone is there for them at a time when they need it the most. Our goals are ever changing—to keep up with technology, change programs as needed, and develop new strategies to improve emergency management in this country.

FEMA and its Federal Insurance Administration embarked on a special campaign to increase the number of flood insurance policies by 20 percent. The goal was reached seven months ahead of schedule and stands at a 22-percent increase. The increase significantly reduces taxpayer dollars and protects the disaster victims, whom we consider to be our customers.

Customer Service. We take customer service very seriously at FEMA. We recently conducted the first ever customer survey of disaster applicants. Eighty percent were satisfied or very satisfied with the service they received. Their responses helped us develop customer service standards. Customer service training is also mandatory for each and every FEMA employee. Nearly everyone has now completed special customer service training.

Our Region 8 office in Denver developed the concept for regional Centers of Excellence and established a center for community relations. The highly trained community relations teams make a huge difference when deployed to disasters to help victims—our customers—understand the programs available to help them.

Streamlining Operations. As far as leadership within the agency is concerned, we streamlined operations by reducing two layers of management and doubling the supervisor-to-employee ratio. We simplified the budget structure to increase flexibility by reducing operating accounts from 47 to just eight elements, which mirrors the new organization and reflects the vision and goals of the agency. We have reduced internal regulations by 30 percent and are on schedule to reduce them by 50 percent by the end of fiscal year 1996. We have greatly improved labor-management relations with the creation of the Labor-Management Partnership Council. We've empowered employees by involving them in the renewal efforts and have changed the agency culture to value employees and their ideas.

James L. Witt
James Lee Witt

General Services Administration
David J. Barram, Acting Administrator

Mission Statement

The mission of the General Services Administration (GSA) is to improve the effectiveness of the federal government by ensuring quality work environments for its employees.

Summary Budget Information

FY 1993 (Actual)		FY 1996 (Budgeted)	
Budget	Staff	Budget	Staff
$419.2 billion	20,249	$242.5 billion	14,780

Reinvention Highlights

The *Washington Post* has called GSA "the bell weather agency for reinventing government." Between 1981 and 1993, GSA's workforce had already been reduced by half. To manage the workload properly with this reduced workforce, GSA had to adopt competitive, businesslike principles. When Roger Johnson became Administrator in 1993, he ensured that GSA would take a leadership role in customer service and cost-effective management.

To date, GSA has streamlined its businesses as a result of the lessons learned in its 15 National Performance Review (NPR) reinvention laboratories and through the results of our Federal Operations Review Model (FORM).

With the help of Arthur Andersen LLP, FORM analyzed all 16 business lines to determine the most cost-effective and efficient ways of delivering services to federal customers. Every alternative was considered, including privatizing operations, creating government corporations, selling operations to employees, or outright elimination.

In 1995, following NPR's recommendation to GSA, we separated our policy and oversight functions from operations by creating a new Office of Governmentwide Policy. This move consolidated all the policy responsibilities that had been scattered throughout the agency, eliminated the Office of Information Technology, and created the Chief Information Officer position.

Today, throughout GSA, we are incorporating new ideas and a new work ethic that empowers employees and unlocks barriers to innovation.

Real Estate Reforms. Public Buildings Service is implementing major reforms in its property management systems. Can't Beat GSA Leasing, the streamlined leasing process developed and tested in our reinvention lab in Auburn, Washington, was introduced to all 700 Public Buildings Service leasing specialists in an intensive training session in July 1996. All of our leasing specialists will incorporate new practices, effective immediately, to turn the GSA leasing program into a lean, effective, and competitive business. We are so confident that our customers will be impressed by our new program and its results that we are opening up leasing competition in October 1996. Our customers will be given the choice of leasing buildings themselves, hiring contractors to provide guidance, or continuing to use Can't Beat GSA Leasing services. We have already saved $300 million with our new leasing practices and expect to save at least that much again.

Some of the many changes at GSA started by just stopping the practices that had been done the same way for 20 years and looking at how the programs could be run using today's technology and other modern advances. A Time Out and Review in the $7 billion federal building program cut $1.36 billion from new real estate projects, including leases.

Streamlining Information Technology Purchases. The Public Buildings Service with an annual budget of $5 billion has traditionally gained more attention from Congress, the media, and past GSA management than has been given to governmentwide spending for computers—which averaged $20 billion a year for the last 10 years. The Time Out on major federal government computer systems avoided spending $7.4 billion for computer systems with cost overruns and other problems.

Savings on Travel. GSA's Federal Supply Service (FSS) encourages federal workers to be innovative in their thinking to break down barriers in their work environment. FSS has saved countless millions for the taxpayers by using the leverage of being a major customer for our vendors and by initiating new technologies. For example, FSS negotiated unrestricted airfares with major airlines that are on average 50-percent lower than commercial rates. A federal employee can now travel round trip between Washington, D.C., and Los Angeles for $242 on short notice without penalties. We lease four-door sedans to agencies for $136 per month. By consolidating vehicles from other federal agencies under our Fleet Management Program, we saved taxpayers $7.2 million; other management improvements have saved an additional $22.8 million.

Congress is considering reforms to travel laws. If passed, savings could amount to nearly $800 million a year and will provide employees who transfer in the interest of the government with more effective and efficient delivery of relocation allowances, while alleviating administrative burdens and costs associated with processing travel and employee relocation.

GSA has forged other new paths on the way to common-sense management. A new contract with American Express Travel Services for government travel enhances savings, simplicity, and scrutiny. For each dollar spent on the Government Travel Card, American Express pays refunds—estimated at $20 million a year—to the federal government to offset travel expenses. Using the card also saves an estimated $250 million a year in administrative costs and increases financial accountability by tracking each transaction to ensure compliance and proper spending.

Reducing the Cost of Phone Calls. Our common sense management of the FTS 2000 long-distance telephone network has drastically cut costs. Federal customers now pay just 5 cents per network minute for domestic long-distance calls, saving taxpayers $200 million a year. Overall costs under FTS 2000 during the past seven years have been reduced by 80 percent, saving nearly $5 billion compared to the previous long-distance program.

Using Technology to Supply the Federal Workforce. We are a leader in expanding electronic commerce, eliminating burdensome and costly paper-driven procurements while increasing accountability. With our new electronic ordering and payment system, GSA Advantage!, federal customers can order supplies via the Internet. And by using the government purchase card (IMPAC/VISA), federal agencies get better, faster service and will save $475 million by eliminating many of the administrative costs associated with buying and paying for goods and services.

Empowering Workers by Providing Internet Access. We have committed to providing the best tools for all employees at GSA by providing them with access to the Internet. The Internet is the fastest growing and most powerful new tool around for connecting people to each other and to unimaginable amounts of content. That is why we made access to the Internet and our own Intranet available to all our employees in June 1996. There is no doubt that access to and use of the Internet will be a big factor enabling GSA employees to compete in the coming years, because this new resource can change the way we do business.

Creating Family-Friendly Workplaces. Not only do we expect GSA employees to have the capability to work with and access the newest technologies, we also expect to improve the work environment by creating family-friendly workplaces with child care and telecommuting centers. Within the federal community, GSA has been an advocate for programs that let employees work at home or change their work hours to help them balance work and family. There are 112 GSA child care centers across the country. With the growing demand for affordable, quality child care, centers continue to multiply—a total of at least 120 centers are expected to be working by the end of 1996. Currently, there are 30 telecommuting centers and numerous governmentwide telecommuting programs operating throughout the country. The goal is to make telecommuting a reality for 60,000 federal workers by 1998.

We have created a culture that seeks opportunity in change. Today's GSA is leaner and delivers more quality products and services in a more timely fashion than ever before in its 46-year history. Since NPR began, through buyouts and attrition

We have reduced our workforce by 28 percent, reduced our operating costs by 21 percent, and found savings or avoided expenditures of $11.7 billion—all while increasing customer satisfaction. We have incorporated the lessons learned from all our activities into our operations to be better, cheaper, faster, easier, and smarter. We are on the course of continuous improvement, and when it no longer makes sense for GSA to perform a service, we will change it or stop doing it.

David J. Barram

Department of Health and Human Services
Donna E. Shalala, Secretary

Mission Statement

The responsibility of the Department of Health and Human Services (HHS) is to protect and promote the health, social, and economic well-being of all Americans and, in particular, those least able to help themselves—children, the elderly, persons with disabilities, and the disadvantaged—by helping them and their families develop and maintain healthy, productive, and independent lives.

Summary Budget Information

FY 1993 (Actual)*		FY 1996 (Budgeted)	
Budget	Staff	Budget	Staff
$591.000 billion	130,366	$325.000 billion	58,924

*Of this amount, $329 billion and 65,386 full-time equivalents were for the Social Security Administration (SSA), which became an independent agency in 1995. The comparable figures for HHS exclusive of SSA in fiscal year 1993 would be $262 billion in budget and 64,980 staff.

Reinvention Highlights

When we came to the Department of Health and Human Services more than three years ago, we made a commitment: we would make bold changes to serve the American people better with fewer resources. Together, we are making good on that promise.

With a powerful combination of courage, creativity, and common sense, our employees are finding new ways to prevent illness, cure diseases, and get new medicines and medical devices to the people who need them. We're forging new partnerships to provide health, social, and community services to all Americans—from children to seniors, and from families to disabled citizens. We're cracking down on health care fraud and abuse, slamming the door on those who would defraud their government, and saving millions of dollars for the American taxpayers. We're reining in the costs of our health care programs, while providing better services to those citizens who rely upon our Medicare, Medicaid, and the Older Americans Act for their care. And we are doing all of this with fewer people and fewer layers of management.

Reforming Food and Drug Regulations. There are historic changes taking place at the Food and Drug Administration. The truth is, drug companies and medical device manufacturers are right to expect faster turnaround times. Researchers are right to expect less paperwork and better service. People afflicted with life-threatening diseases are right to expect expedited approval and improved access to potentially helpful therapies. And that's what we've worked to do. From 1987 to 1995, we slashed the average approval time for new drugs in half. We've virtually eliminated the backlog of routine medical device applications—and our review times for them keep getting faster and faster. We're changing the way we approve cancer drugs, eliminating burdensome regulations, and ensuring that our citizens get the therapies they need—when they need them.

In the last three years alone, we've approved 13 new drugs to combat AIDS and HIV infection, including three extremely promising anti-retroviral drugs called protease inhibitors—all of which were approved in record time.

In fact, it seems that every month, we set another speed record for approving an AIDS drug, including a recent approval that took just 42 days. It has been estimated that the United States is now two years ahead of the European countries in our approval of new AIDS drugs.

To make these historic changes, we didn't just hire consultants or issue reports. We talked to our partners and our customers. We consulted with patients and advocacy groups, with representatives of the pharmaceutical industry, physicians, and researchers. We asked them what works and what doesn't. And we implemented bold new strategies that cut red tape without undermining our commitment to the health and well-being of the American public. That's the same common-sense approach that we're using throughout our Department.

Creating Partnerships and Providing Flexibility. We're changing the way we do business with all our partners, guaranteeing unprecedented flexibility, but demanding accountability for our citizens in return. For example, under waivers the Administration has approved, more than 40 states are experimenting with innovative welfare reforms that are requiring work, rewarding marriage, demanding responsibility, providing child care, and cracking down on child support enforcement. Today, welfare caseloads are down. Child support enforcement is up. And 10 million Americans are involved in welfare reform plans throughout the country—that's about 75 percent of Aid to Families With Dependent Children recipients.

It's the same throughout our Department. Whether it is operating drug abuse prevention and treatment programs, finding a cure for a rare disease, providing a hot meal for a homebound senior, teaching young Head Start children how to play and learn, or providing health care in underserved areas, we are changing the rules and the role of the federal government so our partners spend less time filling out forms and more time helping the people they serve.

We are also working closely with health care providers and intermediaries to improve service to Medicare and Medicaid beneficiaries. Together, we are listening to our customers and making changes to meet their needs better. We are making our rules and forms easier to understand, and we are finding innovative ways to get out important information about preventive services, like flu shots and mammograms, that are covered under Medicare.

Battling Health Care Fraud. As we continue to improve Medicare services and protect the Medicare Trust Funds, we are saving precious resources by cracking down on health care fraud. To do that, the President created a pilot program to focus our efforts in five key states. It's called Operation Restore Trust. In just one year, it has helped us save more than $42 million for the American taxpayers—that's $10 saved for every $1 spent.

Operation Restore Trust works. It makes sense. And the health care reform bill expands it to every state in America.

At the same time, we're working to bring health care information into the 21st century—and into our citizens' homes and lives. Through the Internet and the World Wide Web, the HHS home page can connect you to the Older Americans Act aging network for social services for the elderly; medical information from the National Library of Medicine at the National Institutes of Health; consumer information about Medicare and Medicaid; cutting-edge information from the Centers for Disease Control and Prevention about how to get healthy and stay healthy; and much, much more.

Reorganizing the Department. It's all part of our efforts to create a Department that works better and works smarter—with fewer layers of management and fewer people. For example, in implementing the Vice President's reinventing government program, we streamlined the structure of HHS by merging some of our operations and eliminating entire management layers. And as part of the President's plan to shrink the size of the federal government dramatically, we reduced our staff by nearly 3,300 positions—a full 5 percent—between 1994 and 1995 alone. To meet the President's overall goals, we committed ourselves to a seven-year "right sizing" plan that will reduce the Department's personnel by 7,000 positions (from the 1993 level) by the year 2000. We are a full year ahead of schedule.

In the three years since the first reinventing government report, we have worked hard and met many of our goals. But we still have a long way to go. I know that, working together, we can and will create a Department of Health and Human Services—and a federal government—that always watches the bottom line and delivers excellence in everything we do.

Donna E. Shalala

Department of Housing and Urban Development
Henry G. Cisneros, Secretary

Mission Statement

The mission of the Department of Housing and Urban Development (HUD) is to help people create communities of opportunity. The programs and resources of the Department help Americans create cohesive, economically healthy communities. At the core of this mission is a set of fundamental commitments: to community; to family; to economic lift, to individual rights and responsibilities; and to ending separation by race, national origin, income, disability, age, and class.

To accomplish this mission, we have focused activities at the Department of Housing and Urban Development on three priority objectives:

- **Increase Homeownership.** We build partnerships with the private sector and streamline internal operations to help more Americans become homeowners.
- **Empower Communities.** We make it easier for neighborhood groups and local officials to use federal resources to create jobs, spur economic development, and revitalize neighborhoods.
- **Transform Public and Assisted Housing.** We're breaking with the past, tearing down and replacing dilapidated buildings, cracking down on crime, and asking residents to take on new responsibilities.

Summary Budget Information

FY 1993 (Actual)		FY 1996 (Budgeted)	
Budget	Staff	Budget	Staff
$25.500 billion	13,294	$19.500 billion	11,628

Reinvention Highlights

When I became HUD Secretary in 1993, it was obvious that the traditional top-down, Washington-directed approach to managing housing programs was not getting the job done.

Thick volumes of rules forced administrators to pay more attention to process than performance. HUD programs made passive clients of people, instead of striking an effective balance of rights and responsibilities. Some HUD programs clearly didn't work—as evidenced by America's most distressed public housing.

Tinkering around the edges would not fix HUD. We decided to act boldly, reinventing the Department as a "right-side-up" agency that puts service to our nation's communities first, even while we trim personnel. In 1993, HUD had 13,300 employees. By 1997, we'll be down to

10,400, with a target of 7,500 by 2000. We'll do more with less staff by returning more power to the neighborhoods and communities where people live, by redesigning operations, and by using cutting-edge computer technology.

Our reinvention has been guided at all times by these imperatives from Vice President Gore's National Performance Review:

- Share responsibility and power with communities.
- Build partnerships with the private sector.
- Work with the market instead of against it.
- Simplify programs to improve service to customers.
- Demand quality in public and assisted housing.

These themes drive everything we do through three key strategies:

Increase Homeownership for All Americans. We have united the powerful but segmented homebuilding industry in a drive to make homeownership easier for all Americans. The National Partners in Homeownership's 58 members—representing government agencies and the real estate, construction, lending, and nonprofit sectors—are making an impact: The national homeownership rate has gone up by 1.6 percentage points in the last two years. This is the steepest two-year increase since statistics began to be collected 31 years ago. The new rate, 65.4 percent, is a 15-year high, as some 4.4-million families have become new homeowners since 1993.

Surveys tell us that closing costs are the principal barrier to buying a home. We've cut those costs an average of $1,000 for homebuyers. New paperless transactions at the Federal Housing Administration (FHA) and streamlined operations at Ginnie Mae are speeding service and reducing costs for mortgage firms, resulting in lower costs and faster service for home buyers. And future homebuyers will save as much as $1.5 billion annually because new HUD rules cut funds homeowners are required to place in escrow accounts.

It used to take six weeks to process mortgage insurance applications. The Denver FHA office cut that time down to one day for residents in Rocky Mountain states. Customers will save an estimated $4 million annually, thanks to faster service. We are replicating the Denver center's work across the nation so that all FHA customers can benefit.

More than 70 mortgage bankers have signed "best practices" agreements with us, committing them to increase lending to minority homebuyers, immigrant families, and others who have been underserved in the past. The first firm to sign an agreement increased lending to minorities by 217 percent in one year, proving that fair housing is good business.

Our aggressive mortgage sales initiative has cut the inventory of defaulted, government-owned properties, and returned homes and buildings to private ownership. We've sold more than 30,000 mortgages with an unpaid principal balance of $3.3 billion to private sector buyers at auction, saving taxpayers $650 million in upkeep and maintenance.

Ginnie Mae condensed 42 processes dealing with mortgage-backed securities, saving lenders $50 million annually by eliminating 180,000 sheets of paper that required 400,000 signatures.

Empower Communities. Our Urban Empowerment Zone initiative, begun in July 1995, brings together community leaders, the private sector, and federal and local governments to plot sustainable economic growth strategies for distressed communities. Partners use tax incentives, grants, and loans—and their own ingenuity—to attract private investments worth billions of dollars and to create thousands of jobs. In Boston, Detroit, and other cities, companies have already moved into the zones, bringing jobs and hope where neither existed before.

In the past, local governments submitted separate funding applications for each of 12 HUD community development programs. Now, under our streamlined consolidated plan, our local partners submit a single application for all of the programs. Community partners can skip paperwork altogether by submitting plans in computer files. New software lets applicants pinpoint where funds will affect communities down to the block level. Millions of people have access to the maps through our home page on the World Wide Web (http://www.hud.gov).

The Department that has "Housing" as part of its name must have a special concern for those Americans who have no home. We encouraged and helped develop local coalitions of governments, nonprofit groups, businesses—and the homeless themselves—to design Continuum of Care services that weave together outreach, housing, and needed social programs for homeless individuals. Under Continuum of Care, homeless people have access to more than a cot: they can get off the streets, move into transitional housing, and take control of their lives. Our programs are serving 14 times as many homeless individuals as we did before 1993.

Transform Public and Assisted Housing. The most profound changes in six decades of public housing are occurring right now. Under a flexible program called HOPE VI, officials in Atlanta, Baltimore, Charlotte, and other cities are choosing to demolish their worst public housing developments. Attractive mixed-income, less dense communities of townhouses and apartments are being built in their place. HUD and our partners will have demolished 30,000 units between 1993 and the end of 1996, compared to 20,000 units replaced in the previous 10 years.

Our determination to fix problems at the nation's most poorly managed public housing authorities (PHAs) reduced the number of major PHAs on our "troubled" list from 19 to 12. In Washington, D.C., Philadelphia, Detroit, Kansas City, New Orleans, and San Francisco, HUD works closely with court-appointed receivers or local elected officials to remedy serious management problems. In June 1995, we took direct control of the Chicago Housing Authority. As a result, these housing agencies are providing better housing and better services to residents and streamlining their operations to increase accountability to taxpayers.

A Special Workout Assistance Team (SWAT) created in September 1994 cracks down on negligent landlords and builds viable recovery strategies for run-down, mismanaged, and financially unsound properties in multifamily housing. SWATs withheld federal subsidies worth $62 million to owners of 137 properties until they brought their buildings up to national housing quality standards.

Operation Safe Home—our alliance with local police, the Federal Bureau of Investigation, the Drug Enforcement Agency, and the Bureau of Alcohol, Tobacco and Firearms—thwarts violent crime and drug trafficking in public and assisted housing. We've made 8,040 arrests for crimes involving drugs and weapons, confiscated 1,038 guns—including 119 assault weapons and sawed-off shotguns—and seized drugs valued at over $3 million.

President Clinton's "one strike and you're out" policy helps local housing authorities conduct strict screening and eviction procedures to weed out gang members and drug dealers who threaten the safety of law-abiding families living in public housing. Cities and towns now have the means to enforce zero-tolerance policies and keep developments free from crime and drugs.

These examples of HUD's reinvention are the product of a "clean house" commitment to change the culture of the agency and introduce a can-do attitude in every office. Our field office colleagues tell us they can feel the difference, and our partners in communities remark on the progress.

The reinvented HUD is helping America's cities recognize that they're capable of rebirth and renewal. They're capable of climbing back. One block at a time. One neighborhood at a time. It's happening right before our eyes.

Henry G. Cisneros

103

The Intelligence Community
John Deutch, Director of Central Intelligence

Mission Statement

The United States intelligence effort shall provide the President and the National Security Council with the necessary information on which to base decisions concerning the conduct and development of foreign, defense, and economic policy and the protection of United States national interests from foreign security threats. Specifically, the missions of U.S. intelligence are to:

- provide intelligence support to national level policy makers,
- provide intelligence support to military planning and operations,
- provide intelligence support to law enforcement, and
- counter foreign intelligence activities.

Reinvention Highlights

When I became Director of Central Intelligence, the intelligence community was under siege from those who criticized past intelligence failures and questioned the need for an intelligence capability in the post-Cold War world. There was intense debate over the mission and future of intelligence.

The intelligence community itself had already recognized the need to reexamine and reinvent every aspect of the intelligence process. Many methods used against the Soviet threat were ill-suited to post-Cold War challenges, which included the proliferation of weapons of mass destruction, terrorism, drug trafficking, international organized crime, and the activities of rogue states. Moreover, rapid advances in technology, an explosion in information, changing customer demands, and intense pressure to cut costs had transformed the environment in which we operate. The intelligence community had not only recognized the need to change, but had already begun the process of reinvention.

A year later, the reform process is gaining momentum, and we have a clear direction for the future. We have acknowledged the deficiencies of the past, restored an ethic of accountability, and placed some difficult problems behind us. There is growing recognition that intelligence will continue to be an indispensable part of our national defense. The major studies of the intelligence community undertaken in the last two years—by the Aspin-Brown Commission and others—have come to the common conclusion that our work will be as critical in the next century as it was during the Cold War.

Customer Focus. At the basis of every reform initiative undertaken by the intelligence community is the common goal of better serving policymakers, military commanders, and law enforcement officials who depend on good intelligence to protect our national security. We have focused on improving our knowledge of customer needs and ensuring a fast response to requests. We have put more intelligence officers in policy offices, law enforcement agencies, and military units. We are acquiring and developing technologies that can disseminate higher quality intelligence products to the consumer faster. These efforts have put us in a better position to inform decisionmakers and provide timely warning of potential threats to our national security. Senior policy makers have relied on and praised our intelligence support during crises in Bosnia, the Taiwan Straits, the Aegean, and other areas of the world.

Support to the Military. Soon after becoming Director of Central Intelligence, I created a new position, Associate Director for Military Affairs. This organizational change has been remarkably effective in helping us to improve intelligence support to the military. This task is especially critical now, as a smaller force takes on new and nontraditional challenges in remote and unfamiliar areas of the world. During the Gulf War, technical shortcomings led to slow and low-quality dissemination of intelligence products. Today, National Intelligence Support Teams deployed in Bosnia provide a direct line between the Implementation Force and the intelligence community. We put tailored analysis, imagery, and maps into the hands of military commanders who rely on our daily support.

For the future, we are developing the expertise and technologies to give the military commander an incredible advantage over the enemy—near real-time, all-weather, comprehensive, and continuous view of a battlefield. This dominant battlefield awareness, when combined with improved smart munitions, will be the basis of our future military superiority. An important step toward this goal will be to centralize the production, analysis, and distribution of maps and images—work that is now done in six separate agencies. The proposed National Imagery and Mapping Agency will improve efficiency, save money, and put us in a better position to take advantage of technological breakthroughs.

Support to Law Enforcement. In the past, cooperation between the U.S. intelligence and law enforcement communities was limited. That situation is changing as the responsibilities of intelligence and law enforcement increasingly overlap—particularly in the areas of terrorism, international organized crime, drug trafficking, and proliferation. In the past year, Attorney General Janet Reno and I have made a concerted effort to establish close, routine, and extensive coordination between the intelligence and law enforcement communities. Cooperation, mutual respect, and shared success are replacing old rivalries. Under the auspices of the Intelligence and Law Enforcement Policy Board, we have increased intelligence sharing, better coordinated overseas activities, and engaged in joint technology development. This groundwork has already paid off in a number of joint operations, including the arrest of leaders of the Cali drug cartel.

Reinvigorating Human Intelligence. Espionage will continue to be a critical part of our intelligence capability. The Ames case and shortcomings in Central Intelligence Agency (CIA) activities in Latin America have highlighted problems with CIA's espionage service, the Directorate of Operations. To correct these deficiencies, we put in place new procedures for reporting information relating to human rights abuses and for notifying Congress and country ambassadors. We have also issued new instructions to guide field officers in recruiting, handling, and compensating individuals who have unsavory backgrounds. We now have a reliable system to evaluate such individuals in terms of the value of the information that they provide and their human rights record. I believe that these measures will ensure the integrity of our espionage operations when, as we often find we must, we recruit this type of individual because of the important intelligence they can provide that can protect American lives.

Strengthening the Community. The key to providing better, faster support to customers is often achieving better integration within the intelligence community. When a crisis breaks, our consumers want intelligence that represents the best expertise of the entire intelligence community. Interdisciplinary, interagency centers and task forces have proven the most successful way to bring expertise from across the community to bear on the highest priority intelligence targets. The Balkans Task Force, now in its fourth year, is a superb example. Senior policymakers and military leaders have come to depend on the steady stream of information provided by this round-the-clock team of experts. We have successfully used the Balkan Task Force model to respond quickly to other crises, such as the situation in the Taiwan Straits.

I believe it is essential that the intelligence community become a true community of experts. We are using technology to achieve this goal by setting up our own classified Internet system, called INTELINK, to ensure a constant, productive exchange of information.

Rebuilding the Community Workforce. The future excellence of the intelligence community will depend on its people. We are working to replace the multiple, outdated personnel systems of the intelligence community with a single new human resource management system. The personnel reforms now in process will:

- identify and attract the skills we need for the future,
- foster a community—rather than a single-agency—perspective,
- reward performance rather than longevity,
- insist on continuing education and training, and
- build the next generation of leaders.

When the new system is in place, it will ensure that this nation has a capable, motivated intelligence community workforce by gthe next century.

Improving Resource Management. The intelligence community continues to be on schedule in its goal of downsizing personnel by 23 percent in this decade. Over the same period, our budget will decline 20 percent in real terms. To accommodate these cuts, we have consolidated and restructured organizations with like functions; invested in technology to cut the need for manpower in areas such as communications, training, and data processing and retrieval; and made reductions in selected areas—including support services and collection and analytic resources devoted to the former Soviet military.

To improve use of resources across the intelligence community, the Deputy Secretary of Defense and I have made progress toward instituting a more rigorous resource review process, including a mission-based budget. This system allocates resources to programs that contribute to specific missions—support to the policymakers, military, law enforcement, and the conduct of counterintelligence. This will allow the Director of Central Intelligence to make better decisions on resource tradeoffs, for example, by substituting satellites for aircraft imagery or signals collection. Indeed, these decisions on tradeoffs are already being made. This method of planning will focus our spending on outcomes, rather than inputs, and result in more effective use of our limited resources. Moreover, a new decisionmaking body—the Joint Space Management Board—is working to ensure that both intelligence and military satellite acquisition decisions are made efficiently. Finally, we have worked to repair the financial management of the National Reconnaissance Office and ensure more effective financial accountability in the future.

When President Clinton asked me to be the Director of Central Intelligence, he instructed me to make whatever changes were necessary to ensure that our nation has the best intelligence service in the world and that we carry out our duties with integrity. I believe that the reforms that we are putting in place today will give us a superb intelligence capability for the next century and give the American public confidence that our intelligence activities are carried out in a manner consistent with our national interests and values.

John Deutch

Department of the Interior
Bruce Babbitt, Secretary

Mission Statement

The Department of the Interior's mission is to protect and provide access to our nation's natural and cultural heritage and honor our trust responsibilities to tribes.

In accomplishing our mission, we will:

* restore and maintain the health of federally managed lands, waters, and renewable resources; provide recreational opportunities for the public to enjoy natural and cultural resources; provide for appropriate commercial use and development of federally managed natural resources in an environmentally sound manner; and encourage the preservation of diverse plant and animal species and protect habitat critical to their survival;
* work to transfer federal program operations to tribal governments through Indian self-determination and self-governance agreements, and work with these tribes to enhance education, economic opportunities, and the quality of life for their members;
* provide useful scientific information for sound resource decisionmaking, and advance scientific research and monitoring to improve our understanding of the interaction of natural and human systems in order to reduce the impacts of hazards caused by natural processes and human actions; and
* apply laws and regulations fairly and effectively, placing priority on compliance and enforcement, prevention, and problem solving.

Summary Budget Information

FY 1993 (Actual)		FY 1996 (Budgeted)	
Budget	Staff	Budget	Staff
$7.078 billion	76,880	$6.948 billion	67,150

Reinvention Highlights

In the winter of 1993, I stood before a room packed with land managers who had gathered from all over the Pacific Northwest to try to resolve the timber/spotted owl crisis in the Cascade Mountains.

These would be my first public remarks since taking office only days before, and I looked out over the hushed audience members. They were eager to learn what was expected of them as experienced professionals. Their pride showed in their neatly pressed clothing, and I could make out nearly a dozen different badges on their hats and sleeves: Bureau of Indian Affairs, Oregon Department of Natural Resources, U.S. Forest Service, U.S. Fish and Wildlife Service, U.S. Geological Survey, Bureau of Land Management, Washington Department of Forestry, California Fish and Game Agency, Bureau of Reclamation, and so on.

I knew my words must set the right tone, give them a monumental challenge, and lay out an agenda for them to follow in the critical weeks and months to follow.

I cleared my throat, and said: "Take off your uniforms." Hundreds of jaws dropped, and the earnest expressions on the faces fell. "That's right," I continued. "In your mind, I want you to rip off the uniform badge of the specific agency or bureau that signs your paycheck and sets you apart, because that uniform will only get in the way of the task we have ahead of us. That uniform is too often a barrier to our common goal of protecting and restoring the natural landscape that we all must share and which binds us together."

Call it reinventing government. Call it common sense. Whatever the name, it has been for me and for my Department of the Interior the first order in policy, the first step of many to come. And we haven't turned back once, any more than the 13 loosely affiliated colonies turned back after declaring themselves, for the first time, the United States of America.

Through this process of an open forum, broken bureaucratic walls, unified brainstorming, and the guidance of sound ecological science, we were together able to forge a landmark agreement to protect old-growth forests while adding value to the sustainable logging carried out elsewhere. Independent scientific associations endorsed the plan. Courts backed us 100 percent. And both employment and growth in the region have hit a 30-year high. We were able to restore the Cascades to their sustainable richness and character.

Creating Partnerships. We then turned reinventing government on the Florida Everglades, where the extraordinary plant, fish, and wildlife of that region were dying off at an accelerated rate. True, there were many concerned agencies seeking to resolve the problem. Trouble was, they were each working in complete isolation from one another.

The U.S. Fish and Wildlife Service, in charge of the animals, demanded cleaner water flowing into the National Park, which needed changes from the Florida Sugar Industry, which blamed historic changes on the Army Corps of Engineers, which blamed demands of the South Florida coastal cities, where population had doubled in the last 30 years and needed more water as well.

It was only when we ripped off all the badges, halos, white hats, and uniforms that we were able to build consensus to resolve the 50-year-old battle. We pooled our resources, agreed to a goal, and forged the Everglades Forever Act. Critics called this reinvention a sell-out. We called it a good start. Two years later, we were proved correct, as the momentum shifted to back this initial progress with more funds and resources from all parties involved.

Finally, consider California, where Mark Twain once observed: "whiskey's for drinkin' and water's for fightin'." More than a century later, little had changed. Even federal agencies were opposed to one another, and the state agencies stood apart from them. We set to work at once and chipped away at the walls between organizations and founded a reinvented group we called Club Fed.

By 1995, weary of conflict, failed legislative proposals, and grandiose water export schemes, California's cities, agriculture, and environmental groups came to our table and stayed there until, working together, we hammered out an agreement. Using the Endangered Species Act and Clean Water Act as backstops, we decided how to manage the statewide water system to leave enough "in the stream" to protect salmon runs and migrating waterfowl, and how to restore the fisheries of San Francisco Bay. The result was the Bay Delta Protection Plan, acknowledged by California's governor as the state's equivalent to the Middle East peace accord.

Delegating Authority. By breaking down barriers and building partnerships, our people are working more effectively to get the job done. We are using information technology to save time and money. We are empowering our employees by giving decisionmaking authority to field offices. And we are getting back to basics by concentrating on our core programs, which include managing and protecting our national parks and public lands, providing leadership in natural resource sciences, and fulfilling our trust responsibilities to Native Americans. We are shifting our resources to field offices on the ground to help meet our customers' needs.

For example, the National Park Service has reorganized to move people and resources out of headquarters offices and into the parks. The Park Service has already reduced its central office staff by 25 percent, reduced its 10 regional offices to seven field offices, and moved hundreds of employees out to the parks. The Park Service is putting its resources where they are needed—in the parks, serving visitors.

Here's another example. The Bureau of Reclamation, once the government's premier dam builder, has fundamentally reinvented itself into a customer-oriented water management agency. Reclamation has reduced its budget, tripled its supervisory ratio, and reduced management layers from five to three. What do these changes mean to Reclamation's customers? Water users will see quicker decisions on the certainty of water supplies. Safety inspections of dams throughout the West will happen faster. Projects to aid salmon migration will be planned and built with less delay. In other words, Reclamation's customers will receive quicker, more responsive service, and more decisions will be made by field-level staff who are directly responsible for projects.

These are just a few examples of how we are reinventing the Interior Department. We will continue to embrace the concepts of customer service, empowerment, and partnership as we change the way we do business.

Bruce Babbitt

Department of Justice
Janet Reno, Attorney General

Mission Statement

Our mission at the Department of Justice (DOJ) is to enforce the law and defend the interests of the United States according to the law, provide federal leadership in preventing and controlling crime, seek just punishment for those guilty of unlawful behavior, administer and enforce the nation's immigration laws fairly and effectively, and ensure fair and impartial administration of justice for all Americans.

Summary Budget Information

FY 1993 (Actual)		FY 1996 (Budgeted)	
Budget	Staff	Budget	Staff
$11.209 billion	83,574	$16.392 billion	95,787

Reinvention Highlights

Since March 12, 1993, when I was sworn in as Attorney General, the dedicated employees of the Department of Justice have worked hard to help me meet my pledge to deliver a Justice Department in which the American people can have full faith and confidence—a Department that enforces the law effectively and fairly and uses the taxpayer's money wisely and responsibly. Since that time, I believe we have made real progress in meeting that pledge.

Inspired by the Clinton Administration's call for a government that "works better and costs less," we in the Department of Justice have moved diligently and quickly on several fronts. We have worked to develop strong partnerships with our customers, whether they be fellow law enforcement officers or the general public. We have made sure that federal law enforcement agencies truly coordinate investigative efforts, avoiding self-defeating and costly duplication of effort. We have streamlined our organizations to deliver the highest return with the least investment. And we have sought innovative ways to streamline operations while improving the delivery of services to the public.

Creating Partnerships With States and Localities. As we approach 1997, I am proud of the strides we have made in developing stronger partnerships with states and local communities to fight violent crime. The federal government and local jurisdictions are closer than ever before to becoming full partners in upholding the rule of the law in our communities.

This is a critical time for such partnerships. With passage of the Violent Crime Control Act, the federal government is providing many of the resources necessary to put 100,000 new law enforcement officers on the local beat. To expedite the hiring of these officers, DOJ's Community-Oriented Policing Services (COPS) office dramatically streamlined and simplified the process that local governments use to acquire funds to hire new officers. As a result of the initiatives, $200 million in grants was awarded to 392 state, municipal, county, and tribal law enforcement agencies within two weeks of the bill's enactment.

Many of the customer standards that we have developed over the past three years reflect the Department's focus on relations with our law enforcement brothers and sisters: the Federal Bureau of Investigation has pledged quicker response times to name and fingerprint checks and to National Crime Information Center queries; the Immigration and Naturalization Service (INS) has facilitated contact with its investigations units for other law enforcement bodies; and the Office of Asset Forfeiture has stepped up response time to requests for assets sharing, to mention just a few.

Over the past three years, we have also nurtured partnerships with nonlaw enforcement entities. To this end, we have reduced the burden of reports required from the public by vigorously reinventing and eliminating regulations, and have devised performance measures and customer standards that emphasize grassroots partnerships. The alliances have proven successful. For example, we have worked closely with community leaders and businesses in Southern California as we developed Project SENTRI, a highly regarded pilot project that uses the latest technology to speed the trips of commuters who cross the United States-Mexico border regularly. Elsewhere, the INS Dallas District Office received the prestigious Ford Foundation Award for Excellence for Operation JOBS, an initiative that engages employers, civic leaders, and job placement offices in an effort to replace ineligible alien workers with citizens and persons who are here legally.

Creating Collaboration Among Law Enforcement Agencies. In November 1993, responding to the National Performance Review's recommendation to improve the coordination and structure of federal law enforcement agencies, I established the Office of Investigative Agency Policies to coordinate activities of DOJ law enforcement components. This new office has had a dramatic effect on the way the Department does its business, addressing practical problems of everyday coordination among law enforcement bodies.

Collaboration among our enforcement components has led to the development of the Joint Automated Booking Station (JABS), a prototype in Miami that automates the booking process through the electronic collection, storage, and transmittal of photographic, fingerprint, and biographical information. In its test phase, JABS has significantly improved the manual booking process performed at every agency through which a prisoner passes, reducing processing time by an average of 80 percent and reducing the number of fingerprints returned as unreadable to nearly zero.

Collaboration has also led to the development of the Joint Alien and Prisoner Transportation System (JPATS), which consolidates all detainee air transportation functions performed by INS and the U.S. Marshals Service (USMS). JPATS has permitted more efficient and secure transportation of these aliens: Halfway through fiscal year 1996, INS has moved over 12,000 deportable aliens using JPATS—a 120-percent increase over the same period the previous year.

Streamlining the Department. Recognizing the fiscal responsibility entrusted to the Department by the President, Congress, and the American people, DOJ has been seeking more efficient organizational structures and more innovative ways to streamline operations while improving delivery of services to the public—innovative ways to achieve efficiencies and economies even as our agency realizes budgetary growth.

For example, in the Justice Department's most sweeping reorganization, USMS reduced eight management layers to four, and consolidated 25 organizational units into 11. The result is that USMS will be able to shift significant resources from headquarters to the field and consolidate wide-ranging but related headquarters functions into major divisions for better performance. Other DOJ components have modified their organizational structures on a less ambitious scale. INS, for example, delegated substantial authority for operations to its three newly established regional directors, bringing the work farther from headquarters and closer to the people we serve.

Most improvements within DOJ in the last three years have not been the result of sweeping changes, however. Rather, they have been the result of careful, often laborious, review of DOJ functions and identification of opportunities for improvement. Overseeing much of this activity is the Justice Performance Review (JPR), an organization I established in May 1993 to support the Administration's national effort.

Among its activities, the JPR has developed an ambitious lab program designed to field test more effective and cost-efficient methods of providing services and products. The Department of Justice presently has 16 reinvention labs under way.

All are important. And all represent our commitment to close what Vice President Gore has called government's "trust deficit" with the American people.

Janet Reno

Department of Labor
Robert Reich, Secretary

Mission Statement

The Department of Labor promotes and safeguards the welfare of America's workers. The Department's mandates cover workplace activities for nearly 10 million employers and well over 100 million workers, including preparing workers for new and better jobs; protecting workers' health and safety, wages, employment, and pension rights; promoting equal employment opportunity; and measuring and publishing labor and economic statistics. The state of the American workforce being critical to the future of the nation, the Department of Labor focuses on building opportunities for working Americans.

Summary Budget Information

FY 1993 (Actual)		FY 1996 (Budgeted)	
Budget	Staff	Budget	Staff
$46.892 billion	18,003	$33.879 billion	16,655

Reinvention Highlights

When I became Secretary of Labor in 1993, the challenge was clear: If the Department was to protect and promote the welfare of America's workforce, we would have to reinvent how it operates. We met this challenge by making the Labor Department more efficient and reducing costs—while remaining focused on setting goals and getting results for the American worker.

The results are found in our achievements: greater pension security for Americans, fewer sweatshops, safer and healthier workplaces, and more and better job training. And we did it all with 1,348 fewer employees.

In conjunction with the White House and under Vice President Gore's leadership, the Department developed a reinvention plan. We streamlined our operations and eliminated waste. We already have achieved or exceeded our 1999 goals for reducing employment.

Our reinvention efforts have been recognized with several awards. The Pension Benefit Guaranty Corporation's Early Warning Program and the Occupational Safety and Health Administration's (OSHA's) Maine 200 program each received the prestigious Innovations in American Government Award presented by the Ford Foundation and Harvard University. This year, the Wage and Hour Division's Garment Worker Initiative is a finalist for this award. Labor Department programs have also received more than 20 of the Vice President's Hammer Awards, which recognize reinvention accomplishments.

Our efforts have made a real, significant impact on millions of American workers:

- As a result of the Early Warning Program, $14 billion has been added to underfunded pension plans covering more than one million employees and retirees.
- A total of $9.8 million has been returned to 401(k) plans.
- A total of $8.4 million has been recovered for more than 29,000 garment workers.

113

- Sweatshops are under attack. More than 50 manufacturing firms across the country have committed to monitor their contractors for safe and fair working conditions.
- Employers have the choice of working in partnership with OSHA or facing traditional enforcement. In the Maine 200 program, 65 percent of employers who chose a partnership with OSHA were able to reduce their injury and illness rates, leading to lower workers' compensation costs and fewer lost work days.
- The Family and Medical Leave Act, signed by President Clinton in 1993, is fully implemented.
- The Women's Bureau's Working Women Count! initiative reached out to more than a quarter of a million working women to find out what was right and wrong with their jobs. This effort resulted in the Working Women Count! Honor Roll initiative for businesses and organizations committed to making work better for women and their families. More than 1,300 honor roll pledges have been made for specific new programs that improve pay, make workplaces more family-friendly, and heighten respect and opportunity for one million workers throughout the United States.
- The School to Work Opportunities Act, signed into law in 1994 and administered jointly with the Education Department, eases the transition from secondary education to postsecondary education and the world of work for the 75 percent of America's youth who do not graduate from college. Over 500,000 young people are now participating in these school-to-work opportunities.
- Through the Department's America's Job Bank Internet site, job seekers have access to more than 500,000 jobs across the country every day, for jobs in both government and the private sector.
- One-Stop Career Centers have integrated unemployment insurance, employment, and training services under one roof in a majority of states.

We have also focused on improving service to individual customers:

- Since fiscal year 1993, the Wage and Hour Division's Chicago office has reduced the average time for case resolution from 14 days to two days.
- Following the Oklahoma City bombing tragedy, the Rapid Injury Response Team achieved a same-day establishment of worker's compensation cases and a same-day adjudication of cases, with payments to survivors sent out within nine days.
- The Office of Trade Adjustment Assistance streamlined its investigation procedures, leading to the elimination of a backlog of 100 cases and speeding assistance to eligible dislocated workers.
- OSHA redesigned area offices and streamlined processes so that a worker receives a response to a complaint in about three days, instead of the previous 22 days.

These accomplishments, and many others, have involved all Department of Labor employees, and relied on a partnership with the unions representing those employees. Without that partnership, without the active participation of the frontline employees who actually do the work and serve the customers, we could not have been successful. These efforts were recognized with a National Partnership Award presented to the Department and the National Council of Field Labor Locals (American Federation of Government Employees) by the National Partnership Council.

We have much more to accomplish. But we have kept faith with the National Performance Review and with the American people. We are making government work better and cost less.

Robert Reich

114

National Aeronautics and Space Administration
Daniel S. Goldin, Administrator

Mission Statement

The mission of the National Aeronautics and Space Administration (NASA) encompasses the following:

- explore, use, and enable the development of space for human enterprise;
- advance scientific knowledge and understanding of the Earth, the solar system, and the universe, and use the environment of space for research; and
- research, develop, verify, and transfer advanced aeronautics, space, and related technologies.

The outcomes of NASA's activities contribute significantly to the achievement of America's goals in four key areas:

- **Economic Growth and Security.** We conduct aeronautics and space research and develop technology in partnership with industry, academia, and other federal agencies to keep America capable and competitive.
- **Preserving the Environment.** We study the Earth as a planet and as a system to understand global change, enabling the world to address environmental issues.
- **Educational Excellence.** We involve the educational community in our endeavors to inspire America's students, create learning opportunities, and enlighten inquisitive minds.
- **Peaceful Exploration and Discovery.** We explore the universe to enrich human life by stimulating intellectual curiosity, opening new worlds of opportunity, and uniting nations of the world in this quest.

Summary Budget Information

FY 1993 (Actual)		FY 1996 (Budgeted)	
Budget	Staff	Budget	Staff
$14.305 billion	25,700	$13.821 billion	21,555

Reinvention Highlights

I became NASA's Administrator in 1992, and the agency's budget was $14.3 billion with an average cost overrun of 77 percent as reported by the General Accounting Office. We now have a 5 percent underrun. Congress told me that NASA was out of contact with the fiscal realities of the United States. But it took the elections of 1992 and 1994 for the people's message demanding a smaller, more efficient government really to hit home. When it did, NASA, along with our partners in industry, made real change happen. For example, it used to cost an average of $600 million to build a scientific spacecraft. Today, it costs an average of $200 million, and that price tag will drop to $85 million by the end of this decade.

Better, Faster, Cheaper. Other efforts, specifically work on the reusable launch vehicle, should get the price of a launch down from $10,000 per pound to $1,000 per pound. Two decades ago, NASA and the Department of Defense drove the semiconductor, advance materials, software, computers, and communications industries. Today, we're a fraction of a percent of these markets.

We think a rough measurement of our productivity improvement shows us up 40 percent. We started 21 new programs, even though the budget has come down 36 percent over a five-year budget projection. That means we're going to do more with 55,000 fewer people. We had 25,000 NASA employees in 1992; today, we have about 20,000, and we're reducing further to a target of about 17,500 by the year 2000. We also will lose 47,000 contract employees.

Not only are we going to do more with less people, we're going to do an even better job. The average cycle time to design and develop a scientific spacecraft was eight years. Today, it's four; and in three years, it will be three. Hopefully, by the turn of the century, the average cycle time will be two years. On average, in the early 1990s, NASA launched two scientific robotic spacecraft per year. In the next few years, we'll be launching about eight per year; by the year 2000, we should be launching a dozen robotic spacecraft per year.

To eliminate duplication and overlap, especially at our field centers, and to improve efficiency and effectiveness in the application of diminished resources, NASA has moved to the exciting concept of mission-specific centers. In 1993, we conducted a Zero-Based Review. We told the centers that "Unless you could be best in class, you aren't a world class center; we have to shut you down." So each field center now has a clear mission and area of expertise. For example, the Marshall Space Flight Center is the focal point for launch and propulsion; the Johnson Space Flight Center's mission is Human Space Flight; the Goddard Space Flight Center handles astrophysics and earth science; the Ames Research Center focuses on information technology; and the Lewis Research Center is the center of excellence in turbomachinery.

The impact was considerable. For example, Lewis will focus on building the best jet engines and SCRAM jet engines and RAM jet engines in the world. We haven't canceled programs; we've realigned the infrastructure so we can focus on excellence. And if we find that industry has a better center of excellence, we'll shut ours down and use theirs.

Sharpening Focus on Mission. We're refocusing NASA on being a high-tech research and development agency. We're cutting way back on operations, and we're buying commercial services. We're moving from time-and-materials contracts to performance-based contracts, and we will hold individual CEOs personally accountable for their company's performance while we ensure safety through the features we have in NASA. Not only does this afford us an unbelievable opportunity to cut the budget, reduce the staff, and increase efficiency by partnering with a mature industry, it also affords industry the opportunity to develop new cutting-edge products that they couldn't develop if we held them to time-and-materials contracts.

Accountability and personal responsibility are key themes in NASA's reinvention, but we also are committed to teamwork and partnering within NASA, as well as with our outside partners. To ensure that every member of the team knows what's happening, we established the NASA Program Management Council, which reviews every major program and program commitment agreement (a contract specifying schedules, dollars, and milestones) in NASA at least once a year. And we have no outside consultants helping us do this. That's our rule. We think we have the most capable management team in government, and we don't need outsiders telling us how to manage ourselves.

We have a vision at NASA. We see ourselves as "an investment in America's future. As explorers, pioneers, and innovators, we boldly expand frontiers in air and space to inspire and serve America and to benefit the quality of life on Earth." We also have a strategic plan written by NASA's employees and managers and reviewed by the White House, Congress, civic groups, and scientific groups. Every employee has a copy, and every employee will also have a performance plan in the coming year that links to that strategic plan. We have a focus; we know where we're going. By next year, NASA will have a plan that extends this vision out 25 years. We know what steps to take over the next five years and what our financial performance plan should be for the next year. We've come a long way since 1992.

Daniel S. Goldin

National Science Foundation

Neal Lane, Director

Mission Statement

The National Science Foundation's (NSF's) mission and purpose is to promote the progress of science; to advance the national health, prosperity, and welfare; and to secure the national defense. It does this through:

- basic scientific research and research fundamental to the engineering process,
- programs to strengthen scientific and engineering research potential,
- science and engineering education programs at all levels and in all the various fields of science and engineering,
- programs that provide a source of information for policy formulation, and
- other activities to promote these ends.

Summary Budget Information

FY 1993 (Actual)		FY 1996 (Budgeted)	
Budget	Staff	Budget	Staff
$2.734 billion	1,235	$3.220 billion	1,267

Reinvention Highlights

During my tenure as Director of the National Science Foundation, I have been privileged to preside over widespread reengineering of NSF processes, particularly to take maximum advantage of modern information technology. Both our basic business transactions with the external research and education communities and our internal operations are being transformed.

Reengineering Our Dealings With Customers. NSF's primary business is to fund research and education projects, largely in universities and other academic institutions. We invite competitive proposals, subject those proposals to merit review by peers, and draw on the peer reviews to reach award-or-decline decisions.

NSF already compares favorably with any private foundation in speed of proposal processing and the ratio (around 4 percent) of our administrative costs to our total funds. But we can now apply state-of-the-art information technology to improve service further to those who deal with us, further reduce both their costs and ours, and further speed our processing of proposals and awards. We are doing all those things through what we call Project FastLane.

The basic idea of FastLane is to let citizens and institutions conduct business with NSF easily and quickly using the World Wide Web. To users, FastLane is a World Wide Web home page through which they quickly reach specific applications that help them do business with NSF. Each application comes with online help.

118

Virtually all routine business transactions with NSF either can already be transacted electronically over the Web or are now being tested by external users. Our "customers" in nearly 300 registered institutions already can electronically:

- prepare and submit proposals and proposal forms;
- write proposals using proposal templates;
- submit proposal reviews;
- inquire about proposal review status;
- request cash transfers;
- submit final project reports;
- search NSF awards;
- get from their institution status reports on all actions that are in progress at NSF; and
- assign personal identification numbers, designate authorized organizational representatives, and authorize other organizational officials to access applications from the institution.

FastLane will soon let customers electronically:

- prepare and submit proposal revisions;
- submit reports on project results through a new system that will seamlessly integrate all annual, final, and special project reporting and eliminate repetitious entries;
- submit and process required notifications and requests for NSF approval during the life of an award; and
- prepare and submit quarterly Federal Cash Transaction Reports.

NSF has also established tight coordination with those who are developing similar systems at other federal agencies so that researchers, administrators, and reviewers will encounter much the same interface when dealing with any major agency.

Privatizing the Internet. NSF was well prepared to take a lead role in application of Internet technology to government operations, because we led the development of the Internet itself.

Originally a small network used only by government and university scientists, the Internet came into full bloom under NSF leadership, using the facilities of our NSFNET network. We worked with other federal agencies (especially the Defense Advanced Research Projects Agency which had invented the technology and the network) to develop the fledgling Internet for use by a much broader community of government and university scientists. Then we worked with the other agencies, with industry, and with other governments to open the rapidly growing network to the broader public. As time went on, more and more other networks—including privately operated networks—connected to the Internet, which grew into the Information Superhighway now available and familiar to millions worldwide.

In 1995—in keeping with the emphasis the President and Vice President have placed on a leaner government that performs only those functions that government can perform best, and pursuing a carefully phased plan—NSF spun off the operation of the Internet to commercial suppliers of networking services, and began phasing out NSF support for routine Internet connections and services, which will henceforth be provided and priced commercially.

Reengineering Our Operations. Meanwhile, we have been revamping our own internal operations to take advantage of information technology. All NSF employees have access to the

Internet and the World Wide Web. Internal NSF forms can be filed electronically. And we are now shifting to electronic files—or "jackets," as we call them—for proposals and awards. These jackets already exist and are being tested in 10 NSF programs. For now, we scan in many of the documents in these files from paper submissions. But proposals and other documents filed electronically via FastLane can go directly into the electronic jackets, then go out for review, without ever taking paper form.

We have also set out to improve NSF's basic business processes in other ways. For the past year, we have extensively reexamined the way we review and otherwise process research and education proposals. Teams of staff with input from stakeholders and customers looked at everything from peaks in proposal intake and award outflow to the criteria we and our reviewers apply to determine which proposals should be funded. The recommendations are now being considered and, in most cases, implemented.

Partnership in Education and Research. In its 1995 strategic plan, NSF committed to promoting partnerships to serve society's interest in science and engineering. A model for such partnerships can be found in NSF's programs aimed at educational system reform in science and mathematics: our Statewide Systemic Initiatives, Urban Systemic Initiatives, and Regional Systemic Initiatives. Through these programs, NSF provides catalytic funding that enables states, cities, and regional alliances to move aggressively toward standards-based, discovery-oriented reform in math and science education, leveraging their own funds and those from other federal agencies, state and local governments, and the private sector.

NSF is also part of a significant partnership of federal agencies designed to develop a comprehensive, coordinated approach to managing the federal investment in science and technology. NSF staff have taken a leadership role in many activities of the National Science and Technology Council, partnering with other agencies to identify and eliminate gaps and undesirable overlap in the federal research portfolio. Together, the agencies have reinvented the management of this portfolio.

Neal Lane

Neal Lane

Office of Personnel Management
James B. King, Director

Mission Statement

The Office of Personnel Management (OPM) serves the public by providing human resource management leadership and high-quality services that protect and strengthen the merit system of government in partnership with other federal agencies and their employees, as well as by operating the federal government's highly regarded health, insurance, and retirement programs.

Summary Budget Information

FY 1993 (Actual)		FY 1996 (Budgeted)	
Budget	Staff	Budget	Staff
$452 million	6,208	$377 million	3,557

Reinvention Highlights

From the first, we at OPM took seriously the mandates of the National Performance Review (NPR) and of the Workforce Restructuring Act. The President made clear his goal of a federal workforce that was both reinvented and substantially reduced in size; and we set out to meet this challenge promptly, efficiently, and humanely.

Downsizing OPM to Focus on Core Mission. Our success to date is reflected in the numbers cited above: from fiscal year 1993 through fiscal year 1996 our full-time equivalent workforce decreased by 43 percent while our administrative obligation decreased by 17 percent.

OPM's downsizing was achieved by a combination of attrition, buyouts, privatization, and—as a last resort—involuntary separations. We have decreased the number of supervisors from one for every 7.8 employees to one for every 12 employees and reduced the number of GS-13s through GS-15s by more than half.

However, our goal was not simply to downsize, but to do so with respect and compassion for every employee involved. That is why we assumed leadership in passing the Workforce Restructuring Act, which began a program of separation incentives—or buyouts—to encourage workers to leave government voluntarily.

We have continued to advise agencies on the program, which has provided 34,694 nondefense buyouts through the end of 1995; these buyouts not only will save an estimated $8 billion over five years, they minimized confusion and poor morale during downsizing. We also carried out a career transition program that has helped more than 90 percent of our separated employees find jobs or make another successful transition.

Privatized Units Able to Operate in the Private Sector. We asked ourselves if OPM was doing work that was not basic to our core mission of protecting the merit system. We determined that the work of our training and investigations units, although important, could be performed as well in the private sector. We set out to determine how best to privatize these units while still serving the interests of the American taxpayers, our employees, and our agency customers.

The more than 200 education specialists in our training unit were much-sought-after by existing private sector training programs and told us they wished to explore that option. We helped them negotiate a contract whereby the highly respected, nongovernmental U.S. Department of Agriculture Graduate School hired about 140 members of our training staff at about the same salary and benefits they had been receiving. Others went to work for the Brookings Institution or other first-rate training programs.

Our investigations unit, which conducted government background investigations, was also made up of highly skilled individuals. We presented them with several options, including that of starting an Employee Stock Ownership Plan, a new employee-owned company that would perform many of the same services but in the private sector. We worked with these employees during the complex negotiations that led to the creation of an ESOP called U.S. Investigations Services (USIS), Inc. By July 1996, 681 of the 706 employees who were offered jobs with the new company had accepted them, and USIS, Inc., began operations, aided by an exclusive contract to conduct investigations for OPM.

The creation of USIS, Inc., was the first government privatization of its kind, and we believe it has every prospect for success. A private consulting firm estimated that the action should save the taxpayers $25 million in five years.

Protecting the Merit System. Because of reinvention, we have refocused on our core mission of protecting the merit system. To that end, OPM has strengthened its Office of Merit Systems Oversight and Effectiveness, which works with agencies to ensure that all employees are treated fairly with regard to hiring, pay, leave, promotions, discipline, benefits, and other workplace issues.

OPM has carried out many human resources management reforms recommended by the NPR. For one important example, we decentralized government job recruitment and hiring, so agencies now have the choice of carrying out their own programs or contracting with OPM or others. We have worked with the Interagency Advisory Group of personnel directors (IAG) to exchange ideas and to spread word of new policies and reforms.

Career Transition Services. Working with IAG, OPM has led the way in implementing the President's memorandum of September 12, 1995, directing agencies to provide career transition services to dislocated and surplus employees. In December 1995, OPM issued regulations developed in partnership with agencies and unions implementing this directive. Agencies were to establish career transition services and to set up hiring systems giving preference to dislocated employees for those few vacancies that do occur. OPM is also working with IAG in pooling agency resources to provide career transition assistance to employees. In the field, OPM is working with the Department of Labor, the Federal Executive Boards (FEBs), and the Federal Executive Associations (FEAs) to coordinate agencies' services. Career transition resource materials developed by OPM have been provided to FEBs and FEAs. OPM is also providing direct career transition assistance to a few agencies based on the lessons learned in our own reductions.

Cutting Red Tape and Improving Employee Work Lives. NPR declared war on unnecessary regulations and red tape, and OPM responded with the elimination—a year ahead of schedule—of both the all-but-incomprehensible, 10,000-page Federal Personnel Manual (saving an estimated $30 million) and the complicated Form 171 job application. In most cases, people seeking jobs now can simply submit a resume, or even apply by telephone.

OPM has been a leader in using technology to move government toward the goal of a paperless personnel office. For example, job applications that once took many hours for people to score now are scanned electronically in seconds. Telephones now provide access to current and complete job information. New, automated telephone systems have also improved communications with participants in the federal health and retirement programs.

In response to the President's call for a family-friendly workplace, OPM has supported such initiatives as child care, telecommuting, flexitime, leave-sharing, and a leave bank. In one case, when an employee was seriously ill, her fellow workers donated six months of leave to her. One employee telecommuted from home while he recovered from an automobile accident, and another telecommutes on afternoons when there is no one else to care for her daughter after school. Managers all across government are learning that where someone works is less important than how they work.

In the past three years, we have begun to glimpse the government of the future. It will be smaller, flatter, more focused, more automated, more family-friendly, more customer-oriented, and more market-driven. We at OPM are proud to have played a leading role in this remarkable renaissance in our government.

James B. King

Small Business Administration
Philip Lader, Administrator

Mission Statement

It is the mission of the Small Business Administration (SBA) to champion the entrepreneurial spirit of America's small business community in the most cost-effective manner possible while creating the jobs and opportunities that this country needs to remain competitive in the global marketplace.

To ensure that SBA truly functions as the champion of America's entrepreneurs, President Clinton challenged SBA to meet the following policy goals:

- Free up capital for investment in small businesses; work to end the credit crunch and create jobs.
- Eliminate unnecessary paperwork and regulations that inhibit the growth and productivity of small businesses.
- Reinvigorate SBA to construct a lean, highly motivated organization focused on the needs of small businesses.
- Serve as the President's "eyes and ears" in the small business community.

Summary Budget Information

FY 1993 (Actual)		FY 1996 (Budgeted)	
Budget	Staff	Budget	Staff
$1.10 billion	5,599	$814 million	4,284

These levels include SBA disaster assistance, which fluctuates substantially from year to year in response to assistance needs.

Reinvention Highlights

In 1993, as part of the governmentwide National Performance Review, SBA made a commitment to reinvent the way it works. The challenges seemed daunting: improve access to capital for the small businesses needing it the most while maintaining loan portfolio quality, reduce the regulatory burden on small businesses, cut the agency's budget, reduce the number of SBA employees, and expand the reach of current programs. At SBA, we took the job of reinvention as a challenge.

Doing More With Less. To meet our reinvention goals, the agency needed to accomplish more, with fewer people and with a lower budget. We made a conscious effort to shift resources to the field, where our small business customers operate. We reduced the number of employees in the Washington headquarters by 29 percent and dramatically reduced the staffing in our regional offices. Between fiscal years (FYs) 1992 and 1996, we eliminated 862 full-time positions—an agencywide personnel reduction of over 23 percent—saving more than $250 million in salaries and expenses and exceeding all of our NPR staffing targets.

124

While our personnel levels declined, our loan portfolio expanded. The total volume of SBA-guaranteed loans grew from 24,000 to 56,000 between FYs 1992 and 1995. Support for small business increased for every category of borrower: the number of loans made to minority owned businesses over this period tripled, from 3,680 to 10,380; and the number of women-owned businesses receiving SBA-guaranteed loans quadrupled, from 3,376 to 13,398. As lending has increased, SBA's commercial loss rate has decreased; for FY 1995, it stood at only 1.3 percent, which compares favorably with that of the most conservative lending institutions.

In addition to enlarging our loan portfolio, we also overhauled our Small Business Investment Company program, the country's largest source of venture capital for small businesses. As a result, we have raised more private capital for investment in the last two years than during the previous 15 years combined.

Public-Private Partnerships. Despite restructuring and streamlining, we expanded SBA's current programs to serve more businesses. We were able to do this by working closely with our resource partners—private lenders, nonprofits, educational institutions, state and local governments, corporations, and others. For example, SBA is no longer in the business of direct lending for its largest loan programs. Instead, we work directly with over 7,000 private lenders which provide tens of thousands of small business loans each year.

In addition, SBA partners with the 956 Small Business Development Centers across the country and the 13,000 Service Corps of Retired Executives volunteers to ensure that small businesses have the training and counseling they need to succeed. Over the past three years, we have also worked with state and local governments as well as corporate sponsors to add 35 new Business Information Centers and four new One-Stop Capital Shops, which centralize all the resources a small business would need, from business planning to our full range of loan programs.

Regulatory Reform and Paperwork Reduction. In January 1996, SBA completed a streamlining of all its regulations. The agency converted all of the new rules to plain language, eliminating more than 50 percent of its pages in the Code of Federal Regulations. The regulations that remain are clearer, more understandable, and easier to use.

In 1993, SBA implemented its LowDoc business loan application. This one-page form for loans under $100,000 eliminated a cumbersome predecessor, making the SBA loan process easier and more user-friendly. Most of our brochures have been redesigned and rewritten to appeal to a wider audience. By year's end, our entire 25,000 pages of internal standard operating procedures will also have been streamlined and rewritten in plain English. Thanks to SBA's reinvention work, small businesses now have better information, fewer regulations, and less paperwork.

SBA also has worked to encourage regulatory reform and paperwork reduction at other federal agencies. We have worked closely with the Environmental Protection Agency, the Occupational Safety and Health Administration, the Internal Revenue Service, and others to ease the regulatory burdens they impose on small business owners. We helped pioneer the concept of an electronic regulatory information center (now a key part of the U.S. Business Advisor). We have listened carefully to the needs of our small business customers and have worked hard to meet those needs.

Streamlined Operations and Administration. SBA could not fully reinvent itself without a careful evaluation of its internal operations. Today's SBA is more efficient than ever before. The 10 regional office staffs have each been reduced from an average of 50 full-time employees to three. We closed or converted all 11 of our Post of Duty offices. We are centralizing all of our loan processing into two locations in Little Rock and Fresno and created a centralized preferred lender processing center in Sacramento, CA. (Our most experienced lenders are licensed to participate in the Preferred Lender Program and can approve loans without prior approval from SBA loan officers, saving paperwork and time.) Furthermore, we were recently authorized to pilot the centralized processing of LowDoc loans. This streamlining and centralization has allowed us to reduce our staff while increasing our effectiveness.

Small Business Goes Online. In our effort to reinvent the SBA, we examined every available tool to increase our efficiency, effectiveness, and outreach. As part of this effort, we harnessed the latest technology to put SBA on the Internet and World Wide Web. Getting information is easier and more cost effective than ever for small business owners with our new SBA Online home page. Users can access information instantly on all of SBA's programs. They can even download loan applications to their own computer. Recently, our home page logged over 500,000 hits a week. The U.S. Business Advisor, another online feature, provides instant access to all SBA regulations and over 60 other government agencies. Through the Internet, SBA is more accessible to more of America's small businesses.

Meeting the Challenge. SBA is proud of its achievements. We have streamlined our agency and our regulations while providing record levels of capital to small businesses. We have centralized our resources while creating new programs that extended the reach of these resources. We are smaller and more effective than ever before.

In 1994, we accepted a challenge to reinvent SBA. While some may have doubted that we could succeed, by 1996 it is clear that we have more than met our goals—we have surpassed them.

Philip Lader

Social Security Administration
Shirley S. Chater, Commissioner

Mission Statement

The mission of the Social Security Administration (SSA) is to administer national Social Security programs as prescribed by legislation in an equitable, effective, efficient, and caring manner.

Summary Budget Information

FY 1993 (Actual)		FY 1996 (Budgeted)	
Budget	Staff*	Budget	Staff
$4.905 billion	66,101	$5.890 billion	64,752

(The Social Security Administration was part of the Department of Health and Human Services until 1995. These budgetary figures represent only SSA's operating costs, not program benefits.)
*1993 Actual is adjusted for comparability to 1996 by inclusion of an estimated $53 million and 1,254 FTEs related to independent agency functions transferred from HHS to SSA in 1995.

Reinvention Highlights

Since President Franklin D. Roosevelt signed it into law more than 60 years ago, Social Security has been a source of pride for all Americans, and an essential source of income for millions. Whether an older American receiving insurance benefits, a family needing disability or survivors' insurance benefits, or a lower income elderly or disabled person needing Supplemental Security Income, about 48 million people currently receive some form of Social Security payment. Today 141 million workers—95 percent of the American workforce—are covered by Social Security insurance.

With a program touching so many lives, it is essential that the American public have absolute confidence in the Social Security program. In 1994, President Clinton signed into law legislation creating the Social Security Administration as an independent agency. The Commissioner reports directly to the President on the administration of its programs.

Creating World-Class Customer Service. Given the size and scope of its responsibilities, it is vital that the agency strive to provide nothing less than world-class service. When President Clinton and Vice President Gore announced the Administration's National Performance Review (NPR) initiative in 1993, SSA welcomed this new approach. We were determined at the outset to make NPR's focus on customer service an SSA hallmark.

We began our reinvention effort by listening to our customers, employees, stakeholders, Congress, and advocacy groups to find out what we did right and what we could improve upon. We interviewed more than 10,000 customers. We called beneficiaries on the phone; we sent out 26,000 comment cards. We met with employees and stakeholders one-on-one and in larger groups. We drafted proposals for change, then had customers and our staff review them to see what more we could do. Since there is always room for improvement, these efforts continue today.

SSA has achieved a level of world-class customer service about which we can all be proud. You should notice the difference the moment you walk into an SSA office. We've modernized payment delivery through electronic banking. We've increased the number of bilingual employees to make sure our non-English-speaking customers receive the same high quality of service. We are streamlining and automating claims; in one state, individuals can now apply for several government programs with a single application and interview. We've even worked to cut down the waiting time to see an SSA representative.

You may notice the high quality of service without actually having to go to an office at all. Instead of making people who need assistance come to an office, we are going to them. In partnerships with local, state, and federal agencies, there are now SSA representatives at Immigration and Naturalization Service offices, and many other locations such as city and county hospitals.

You should notice our commitment to world-class service when you call us at our toll-free number, 1-800-772-1213. We've changed two of our three data operations centers from data processing to customer telephone service. We've hired additional representatives to take your calls during the busiest times of the year. And we've installed a 24-hour automated service for routine inquiries.

Is all this making a difference? In a word, yes. In 1995, we handled more than 42-million telephone calls. In 1996, we expect to handle more than 50 million. But it is customer service we are providing, not customer processing. While the volume of inquiries alone is impressive, it is the ability to answer the questions that is the real measure of our success. In 1995, an independent financial services company, Dalbar, Inc., did that measurement for us. Dalbar compared SSA's 800 number phone service along with companies renowned for customer service, such as Disney, Nordstrom, and L.L. Bean. SSA was rated as having the best service.

Throughout SSA, we've reviewed every line of our regulations in order to streamline and clarify them. Our review of the disability claims program was particularly exciting. Reviewing more than 6,000 comments from beneficiaries, we studied every element of the claims process. By FY 2001, we anticipate a major redesign of the disability claims process that will mean that our customers have a faster, more efficient process that is easier to use.

It's More Than Retirement. While streamlining our services, we also began actively educating the public about SSA's programs. By the end of this year, we will have sent a Personal Earnings and Benefits Estimate Statement to every worker over the age of 58, and anyone else requesting information. The statement includes all past earnings in SSA records, as well as the recipient's estimated retirement, disability, and survivor benefits. We sent out over 10.7 million statements in FY 1995. By FY 2000, we will be sending annual statements to all workers over the age of 25—more than 120 million people.

Social Security isn't just a retirement program; it is a family program as well. So to make sure our younger citizens understand programs such as the agency's aid to the disabled and those who have lost a loved one, we've spoken at colleges, universities, and other organizations; we have provided information to more than 17,000 high schools around the country.

Since we realize that effective communication between our customers and staff is essential, we are eager to pursue every avenue possible. Video programming, satellite broadcasts, and the Internet are just a few of the new venues we are using. Our Web site, Social Security Online, offers interactive access to 600 documents; industry publications herald the site as one of the best. And we are using the technology internally as well; we use electronic messaging, videoconferencing, and interactive training technology within SSA on a daily basis.

Using technology of the future is just the latest step in preparing SSA for the future. The changes that we have already made provide better customer service to our beneficiaries now. These changes will also make a difference in service for years to come. Because preparing for our customers' future is what Social Security is all about.

Shirley Chater

Department of State
Warren Christopher, Secretary

Mission Statement

The Department of State—the flagship institution of American foreign policy—promotes American interests and assists American citizens around the world. Drawing on our nation's democratic values and military strength, the State Department seeks to foster a stable and peaceful international environment that ensures the security and prosperity of the American people. As the President's principal foreign policy advisor, the Secretary of State is responsible for the overall coordination and management of U.S. government activities abroad.

The State Department leads the U.S. government in defining American priorities and promoting American interests through unilateral actions, alliances, bilateral and multilateral relations, and international organizations. It directs diplomatic resources to prevent, manage, and resolve crises. It carries out statutory consular functions to protect U.S. borders and assist American citizens. The department also coordinates the activities of U.S. government agencies overseas and provides facilities and services that serve as the overseas diplomatic and administrative platform for their operations.

Summary Budget Information

FY 1993 (Actual)		FY 1996 (Budgeted)	
Budget	Staff	Budget	Staff
$5.000 billion	26,000	$4.800 billion	23,700

Reinvention Highlights

The foreign policy record of this Administration is one in which all Americans can take great pride. Our efforts have been guided by four principles:

- the imperative of American leadership in the world,
- the need to maintain effective relations with the world's most powerful nations,
- the importance of adapting and building institutions that will promote economic and security cooperation, and
- the need to continue to support democracy and human rights.

We have accomplished much over the past three years. We ended the fighting in Bosnia, and eliminated the threat it posed to European security. We are bringing together former adversaries in the Partnership for Peace, and we are moving ahead with the historic process of NATO enlargement. We stopped the flight of Haitian refugees to our shores, and gave that nation a chance to build democracy. We achieved the indefinite and unconditional extension of the

Nuclear Non-Proliferation Treaty. We froze North Korea's nuclear program and put it on the road to the scrap heap. We stemmed a destabilizing financial crisis in Mexico and damage to other emerging markets in this hemisphere and around the world. Our economic diplomacy has produced more than 200 trade agreements which have helped to fuel an export boom, creating more than one million high-paying American jobs. These achievements would not have been possible without President Clinton's determined leadership and the bipartisan support that has sustained American dipomacy over the last half-century.

We know that without continued American leadership, we cannot hope to seize the opportunities or confront the threats of the complex post-Cold War world. We also know that in an era of scarce resources, we have an obligation to the American people to apply the most rigorous standards in spending their tax dollars. As we meet our fundamental responsibilities to safeguard our national security and advance our enduring interests, the State Department will continue doing its part to give the nation a government that works better and costs less.

Increasing Productivity and Streamlining. We will continue our efforts to increase our productivity and streamline our organization, efforts that were begun under the auspices of the National Performance Review. Strengthening our diplomacy by making it more efficient and effective has been a focus of the Department's attention. Some of our more noteworthy accomplishments over the past three years have been:

- an estimated reduction in our administrative expenses of $139 million;
- the closure of more than 30 posts overseas;
- the absorption of a 40-percent increase in passport workload with no increase in staff;
- the development of new management tools, such as the "overseas staffing model" and a new interagency administrative cost-sharing system that will enable us to rationalize our overseas staffing and its related costs;
- the reduction of a number of middle management positions, such as a 25-percent cut in the number of deputy assistant secretary jobs; and
- a roughly 20-percent reduction in real resources (adjusted for inflation) since the beginning of the Administration.

Improving Service. Last year, as part of the Department's reinvention efforts, I launched a strategic management initiative that created teams of State Department employees to examine ways of improving our service to the American people at a lower overall cost. For example, we set up an 800 number for consular crises and made travel information more available by fax-on-demand and through the Internet. And we launched interagency teams to pursue priorities such as expanding trade and combating crime more aggressively. We eliminated redundancy by combining some administrative services like warehousing and printing with other foreign affairs agencies. We also broadened our job-sharing programs and opened a child care center to make sure that we retain the most skilled and diverse workforce possible.

As Secretary of State, I am proud of our record on downsizing, streamlining, and reinventing how we do business. We have instilled a strong customer service ethic among our employees, toward both the American public and the other government agencies with which we work. Our employees have been enthusiastic participants and leaders in this process, becoming even more aware of how the line that used to separate domestic and foreign policy has all but vanished. We clearly recognize that our strength at home is inseparable from our strength abroad.

I have committed the Department of State to continue responsible efforts to increase our productivity, keep our diplomatic institutions strong and effective, and maintain an efficient, universal diplomatic presence. We will do so on behalf of the growing number of American travelers and workers, students, and business people who rely on our efforts overseas and on behalf of the American people who count on us to protect their security and prosperity at home.

Warren Christopher

Department of Transportation
Federico Peña, Secretary

Mission Statement

The Department of Transportation (DOT) is vital to our economy and quality of life. DOT will Tie America Together with a safe, technologically advanced, and efficient transportation system that promotes economic growth and international competitiveness now and in the future and that contributes to a healthy and secure environment.

To accomplish this overall mission, DOT has identified seven primary goals:

- Tie America Together through an effective intermodal transportation system;
- invest strategically in transportation infrastructure, which will increase productivity, stimulate the economy, and create jobs;
- create a new alliance between the nation's transportation and technology industries, to make them both more efficient and internationally competitive;
- promote safe and secure transportation;
- actively enhance our environment through wise transportation decisions;
- put people first in our transportation system by making it relevant and accessible to users; and
- transform DOT by empowering employees in a new team effort to achieve our goals.

Summary Budget Information

FY 1993 (Actual)		FY 1996 (Budgeted)	
Budget	Staff	Budget	Staff
$36.681 billion	109,242	$37.504 billion	101,232

Reinvention Highlights

Today, the U.S. Department of Transportation provides safety oversight and infrastructure and technology investment that keep the U.S. transportation system the safest and most efficient in the world.

When President Clinton took office, the Department's ability to maintain this leadership was under stress. Red tape, outdated programs, and misplaced requirements wasted money, burdened our partners, and hindered our ability to serve the American people. Major project delays and cost overruns, like those of the initiative to automate air traffic control technology, were only the most visible problems.

I saw that we needed to do two things. First, clearly define the Department's mission to focus our resources on core responsibilities. Second, change the Department's culture to one that views transportation system users, state and local governments, and the American people themselves as our customers.

Redefining Mission. I developed a strategic plan that clarified the Department's mission, outlined the challenges we faced to fulfill that mission, and then set seven primary goals to meet those challenges. This strategic plan is focused on results, not process, and has guided us in everything we've since done to help America's transportation systems prepare for the 21st century.

The plan's results can be seen in many ways: the increase of infrastructure and research investment to its highest levels ever, the establishment of three-dozen international aviation agreements to open markets and create jobs for American airlines, to increase opportunities for travelers, and to improve in the health of America's aerospace and shipbuilding industries.

Changing the Culture. The effort to change our culture is based on Vice President Gore's National Performance Review, which focuses on making the federal government work better, cost less, and be more responsive to its customers. To do so, we're implementing a wide range of new initiatives and operational improvements.

The most dramatic of these is a restructuring of the Department to put front line service as our top priority. The Federal Highway, Transit, and Railroad Administrations and the National Highway Traffic Safety Administration—which have many functions in common—are streamlining their field offices to provide one-stop shopping for our customers and move us towards a seamless system in which the different forms of transportation are fully integrated.

The Coast Guard is carrying out a streamlining that will eliminate layers and better align its programs and command structure. Shifting headquarters staff to the field, decommissioning inefficient older ships and aircraft, and consolidating unneeded offices will not only improve performance but also save $400 million from 1994 to 1998 while freeing hundreds of millions of dollars in property for other uses.

The Federal Aviation Administration (FAA) is streamlining its operations to focus on key areas such as air traffic control and aircraft safety inspections and is making sure that the right people are in the right jobs right away. Personnel reforms are cutting outside hiring times from seven months to six weeks, reducing 155,000 job descriptions to fewer than 2,000, and replacing a foot-thick stack of personnel rules with a 41-page booklet.

Focusing on Customers and Results. Improving customer service through streamlining has allowed us to reduce our workforce by more than 8,000 overall, saving hundreds of millions of dollars a year in salaries and overhead. However, our focus on improving customer service goes beyond restructuring.

- **We're Listening to Our Customers.** For example, the Intermodal Surface Transportation Efficiency Act, which authorizes federal highway, highway safety, and transit programs expires in 1997. We're already holding numerous public forums and meetings with our customers so that our proposals for reauthorization meet their needs.
- **We're Changing Our Focus From Process to Results.** The FAA's flexible new procurement system cuts the time and cost of buying systems and services. Paperwork has been slashed from 233 documents to fewer than 50 and the time required to award contracts has been reduced by half, cutting the cost to vendors—and, ultimately, to taxpayers. Most importantly, new technologies will come on line sooner to make our skies safer.
- **We're Managing by Performance.** We've built on the Government Performance and Results Act to target our resources better and are developing specific, measurable goals and plans to achieve them. The Coast Guard threw out its old "activity standards" and held its field offices accountable for specific results such as a five-year, 20-percent reduction in accidental maritime workers deaths and injuries. Focusing on specifics in this way has already freed up a half-million work hours.

133

- **We're Introducing Common Sense to Our Operations.** Our telephone directory "blue pages" are no longer based on bureaucratic organizational charts but on things people can logically relate to. A businesswoman calling about hazardous materials can look up "HazMat," and not waste time by figuring out she needs to call our Research and Special Programs Administration.
- **We're Slashing Red Tape.** We've already cut more than 1,200 pages of unnecessary public regulations, such as rules about how a truck driver should climb into his sleeper berth. An additional 3,000 pages have been simplified or improved. All told, nearly half of the Department's regulations are being cut or reworked, and new regulations are being developed in partnership with industry through negotiated rulemaking instead of by fiat.
- **We're Building New Partnerships to Pay for Infrastructure.** Our Partnership for Transportation Investment uses innovative financing methods to cut red tape and stretch federal dollars by attracting private funds. In Michigan, the owners of an industrial park are putting up part of the funding for a nearby highway interchange, letting work get under way faster and freeing state funds for other projects. We have 74 such projects, worth about $4 billion, under way in 35 states. More advanced concepts, such as infrastructure banks, will enable states to use federal seed money to leverage private funds. These strategies can be used not only for infrastructure but also in other areas in which public funding could be limited, such as technology research and development.

The examples I've cited are only a few of the ways the Department of Transportation is reinventing its operations to focus on its core mission and to improve customer service. As we continue these initiatives, we're keeping our eye on the goal: a leaner, less costly government that better serves the American people. I'm proud to say that we're well on the way to doing that.

Federico Peña

Department of the Treasury
Robert Rubin, Secretary

Mission Statement

The mission of the Department of the Treasury is to formulate and recommend economic, fiscal, and tax policies; serve as the financial agent of the government; enforce the law; protect the President and other officials; and manufacture coins and currency. Treasury's functions are broad and critical to the nation's well-being and include the following:

- Serve as the President's principal advisor in formulating international monetary, financial, and trade policies.
- Develop policies that consider economic effects of tax and budget policy.
- Regulate national banks, the government securities markets, and federal- and state-chartered thrifts.
- Sell securities needed to finance the federal government, and report on the government's financial condition.
- Collect the proper amount of income tax revenue at the least cost to the public and with the highest degree of public confidence.
- Collect revenue from imports and excise taxes on alcoholic beverages and tobacco products.
- Improve government-wide financial management.
- Disburse payments to over 100-million citizens annually.
- Enforce laws related to:
    - smuggling drugs and contraband;
    - trade, tax, and financial institution and telecommunications fraud;
    - exports of high technology and munitions;
    - counterfeiting and money laundering;
    - alcohol, tobacco, firearms, explosives, and violent crimes; and
    - the protection of the President, Vice President and others.
- Train law enforcement officers.
- Manufacture currency, coins, and stamps for the nation's commerce.

Summary Budget Information

FY 1993 (Actual)		FY 1996 (Budgeted)	
Budget	Staff	Budget	Staff
$10.131 billion	161,100	$10.402 billion	153,319

Reinvention Highlights

For over two hundred years, the Treasury Department has been a symbol of stability for the federal government and the nation. But being an old-line agency does not mean we are not open to new ideas. In the last three years, we have taken a hard look at some of our traditional ways of doing things and have begun reinventing Treasury. We are using new approaches and new technology to work more efficiently and serve the public better. We are handling monetary transactions electronically, reducing our regulations, and treating the businesses we regulate as partners. And we are doing these things with fewer people. In 1993, our baseline employment was 161,100 compared to about 153,000 today, a decrease of nearly 8,000 employees in three years. Our budget has stayed basically at the same level—$10 billion in 1993, $10 billion in 1996. Taking into account the effects of inflation, our budget has dropped. We are now doing more with less.

Handling Our Money Electronically. Whether it is collecting taxes and import duties or making federal payments, Treasury has the world's largest cash flow—about $3 trillion annually. Until recently, most of the 840-million federal checks going out each year, and the over 200-million tax returns coming in, were paper instead of electronic or wire transactions. Handling all this paper costs more, takes longer, and is not as reliable or secure as doing it electronically. We are bringing the nation's financial management into the information age—in both collecting money and paying it out.

Taxpayers with simple tax returns are now able to file electronically by phone; about three-million people filed their 1995 returns this way. This year, instead of making a trip to the public library or Internal Revenue Service office to get tax forms, taxpayers were able to download forms instantly through the IRS home page on the World Wide Web. Over 100,000 files were downloaded on just one day—April 15. The next step will be to let taxpayers with home computers file their returns directly via their computer modem—and we are working on that.

We are cutting business taxpayers' paperwork as we switch to electronic tax collection. For more than 40 years employers deposited their federal withholding and employment taxes sending a special form and check to their bank. A 1995 law required a small number of employers (1,500) to start making their deposits electronically, but more than 64,000 employers—depositing over $300 billion—have voluntarily joined the program as of June 1996.

Our Financial Management Service is also delivering 425-million payments valued at nearly $700 billion electronically this year. This represents over half its total payment transaction volume and nearly 70 percent of its total dollar volume. Electronic payments are faster, safer, more reliable, and cheaper. An electronic payment costs 2 cents, but cutting and sending a check costs 45 cents (not including the costs to agencies and the banking industy of handling lost, stolen, or forged checks). We expect this to save the government about $500 million over the next five years, and the banking industry estimates it will save almost $400 million each year.

Starting in July 1996, people or businesses receiving new payments from the federal government who have bank accounts will be required to have their payments deposited electronically into those accounts. By January 1, 1999, we are required by law to deliver all payments, except tax refunds, electronically. This includes having in place a convenient, low-cost way to get payments to people who do not have a bank account. To that end, we have been experimenting for the past seven years with giving nearly 30,000 people a plastic card for their benefit payments, which they can use to get their money from an automated teller machine or point-of-sale terminal. We have also begun to deliver tax refunds electronically, even though this will not be required by law.

Regulatory Partners, Not Adversaries. Treasury investigates crimes and enforces laws and regulations involving firearms and explosives, money laundering, counterfeiting, banks, trade, and taxes. As regulators, we are cutting down on our regulations. We are changing our approach by taking a position of trusting those we regulate to do the right thing and by treating them as honest citizens and business people who do want to comply with the law.

To protect people's bank deposits, Treasury regulates national banks and thrift savings institutions to see that their operations are safe and sound. In the past three years, the Office of Thrift Supervision and the Comptroller of the Currency reinvented their approach to supervising thrifts and banks. For example, officials of the Office of Thrift Supervision personally met with numerous people in the thrift industry to get their perspective. Acting on the feedback they received in these meetings, they cut out 40 percent of the paperwork required in the thrifts' quarterly reports and agreed to do a better job in coordinating their examinations. They canceled useless regulations and overhauled 70 percent of the remaining regulations by reviewing, reorganizing, and rewriting them in plain English. The Comptroller of the Currency did the same with all its bank regulations from A to Z. In fact, last year all Treasury bureaus with regulatory responsibilities set goals to eliminate regulations. Treasury's total target was to eliminate 500 pages of regulations. As of June 30, we had cut out nearly 400 pages of rules.

If a regulatory agency wants to get results, it needs cooperation from the industry it regulates. Some gun dealers told us that in the past, there was a wall between legitimate gun dealers and the Bureau of Alcohol, Tobacco and Firearms (ATF). In 1993, the new chief of the Firearms Regulatory Division phoned the executive director of a key association of gun store owners. When he suggested they talk about industry/regulatory problems, the association executive was astonished. This was a whole new ball game. They began talking—exchanging information, airing their differences, and building a new relationship. This year, the National Alliance of Stocking Gun Dealers recognized ATF's leadership with an award for forging this new partnership with legitimate gun dealers.

This is just one example of ATF's new approach in working with gun dealers, importers, and manufacturers. The industry has profited by becoming part of the process under which they're regulated. ATF now gets better industry cooperation than before. State and local police get help in solving violent crimes as ATF, gun manufacturers, and distributors work with them. We have learned that when you trust those you regulate to do the right thing and work with them, the result is increased cooperation and better compliance with the law.

Doing More With Less. We are doing all these things with a workforce that is significantly smaller than it was in 1993—we have cut our numbers from about 161,000 to just over 153,000—a reduction of nearly 8,000 employees. At the same time we cut staffing, we have become more productive and done more with less. For example, when we introduced the redesigned $100 bill this past spring (to stay ahead of advances in counterfeiting technology), we did not have to set up a big bureaucracy to do it. A core team of five people, working with an outside contractor and several other federal agencies, designed a worldwide education campaign to make sure people in all countries around the world recognized and accepted our new currency. Our $100 note is the most widely circulated bill in the world. When the new currency came out, it happened without a hitch. There were no problems with people rushing to trade in their old bills for new ones or to exchange their U.S. currency for another country's currency. This successful story is just one example of how we have used minimum resources to get maximum benefit.

Treasury is reinventing the way we do things because we want government to serve the people, not the other way around. We are trying to use good judgment and common sense in dealing with those we regulate, and we are cutting back on the number of our regulations. We are trying new ways to be more efficient and save the taxpayers money. We are doing more with less. The bottom line is that reinventing Treasury is about dollars and common sense.

Robert Rubin

137

U.S. Agency for International Development
J. Brian Atwood, Administrator

Mission Statement

The U.S. Agency for International Development's (USAID's) principal mission is to advance U.S. interests by:

- promoting sustainable development and addressing global problems;
- providing humanitarian relief; and
- helping countries make the transition to becoming stable, free democracies and long-term trading partners for the United States.

Summary Budget Information

FY 1993 (Actual)		FY 1996 (Budgeted)	
Budget	Staff	Budget	Staff
$7.942 billion	3,928	$7.443 billion	3,246

Reinvention Highlights

When I became Administrator in 1993, the USAID was a troubled organization. A presidential commission appointed at the behest of Congress to study the agency had reported in 1992 that USAID was "hamstrung by waste, poor communication, and just plain bad management."

Over the years, Congress had piled on too many responsibilities and objectives for an agency with limited personnel and resources. USAID was top-heavy with managers who put more emphasis on how much money went into assistance and how many people were trained than it did on getting actual development results.

USAID employees are among the most motivated and committed people in the federal workforce. Many are former Peace Corps volunteers. In the course of doing their jobs, they have braved earthquakes, floods, epidemics of terrible diseases, coups, and civil wars. They are dedicated to helping people and accustomed to overcoming obstacles and inconveniences as they take practical action to build a more peaceful, just, and prosperous world. Often, however, their efforts had been frustrated by thousands and thousands of pages of regulations, and uncoordinated, antiquated communications and management systems.

The problems went beyond management and red-tape to a more fundamental concern: the world had changed suddenly and dramatically with the collapse of the Soviet Union. USAID needed to clarify its mission and refocus its programs on the new threats and opportunities of the post-Cold War period.

Focusing on Fewer, Obtainable Goals. I eagerly volunteered our whole agency as an experimental laboratory in Vice President Al Gore's reinvention of government program. I promised to focus USAID on fewer, more obtainable goals and to be accountable for measurable results.

Three years into the effort, most of the refocusing and reengineering has been done. The results have been so dramatic that when the chairman of the commission appointed by President Bush—which had been so critical in 1992—came back last year, he declared, "This is the most remarkable transformation of a government agency I have ever seen."

We are proud of that transformation. Among other things, we have accomplished the following:

- We reorganized the agency to make it more responsive to the development challenges of today, removing unnecessary layers of management, eliminating duplication and overlap.
- We made procurement easier and quicker. We replaced stacks of manuals with a single CD-ROM that allows both the agency and contractors to retrieve desired information within minutes.
- We developed integrated systems for communications and management of all core business systems—accounting, procurement, budgeting, and personnel. USAID is now a resource for other agencies developing standards for electronic recordkeeping.
- We reformed basic program operations to improve delivery of assistance; rewarded team performance and empowered employees; improved coordination with other donors; and encouraged those whose lives are affected by our aid to participate in all aspects of the process, from initial planning through execution of projects.
- We reduced the number of country programs and field missions to focus our resources better where we can achieve sustainable development results. By the end of fiscal year (FY) 1996, we will have closed 23 of our missions. At the same time, we have reduced our payroll 17 percent since FY 1993.
- We are closing three categories of missions: very small ones with high administrative costs, missions that do not get results because the host country does not share our development goals or is unwilling to invest its own money, and missions in countries that are ready to graduate from USAID programs. These last include traditional developing nations as well as countries making the transition to democracy and free enterprise after years of communist oppression.

Serving Customers Better. Reengineering is not just cost cutting. We have also added new activities that enable us to serve our customers better:
- We launched Lessons Without Borders to share with U.S. cities and rural communities some of the lessons USAID has learned in 30 years of development work.
- We put contract information—and information about USAID programs—on the Internet, which serve more than 65-million computer users worldwide.
- We have already received awards for having one of the top Web sites in government.

We are giving better service to our ultimate customers—the people in developing nations and the U.S. taxpayers. These reforms and consolidations will allow us to focus our limited financial and human resources where the agency can make a real difference. They are essential steps to carrying out the goals of USAID:
- to help establish the conditions for democracy and free enterprise in partner countries;
- to provide humanitarian relief in situations of natural or manmade disasters in a manner that advances long-term development goals;
- to move nations to self-sufficiency in order to promote stability and create markets for U.S. goods, thereby advancing U.S. national security interests and the U.S. economic and trade position; and

- to address global problems that could directly threaten U.S. security and national interests, such as diseases, food supply, climate change, rapid population growth, or depletion of environmental quality or biodiversity.

To carry out these goals, USAID will support programs in four areas that are fundamental to sustainable development: broad-based economic growth, environment, population and health, and democracy. These efforts reinforce each other.

I am proud of what the agency has accomplished and of the teams of USAID people who have made it possible. We are committed to continue improving what we do and how we do it. By harnessing new technologies and listening to new ideas, we can do an even better job of promoting the long-term interests of the United States abroad; improving the lives of millions of individuals; and building a safer, more peaceful world for all.

J. Brian Atwood

United States Information Agency
Joseph Duffey, Director

Mission Statement

The mission of the United States Information Agency (USIA) is to understand, inform, and influence foreign publics in promotion of the U.S. national interest, and to broaden the dialogue between Americans and U.S. institutions and their counterparts abroad. Its goals are as follows:

- Increase understanding and acceptance of U.S. policies and U.S. society by foreign audiences.
- Broaden dialog between Americans and U.S. institutions and their counterparts overseas.
- Increase U.S. government knowledge and understanding of foreign attitudes and their implications for U.S. foreign policy.

Summary Budget Information

FY 1993 (Actual)*		FY 1996 (Budgeted)	
Budget	Staff	Budget	Staff
$1.409 billion	8,470	$1.077 billion	7,311

*Includes funding and staff for the Board for International Broadcasting for comparability between 1993 and 1996 figures. The functions of the Board, and associated funding, are now within USIA as a result of reinvention.

Reinvention Highlights

Public diplomacy, USIA's core mission, is a future-oriented foreign policy tool that helps ensure America's continued global leadership.

The communications revolution, the demise of the Soviet bloc, and the removal of political barriers in other nations have increased greatly the flow of information to other peoples. They also have created, however, a cacophony of voices. Cutting through this noise, USIA ensures that the U.S. message is heard and understood abroad.

Creating the Bureau of Information. USIA's most comprehensive restructuring has occurred in press, publications, and speaker programs, where an entire bureau—the Bureau of Information—was created to take full advantage of the information revolution. Three factors were indispensable to this reinvention: a vision of the future, determination to focus on the most vital programs, and employee involvement in structuring the new organization.

The metamorphosis began in 1993, when I decided to take a 30-percent reduction from a single bureau, rather than 3-percent cuts across the entire agency. More than 100 employees comprising USIA's Restructuring Partnership Team developed a blueprint for implementing reductions. Traditional hierarchical structures were replaced by a decentralized, team-based, customer-oriented, flexible organization. Employees were made accountable and empowered to be bold, take risks, and produce ever more timely products and services.

Staff was cut from more than 600 full-time positions to fewer than 400, and the labor-management ratio was increased from 3-to-1 to 11-to-1. Programs such as worldwide printed magazines were discontinued because they were no longer the most effective means of influencing foreign opinion.

A steering committee of management and union representatives guided the development of a clearly defined mission and culture. Simultaneously, a design team of employees managed the development of new or improved products. For these efforts, in 1994, the Vice President awarded USIA a Hammer Award recognizing the agency's leadership in reinvention.

Reconfiguring Overseas Offices. Our overseas posts are staffed by foreign service officers who serve as the spokespersons for U.S. diplomatic missions and manage highly targeted programs of information and educational exchange. Over the past two years, we have begun deploying field resources in accordance with post-Cold War realities, in which economic factors and the new democratic marketplaces of ideas are increasingly important to U.S. national security. USIA's overseas operations—which provide the crucial human connection with foreign publics—have experienced a 14-percent cut in foreign service officer staffing and a 16-percent cut in foreign national staffing in fiscal year (FY) 1996 alone. We no longer maintain the principle of universal presence. Instead, overseas reductions are guided by a rigorous analysis of each post's contribution to U.S. foreign policy. It is a dynamic model for allocating resources in which adjustments are being made for changing circumstances.

During my three-and-a-half year tenure, USIA has embraced a strategy of rational downsizing. Cost cutting has been the impetus for carefully paring and refining USIA's public diplomacy priorities. Our reinvention efforts have been driven by the need to advance U.S. foreign policy interests to embrace advanced communications technologies, as well as to cut costs.

USIA's agility in meeting the challenges of geopolitical change has been demonstrated by our closing 28 field offices while opening new posts in the new independent states of the former Soviet Union and in the former Yugoslavia. In FY 1996 alone, we are closing 15 field offices, including ones in Libreville, Gabon; Kyoto, Japan; Melbourne, Australia; and Poznan, Poland.

Consolidating Overseas Broadcasting Operations. Profound changes also have occurred in America's global broadcasting operations. Last year's inauguration of the Broadcasting Board of Governors, established by 1994 legislation, consolidates—for the first time—the responsibility for all nonmilitary U.S. government international broadcasting, including USIA's Voice of America, Radio and TV Martí, and WORLDNET television, as well as the independent grantees, Radio Free Europe/Radio Liberty, and the new Asia Pacific Network.

All engineering and technical operations of USIA's Voice of America and the surrogate international broadcast services Radio Free Europe/Radio Liberty have been integrated. Overlapping programs in the same language have been eliminated, while each operation's program strengths have been retained. New professional relationships with affiliate stations and cable networks have increased listenership and reduced costs.

Consolidation of broadcasting has resulted in savings of over $400 million during the 1994-97 period, including a 31-percent reduction in staff and the elimination of over 400 direct broadcast programming hours via short—or medium—wave transmitters. These cuts were not taken across the board, however. Taking into account the end of the bipolar world order and an upsurge in regional conflicts and terrorism, we increased broadcasting and opened new relay stations in Asia, the Middle East, and Africa; we closed stations in Europe.

142

Expanding the Use of Technology. Technology will play a vital role in keeping the United States in the forefront of international communications. USIA's strategic plan envisions the creation of a two-way, high-speed worldwide digital information platform that will serve all agency divisions in the 21st century.

Innovative use of the Internet has expanded USIA's reach overseas. Our award-winning World Wide Web sites, new electronic journals, and database search capabilities offer people in many countries the latest information about the United States. Long-standing USIA products, such as the daily wire service of key documents and background articles, are posted on the Internet almost hourly. With this technology, customers can call upon USIA's authoritative information sources whenever they need them. Wide-ranging information technologies are used to perform traditional program functions more economically. Through digital videoconferencing, for example, a top U.S. trade official recently discussed U.S. objectives for the Asia-Pacific Economic Cooperation forum in a face-to-face dialog with journalists in two Japanese cities—without ever leaving USIA's Washington headquarters.

Restructuring the Bureau of Education and Cultural Affairs. Technology alone could never take the place of USIA's programs that provide direct experiences with American values, ideas, and traditions, however. To that end, USIA's Bureau of Educational and Cultural Affairs enhances the knowledge, understanding, and skills of people abroad through person-to-person exchange programs with their counterparts in the United States. Recently, I approved the broad outline of a restructuring plan for that bureau: cutting the number of its major elements from seven to four; reducing supervisory levels; increasing team work, staff cohesion, and communication across functional lines; and reducing total positions.

In FY 1996, the Bureau of Educational and Cultural Affairs cut personnel by about 12 percent. A further reduction is projected for FY 1997. Meanwhile, four Reorganization Working Groups of employees are developing detailed restructuring plans to improve efficiency and effectiveness.

USIA's Bureau of Educational and Cultural Affairs and field offices are spearheading new partnerships with the private sector. These allow us to share expertise with private sector individuals and firms, while leveraging shrinking federal dollars. Creative new initiatives, such as USIA's Business for Russia program, bring together individuals from that society crucial to the long-term development of democratic institutions and free markets with relevant American organizations and businesses. Fully one-fourth of the Business for Russia program funds comes from sources outside the U.S. government.

Finally, we have restructured our Office of Research and Media Reaction, making a 25-percent cut in the office's staff and a 15-percent cut in its budget over the past two years. USIA Foreign Media Reaction Reports are now available on the Internet (World Wide Web site), and the distribution of our foreign Opinion Analysis papers has been expanded to include—for the first time—nongovernmental organizations.

Ensuring Results. USIA reinvention—a constant and purposeful evolution—will help ensure that public diplomacy continues to advance the U.S. national interest effectively by nurturing relationships with people around the world who can affect our well-being.

Joseph Duffey

Department of Veterans Affairs

Jesse Brown, Secretary

Mission Statement

The mission of the Department of Veterans Affairs (VA) is to serve America's 26.5 million veterans and their families with dignity and compassion and to be their principal advocate in ensuring that they receive the care, support, and recognition earned in service to this nation.

Summary Budget Information

FY 1993 (Actual)		FY 1996 (Budgeted)	
Budget	Staff	Budget	Staff
$36.019 billion	234,428	$38.608 billion	223,727

Reinvention Highlights

In three short years, the road to reinvention has taken the VA from doing business as usual to performance that is striving to be the best in the business. Upon taking the helm of the second-largest federal agency in 1993, I introduced a new mission focus for each of the department's employees with the slogan Putting Veterans First. The phrase came to permeate not only VA rhetoric, but thinking and planning as well. It meshed mission and customer at all levels and provided a sturdy platform from which to launch Vice President Gore's National Performance Review (NPR) the government reinvention program. The Putting Veterans First philosophy was implemented at all VA facilities through mandatory training for each employee that focused on courtesy, caring, and respect.

VA reinvention labs set the pace for NPR innovation early on. The New York VA Benefits Office launched a major effort to focus on customers. Employees surveyed customers and benchmarked against commercial businesses to redesign benefits processing and delivery procedures. When Vice President Gore presented his very first Hammer Award to the New York VA office, he said, "Veterans are happier... The employees are also happier." As Gale Noble, a VA case technician, put it, "The satisfaction is in greeting the veteran, actually seeing first-hand these men and women who served this country so that we all would be here... Now, I actually can talk to them, make them laugh, give them a friendly smile, and they leave very happy." Since then, VA facility and program office reinvention teams have been honored with 46 of the Vice President's Hammer Awards for leading the way in creating a government that works better (for veterans) and costs less.

Creating a Customer Focus. VA published department-wide customer service standards in September 1994 to put both veterans and VA employees on notice that nothing is more important to our success than veterans' satisfaction. These were quickly followed by specific standards of service for each VA operational branch and service facility. VA customers were told the maximum amount of time they should expect to wait for service at each facility; the steps VA employees would take to ensure their understanding and satisfaction with VA response to their needs; and the avenues open to them for comment, complaint, and follow-up.

Reinventing VA's Health Care. The Veterans Health Administration's (VHA's) 22 new Veterans Integrated Service Networks (VISNs) have streamlined middle management and positioned VA to focus its resources on maintaining veterans' health rather than maintaining veterans' hospitals. The VISN concept is a result of benchmarking against private-sector hospitals, health care systems, and health maintenance organizations. VISN will take a far more active role than former regional offices in assessing VA field resources against customer needs and distributing resources accordingly. As in the private sector, VA health care resource allocation decisions soon will be totally driven by customer demand rather than facility maintenance budgets, as VISNs adopt capitated budgets by 1998.

VA medical facilities, in line with private sector health care providers, are shifting emphasis from hospital-based to outpatient care and to more customer-focused primary health care teams. The veteran receives all basic health care from a team of doctors, nurses, and other health-care providers who work with the veteran on a continuing basis to maintain his/her health. All VA facilities will use primary care teams by the end of 1996.

The need for costly inpatient hospital beds is decreasing as VHA expands outpatient care to reduce costs of medical care delivery while increasing access to that care. Customer access has been aided through administrative innovation as well. The basic medical care application form is being reduced from 93 to fewer than 20 questions, and VA has eliminated 887 other redundant forms to improve timely access to care for veteran patients. A Veterans Universal Access Identification Card is currently being piloted at six VA medical centers. Among this state-of-the-art "smart" card's features are a bar code and a magnetic strip containing basic patient data such as name, Social Security number, date of birth, veteran status, and service-connected indicator, as well as a photo of the veteran. Use of the card will eliminate a significant amount of paperwork and reduce waiting times for veterans. Access is also being increased through more VA sharing agreements with Department of Defense (DOD) and community health care providers.

Patient Maurice E. Lewis was inspired to send a letter to the editor of the Arkansas Democrat-Gazette in which he wrote, "The positive changes in VA services are too numerous to mention and the attitude and morale of VA employees have improved drastically. I know this to be true because I have used the VA medical system for the past seven years. I have never been treated better by any medical system, hospital, or doctor."

Reinventing Veterans Benefits. The Veterans Benefits Administration (VBA) began its reinvention effort by conducting employee-customer focus groups and customer satisfaction surveys to evaluate core services and provide data to monitor and refine VBA customer service standards. Loan Guaranty Service used similar tools to evaluate service to both veterans and business clients in the banking industry. Early results were used to improve communication with lenders, reduce the need for them to contact field facilities, and cut the time needed to close VA home loans.

VBA outreach services complemented customer service initiatives. Toll-free telephone service (a dozen toll-free services provide information and referral for specific groups, including women veterans and Persian Gulf War veterans) and new electronic bulletin boards and World Wide Web home pages supported VA outreach to a variety of special needs customer groups.

The VA Insurance Center designed a new simplified statement for its policyholders after evaluating private sector formats and listening to customer feedback. The statement gives a complete status of an individual veteran's policy and reduces the amount of time the veteran spends calling VA for more information—as well as the staff time needed to respond.

Each of VBA's four regional headquarters consolidated widespread human resources management services into single offices serving each region. Reduced overhead allowed more resources for customer service and benefits delivery while improving the region's employee-supervisor ratio to more than 15-to-1.

Similar benefits are on tap as VBA consolidates specific operational functions into processing centers. This has already been done with Montgomery GI Bill Educational Benefits and Persian Gulf War compensation claims and will continue as new automated data processing networks allow immediate electronic access to records, certifying agencies, and veterans. A recent example is an electronic data interface established with the Social Security Administration (SSA) which greatly improves the timeliness of compensation and pension benefits claims processing requiring SSA data. VBA regional offices can now communicate with SSA on veterans' Social Security numbers and verification of security assistance payments within 24 hours. Such transactions used to take up to 10 weeks by mail. Similar VBA-DOD collaboration streamlined the processing of DOD's death gratuity benefit to survivors. Consolidated processing in the Cleveland VA Regional Benefits Office, collocated with the DOD Defense Finance and Accounting Service, cut award payment time from six months to a few weeks. VA and DOD also are working together on a pilot project to link military discharge physicals with the processing of VA disability compensation claims.

The Muskogee VA Regional Office focused on the implementation of self-directed employee work teams not only to do the work better, but in entirely new ways focused on customer need rather than institutional process. The work team concept has vastly improved performance and customer service: Claims processing time has dropped an average of 50 percent; supervisor-staff ratios have improved and saved $1.4 million a year in salaries; widows' pension claims presented in person are processed within one hour. Muskogee received both a Hammer Award and, this year, a Presidential Award for Quality Achievement for its pioneering work in employee-directed work team implementation.

Cutting Red Tape. VA has moved to reduce red tape, redundancies, and bureaucracy that interfere with the private sector's awareness of and ability to compete for VA contracts. VA's Financial Operations Team received a Hammer Award for designing and implementing a 1994 electronic commerce agreement with the Department ofj126 the Treasury calling for enhancement of every major VA benefit, administrative, and vendor payment system. All initiatives were successfully implemented, including the first check intercept system allowing the Federal Reserve to withhold checks to deceased payees, a national direct deposit enrollment program, and electronic linkages for transmission of all payment data between the two departments.

VA continues to expand electronic commerce, from increasing employee and beneficiary use of direct deposit of paychecks to 92-percent participation to developing software that enables small business personal computers to deal with VA on contract information and procurement matters. VA's Vendor Inquiry System allows more than 300,000 VA vendors to access their VA payment data electronically, saving thousands of phone inquiries and associated staff time.

VA developed new distributor agreements under its Medical/Surgical Prime Vendor program, which established 25 regional clusters for contract awards covering 173 VA medical centers. This improved procurement access to contractors around the country—particularly to small disadvantaged business owners who were guaranteed access to VA contracts under the program.

Listening to Our People. In May 1995, I joined Vice President Gore in announcing far-reaching VA reinvention initiatives that will continue to improve service to our veterans and make VA more efficient. Virtually all of those initiatives have been or are being implemented, and there is more to come as VA employees and their customers listen more intently to each other and work together.

"It's significant," said Vice President Gore at that announcement, "that the very first reinventing government award given any team in federal government was given right here in Veterans Affairs [to the New York Benefits Office]. . . In our effort to reinvent government, we've found one secret that's more important than any other: you've got to listen to the people who actually do the work; in this case, the people who deal first hand with America's veterans. Ask them what's going on; what needs to be changed; what needs to be improved. And they will tell you!"

Jesse Brown

APPENDIX B:
STATUS OF MAJOR RECOMMENDATIONS AFFECTING GOVERNMENTAL SYSTEMS

The September 7, 1993, report of the National Performance Review (NPR) contains 130 major recommendations affecting governmentwide management systems such as budget, procurement, financial management, and personnel. Separate accompanying reports delineate these recommendations, breaking them into 430 specific action items. Now, three years later, agencies report that 38 percent of these action items are complete, 49 percent are in progress, and the remainder are on hold or not making expected progress. Following are highlights of these governmentwide system reinvention efforts. Additional information on the status of these recommendations may be found on NPR's World Wide Web home page (http://www.npr.gov).

Creating Quality Leadership and Management

NPR Recommendations

QUAL01	Provide Improved Leadership and Management of the Executive Branch
QUAL02	Improve Government Performance Through Strategic and Quality Management
QUAL03	Strengthen the Corps of Senior Leaders
QUAL04	Improve Legislative-Executive Branch Relations

Progress to Date

The President and his Administration continue to provide leadership on management issues. Vice President Gore spearheads the reinvention initiative. The President's Management Council—which was created three years ago as recommended by NPR—has become a pivotal and effective force in the coordination of governmentwide reform initiatives, including customer service improvement, streamlining, and civil service reform.

Cabinet secretaries and agency heads have made a visible commitment to leading and managing in accordance with the Malcolm Baldrige National Quality Award criteria; in fact, a 1995 survey showed that 18 of the 24 largest agencies had created top-level quality councils to help lead their efforts. Although NPR recommended that a category be created within the Baldrige Award for federal government agencies, this has not been done. However, agencies are still committed to training their staff on quality management.

The Office of Personnel Management (OPM) has taken a leadership role in strengthening the corps of senior leaders by improving the selection process for senior executives and providing orientations for new political as well as career leaders in the government.

Streamlining Management Control

NPR Recommendations

SMC01	Implement a Systems Design Approach to Management Controls
SMC02	Streamline the Internal Controls Program to Make It an Efficient and Effective Management Tool
SMC03	Change the Focus of the Inspectors General
SMC04	Increase the Effectiveness of Offices of General Counsel
SMC05	Improve the Effectiveness of the General Accounting Office Through Increased Customer Feedback
SMC06	Reduce the Burden of Congressionally Mandated Reports
SMC07	Reduce Internal Regulations by More Than 50 Percent
SMC08	Expand the Use of Waivers to Encourage Innovation

Progress to Date

The Office of Management and Budget (OMB) continues to provide leadership in streamlining management control systems through its efforts to consolidate multiple reporting systems and integrate planning, budget, financial management, and performance reporting systems. For example, it is working on accountability reports in six agencies that consolidate a series of separate reports. This will provide decisionmakers with a clearer picture of agency operations—with less work involved.

Agency inspectors general continue to implement their January 1994 report, *Vision and Strategies to Apply Our Reinvention Principles*. In addition, they have developed a guide to help measure their performance and effectiveness. Also, selected units in the General Accounting Office are documenting best practices, and that office is beginning to use feedback loops more broadly.

The Federal Reports Elimination and Sunset Act of 1995 (Public Law 104-66) eliminated or modified more than 200 outdated or unnecessary congressionally mandated reporting requirements. It also automatically terminates, after four years, an estimated 4,800 additional reports with annual, semiannual, or other periodic reporting requirements unless Congress specifically renews them.

In September 1993, President Clinton directed agencies to cut their internal regulations in half by October 1996. A preliminary survey shows that 19 of the 24 largest agencies have already met this goal; the remaining five are making significant progress. Four agencies alone cut more than 315,000 pages. The Defense Department canceled 3,300—about 188,000 pages—of its 7,000 regulations. The Department of Transportation eliminated 89,367 pages of regulations, the Department of Veterans Affairs cut 25,799 pages, and the Department of Labor will cut 12,264 pages.

Transforming Organizational Structures

NPR Recommendations

ORG01	Reduce the Costs and Numbers of Positions Associated With Management Control Structures by Half
ORG02	Use Multi-Year Performance Agreements Between the President and Agency Heads to Guide Downsizing Strategies
ORG03	Establish a List of Specific Field Offices to Be Closed
ORG04	The President Should Request Authority to Reorganize Agencies
ORG05	Sponsor Three or More Cross-Departmental Initiatives Addressing Common Issues or Customers
ORG06	Identify and Change Legislative Barriers to Cross-Organizational Cooperation

Progress to Date

All agencies have developed plans for internal streamlining and reducing their workforces. Agencies are more than a year ahead of the statutory timetable for cutting 272,900 positions by 1999. Also, the President's Management Council completed a study on strategies for closing field offices and is sponsoring a benchmarking study on this. Individual agencies have examined their field offices and propose closing about 2,000.

However, most agencies have not yet targeted their personnel reductions in order to cut their management control costs in half over a six-year period, as recommended by NPR in 1993. However, six agencies are making significant reductions in this area and plan to continue to do so. Appendix H provides additional details.

The Administration continues to sponsor cross-departmental initiatives addressing common issues and customers. In all, the Administration is sponsoring at least 25 significant cross-cutting initiatives, such as better coordination of governmental statistics. In addition, it is piloting multi-agency "one-stop" offices for small business and other government services in several locations around the country. It has created the U.S. Business Advisor as a one-stop electronic link to government for business, so individuals can more easily search federal rules and obtain information.

The President has not asked Congress for authority to reorganize agencies, as recommended by NPR, but is instead achieving the efficiencies and other results desired through streamlining and joint agency efforts, such as the Federal Electronic Benefits Task Force. Further, Congress has not reduced barriers to cross-organizational cooperation, as recommended.

Improving Customer Service

NPR Recommendations

ICS01	Create Customer-Driven Programs in All Departments and Agencies That Provide Services Directly to the Public.
ICS02	Customer Service Performance Standards—Internal Revenue Service
ICS03	Customer Service Performance Standards—Social Security Administration

ICS04   Customer Service Performance Standards—Postal Service

ICS05   Streamline Ways to Collect Customer Satisfaction and Other Information From the Public

Progress to Date

In September 1993, President Clinton directed agencies to set customer service standards. To date, 214 agencies have published more than 3,000 standards telling their customers what kind of service to expect. The standards were developed by asking customers what they want; they are part of the agencies' response to Presidential Executive Order 12862 to build a customer-driven government. In his order, the President set an overall service goal to "equal the best in business."

Once their standards were issued, the agencies went to work to make good on their promises to be courteous, quick, accurate, and accessible. For example, each quarter, the Postal Service now publishes on-time delivery percentages in local papers around the country. In mid-1996, it achieved a historic high of 90 percent across the country. Counter service in five minutes or less is a national Postal Service goal, with signs posted in those local offices that have committed to fulfill the standard. A 1-800 service has been available since 1994 to respond to customer inquiries.

Agencies also are applying information technology to deliver better service. This past year, the Internal Revenue Service made tax forms available on the Internet—filling a huge demand as April 15th approached. Agencies have developed new ways to serve as well. A one-stop U.S. General Store for Small Business opened in Houston in 1995, providing links to services offered by dozens of government agencies. That pilot was so successful that a second store was opened in Atlanta in the spring of 1996.

The President also directed agencies to measure their results and report them to their customers. To date, more than one million customers have participated in voluntary surveys of satisfaction. The results of these surveys are being used to improve both service and standards.

Mission-Driven, Results-Oriented Budgeting

NPR Recommendations

BGT01   Develop Performance Agreements With Senior Political Leadership That Reflect Organizational and Policy Goals

BGT02   Effectively Implement the Government Performance and Results Act of 1993

BGT03   Empower Managers to Perform

BGT04   Eliminate Employment Ceilings and Floors by Managing Within Budget

BGT05   Provide Line Managers With Greater Flexibility to Achieve Results

BGT06   Streamline Budget Development

BGT07   Institute Biennial Budgets and Appropriations

BGT08   Seek Enactment of Expedited Rescission Procedures

Progress to Date

As part of the shift to greater accountability for results, President Clinton and the heads of major agencies have signed performance agreements as a way of clarifying priorities. To date, ten agency heads have negotiated annual agreements. The Secretaries of the Departments of Energy, Veterans Affairs, Transportation, and Housing and Urban Development have signed performance agreements for fiscal year (FY) 1996. The delay in receiving FY 1996 appropriations disrupted the development of additional performance agreements. However, all agencies are using other means for increasing accountability for results by, for example, developing goals, objectives, and performance measures as required by the Government Performance and Results Act (GPRA) (Public Law 103-62).

All agencies are working to develop the performance information that GPRA requires. OMB is leading the development process and increasing emphasis on the use of such information in the formulation of the FY 1997 budget. It is using the FY 1998 budget process to focus on the performance goals and measures that will be needed for full GPRA implementation in FY 1999.

As recommended by NPR, Congress allowed carryover authority of unobligated year-end balances for some agencies in FYs 1994 and 1995 but withdrew this authority in following years. Six agencies historically have had multi-year funding authority and are able to carry over funds, but the remainder do not. This continues to create an incentive for year-end spending rushes in some agencies.

Congress granted the President line item veto authority beginning in 1997 (Public Law 104-130). This provides an important tool for cutting wasteful spending. In addition, several congressional committees have begun exploring streamlining of the budget process, including converting to a biennial budget as proposed by NPR.

Improving Financial Management

NPR Recommendations

FM01	Accelerate the Issuance of Federal Accounting Standards
FM02	Clarify and Strengthen the Financial Management Roles of OMB and Treasury
FM03	Fully Integrate Budget, Financial, and Program Information
FM04	Increase the Use of Technology to Streamline Financial Services
FM05	Use the Chief Financial Officers (CFO) Act to Improve Financial Services
FM06	"Franchise" Internal Services
FM07	Create Innovation Funds
FM08	Reduce Financial Regulations and Requirements
FM09	Simplify the Financial Reporting Process
FM10	Provide an Annual Financial Report to the Public
FM11	Strengthen Debt Collection Programs
FM12	Manage Fixed Asset Investments for the Long Term
FM13	Charge Agencies for the Full Cost of Employee Benefits

Progress to Date

In June 1996, the first set of accounting standards was issued for the federal government, and a financial systems framework was established.

Through the Chief Financial Officers Council, financial managers and oversight organizations have developed a uniform vision, a set of priorities, and a program plan. FinanceNet, an Internet-based forum operated by the National Science Foundation, has been institutionalized by the CFO Council and the Joint Financial Management Improvement Program as a mechanism for professional interchange for improving financial services. The network's usefulness has been recognized across the federal government, by state and local organizations, and by other nations as well.

Five pilot franchise funds authorized by the Government Management Reform Act of 1994 (Public Law 103-356) have been approved for operation and are under way. Also, as authorized by the act, OMB is working with agencies to develop a single annual planning report each fall and a single accountability report each spring to replace the myriad financial reports currently required throughout the year. This approach is designed to ease agencies' reporting burden and provide information to decisionmakers rather than just data. These pilots are under way in six agencies.

A comprehensive debt collection management initiative was passed by Congress and signed by the President in April 1996 (Public Law 104-134). This will allow agencies to finance their debt collection activities with the revenues generated from their collection efforts. In addition, it will let agencies keep up to 5 percent of any increased collections of delinquent debt. The legislation authorizes the Department of the Treasury to offset payments to individuals and entities that are seriously delinquent in their debts to the federal government; it also authorizes an electronic screening process that will track borrowers governmentwide to bar seriously delinquent debtors from receiving additional credit.

The Administration also submitted legislation to Congress to charge agencies for the full cost of employee benefits. Currently, OPM shares part of these costs, thereby indirectly subsidizing agency operating costs.

Reinventing Human Resource Management

NPR Recommendations

HRM01	Create a Flexible and Responsive Hiring System
HRM02	Reform the General Schedule Classification and Basic Pay System
HRM03	Authorize Agencies to Develop Programs for Improvement of Individual and Organizational Performance
HRM04	Authorize Agencies to Develop Incentive Award and Bonus Systems to Improve Individual and Organizational Performance
HRM05	Strengthen Systems to Support Management in Dealing With Poor Performers
HRM06	Clearly Define the Objective of Training as the Improvement of Individual and Organizational Performance; Make Training More Market-Driven

HRM07	Enhance Programs to Provide Family-Friendly Workplaces
HRM08	Improve Processes and Procedures Established to Provide Workplace Due Process for Employees
HRM09	Improve Accountability for Equal Employment Opportunity Goals and Accomplishments
HRM10	Improve Interagency Collaboration and Cross-Training of Human Resource Professionals
HRM11	Strengthen the Senior Executive Service So That It Becomes a Key Element in the Governmentwide Culture Change Effort
HRM12	Eliminate Excessive Red Tape and Automate Functions and Information
HRM13	Form Labor-Management Partnerships for Success
HRM14	Provide Incentives to Encourage Voluntary Separations

Progress to Date

Substantial progress in reforming the human resource management process has been made through a number of incremental legislative and administrative steps. For example, in early 1996, Congress authorized OPM to delegate hiring authority to agencies (Public Law 104-52). Also, in May 1996, the Administration introduced H.R. 3483, which would dramatically expand the current demonstration authority and also streamline the process by which personnel demonstrations become permanent. Use of demonstration authority would allow agencies to implement a series of NPR's human resource recommendations, including a flexible and responsive hiring system, reforms to the classification schedule and pay system, development of performance management programs, use of award systems, and strengthening systems to deal with poor performers.

In response to another NPR recommendation, OPM in late 1995 issued regulations to decentralize performance management systems. To date, OPM has approved 17 agency systems and published a Performance Management Programs Handbook. OPM continues bimonthly publications of *Workforce Performance*, a newsletter that provides agencies with information on program design and development issues. As they reform their performance management systems, 20 of the larger agencies are using this opportunity to redesign their systems for dealing more effectively with poor performers.

A series of initiatives is under way to provide family-friendly workplaces. In 1995, Congress passed laws and OPM issued regulations to implement family-friendly leave policies. Federal employees can now use sick leave to adopt a child, serve as a bone-marrow or organ donor, and care for family members or attend their funerals. The limitation on recrediting sick leave has been removed for former federal employees who return to government service. Separately, an Interagency Adult Dependent Care Working Group has been established to promote awareness of federal elder care programs and related activities. In addition, the use of telecommuting is being expanded; pending legislation would expand agencies' authority to allow their employees to telecommute.

Following the recommendations of an interagency workgroup, an Executive Succession Planning Tool Kit has been developed. This uses a corporate model to address the challenges of changes in the executive levels of the civil service. Tool kits have been printed and mailed to heads of departments and agencies, directors of personnel, and senior executive contacts.

Considerable progress in creating labor-management partnerships has been made. To date, about 650 such partnerships have been established. Surveys show that these are beginning to make important differences in agency efficiency and worker satisfaction by addressing issues such as downsizing, customer service, and working conditions. Agencies are identifying measurable savings in legal costs and increased productivity as a result of better working relationships.

To address the challenges of downsizing, President Clinton directed agency heads in September 1995 to establish career transition programs. Consistent with the regulations implementing this direction, 51 agencies have completed career transition assistance plans and submitted them to OPM for review and feedback. Three others have submitted draft plans, and 10 have yet to submit plans. Additionally, OPM, in conjunction with other agencies and local governments in the metropolitan Washington area, has established a career transition center for use by locally based employees. Other centers are being created across the country.

Reinventing Federal Procurement

NPR Recommendations

PROC01	Reframe Acquisition Policy
PROC02	Build an Innovative Procurement Workforce
PROC03	Encourage More Procurement Innovation
PROC04	Establish New Simplified Acquisition Threshold and Procedures
PROC05	Reform Labor Laws and Transform the Labor Department Into an Efficient Partner for Meeting Public Policy Goals
PROC06	Amend Protest Rules
PROC07	Enhance Programs for Small Business and Small Disadvantaged Business Concerns
PROC08	Reform Information Technology Procurement
PROC09	Lower Costs and Reduce Bureaucracy in Small Purchases Through the Use of Purchase Cards
PROC10	Ensure Customer Focus in Procurement
PROC11	Improve Procurement Ethics Laws
PROC12	Allow for Expanded Choice and Cooperation in the Use of Supply Schedules
PROC13	Foster Reliance on the Commercial Marketplace
PROC14	Expand Electronic Commerce for Federal Acquisition
PROC15	Encourage Best Value Procurement
PROC16	Promote Excellence in Vendor Performance
PROC17	Authorize a Two-Phase Competitive Source Selection Process
PROC18	Authorize Multi-Year Contracts
PROC19	Conform Certain Statutory Requirements for Civilian Agencies to Those of Defense Agencies
PROC20	Streamline Buying for the Environment

Progress to Date

The Administration continues to make substantial progress in improving the procurement process. In April 1996, the Federal Acquisition Reform Act (FARA) and the Information Technology Management Reform Act (ITMRA) passed with bipartisan congressional support and the full support of the Administration (both are contained in Public Law 104-106). These laws will enable the federal procurement system to emulate many of the most successful buying practices used in the commercial marketplace. Building on the important reforms made by the Federal Acquisition Streamlining Act of 1994 (Public Law 103-355)—which focused largely on the purchase of commercial items and smaller dollar buys (those under $100,000)—FARA and ITMRA are reforming the way the government makes larger dollar purchases and acquires information technology.

In particular, these laws streamline the contract award process by allowing contracting officials—after reviewing initial proposals—to reduce the number of suppliers with whom they must negotiate. They authorize the use of simplified source selection procedures for commercial–item acquisitions up to $5 million. They permit agencies to manage their own information technology investments, and they repeal unique and time-consuming approval procedures that were required by the Brooks Act as well as the intrusive and disruptive protest process authorized by that act. In addition, these laws authorize OMB's Office of Federal Procurement Policy (OFPP) to initiate pilot programs immediately and grant the statutory waivers needed to test innovative procurement concepts.

Several related administrative initiatives are under way to make the procurement system more responsive to government customer needs, reduce bureaucracy, and seize the opportunities provided by advances in information technology. For example, a final rule to incorporate a statement of guiding principles in the Federal Acquisition Regulation was published in July 1995. A *Guide to Best Practices for Performance-Based Service Contracting* was developed and issued by OFPP in April 1996 to encourage greater use of performance-based service contracting. The guide is designed to assist agencies in defining their requirements in terms of performance standards—rather than in terms of how the work is to be done. This practice has significantly reduced the cost of large service contracts.

OFPP is also encouraging agencies to consider use of oral presentations in lieu of detailed written proposals to streamline the negotiation process and reduce costs associated with preparing and evaluating proposals. These types of reforms, in combination with the additional flexibilities authorized by FARA and ITMRA, are enabling government buyers to maximize the return on taxpayer dollars.

The Department of Defense (DOD) and the General Services Administration (GSA) are developing acquisition workforce education and training materials and opportunities to encourage innovation among the acquisition workforce. In addition, OFPP—in a joint partnership with NPR, GSA, DOD, Lawrence Livermore National Laboratory, and the nonprofit Council for Excellence in Government—has developed the Acquisition Reform Network. This Internet Web site provides both public and private sectors with access to federal acquisition information, including a reference material tool kit, an electronic conferencing forum, training packages, descriptions of acquisition best practices, and acquisition opportunity links. Also, the Administration is strongly committed to streamlining procurement through electronic commerce and is heavily involved in promoting electronic dissemination via mechanisms such as electronic catalogs, purchase cards, and the Acquisition Reform Network.

In addition, the President's Management Council led efforts to provide a performance management focus to the procurement system. A council subgroup shared knowledge and innovative practices across government and developed a set of procurement performance measures that will shift the system from a focus on process to a focus on outcomes. Agencies have agreed to develop performance measurement plans by October 1996 and to begin using them to measure quality, timeliness, price, and productivity of the procurement system.

Reinventing Support Services

NPR Recommendations

SUP01	Authorize the Executive Branch to Establish a Printing Policy That Will Eliminate the Current Printing Monopoly
SUP02	Assure Public Access to Federal Information
SUP03	Improve Distribution Systems to Reduce Costly Inventories
SUP04	Streamline and Improve Contracting Strategies for the Multiple Award Schedule Program
SUP05	Expand Agency Authority and Eliminate Congressional Control Over Federal Vehicle Fleet Management
SUP06	Give Agencies Authority and Incentive for Personal Property Management and Disposal
SUP07	Simplify Travel and Increase Competition
SUP08	Give Customers Choices and Create Real Property Enterprises That Promote Sound Real Property Asset Management
SUP09	Simplify Procedures for Acquiring Small Blocks of Space to House Federal Agencies
SUP10	Establish New Contracting Procedures for the Continued Occupancy of Leased Office Space
SUP11	Reduce Postage Costs Through Improved Mail Management

Progress to Date

Significant progress has been made in eliminating internal government monopolies on services. After a one-year pilot program, and guided by participant evaluations, GSA announced in July 1996 that, beginning this October, federal agencies will be allowed to acquire new leased space on their own if government-owned space is not available or does not meet the agency's needs. In addition, GSA granted agencies the authority to use its supply services or seek alternative sources. GSA also now allows agencies to dispose of excess personal property independently. Progress is being made legislatively to eliminate the Federal Prison Industries as a mandatory supply source for federal agencies. Finally, the recent Information Technology Management Reform Act delegated procurement of large information technology systems from GSA to the agencies.

In an effort to reduce agencies' dependence on supply depot systems and improve distribution systems, GSA compared itself with commercial supply distribution systems. This comparison showed that recent changes to the Federal Supply Service—direct vendor delivery, the elimination of specialized government specifications, the use of electronic data interchange to simplify ordering in near real-time, and the use of GSA's ADVANTAGE information system for the Federal Supply Service's catalog—has made the agency both cost effective and competitive. Benchmarking will continue to be used as a valuable tool in furthering savings.

Significant progress has been made on statutory and nonstatutory efforts to simplify travel regulations. In separate legislation, both houses of Congress have passed major reforms to the federal travel system. To complement this effort, GSA and the Joint Financial Management Improvement Program are streamlining the Federal Travel Regulation, which sets government-wide travel policies. These reforms have the potential for saving more than $800 million a year in administrative costs currently required by law.

Reengineering Through Information Technology

NPR Recommendations

IT01	Provide Clear, Strong Leadership to Integrate Information Technology Into the Business of Government
IT02	Implement Nationwide, Integrated Electronic Benefit Transfer
IT03	Develop Integrated Electronic Access to Government Information and Services
IT04	Establish a National Law Enforcement/Public Safety Network
IT05	Provide Intergovernmental Tax Filing, Reporting, and Payments Processing
IT06	Establish an International Trade Data System
IT07	Create a National Environmental Data Index
IT08	Plan, Demonstrate, and Provide Governmentwide Electronic Mail
IT09	Improve Government's Information Infrastructure
IT10	Develop Systems and Mechanisms to Ensure Privacy and Security
IT11	Improve Methods of Information Technology Acquisition
IT12	Provide Incentives for Innovation
IT13	Provide Training and Technical Assistance in Information Technology to Federal Employees

Progress to Date

As part of the Information Technology Management Reform Act of 1996—which substantially improved methods for acquiring information technology—agencies are required to designate chief information officers to provide leadership in the use of information technology. As this provision is implemented, information technology systems should be more effectively managed to achieve mission results. To help implement the act, President Clinton issued Executive Order 13011 in July 1996 to establish a Chief Information Officers Council as a forum to share ideas and make recommendations for the entire government. The order also sets up a Government

Information Technology Services Board to see that NPR's information technology recommendations continue to be implemented.

Substantial progress has been made on all recommendations. For example, the Federal Information Center developed by GSA to integrate governmentwide information to the public is up and running. This year, the program has expanded the center's service to 13 additional metropolitan areas, thereby providing service to all 50 states. A single toll-free number is in use (1-800-688-9889). In another effort to improve the government's information infrastructure, a governmentwide one-stop electronic bulletin board system was created to improve links among agencies.

Meetings of the Governmentwide Electronic Online Service Task Force are held on a monthly basis, with active and regular participation of online information principals from a wide range of executive and legislative branch agencies. Topics have included templates for user instruction, automated grants processes, and Mosaic technology. A most useful technical and "what's new" information exchange has developed among participants. The task force actively participated in a review of the White House World Wide Web home page and the roll-out of the Government Information Listing Service.

As more information is accessible online, concerns have grown over the security of governmental information. In response, the Administration's Information Infrastructure Task Force created a subgroup which established uniform privacy protection practices and generally acceptable implementation methods for these practices. In February 1996, OMB revised Circular A-130, Appendix III, to address better the security of federal automated information. This revision (1) requires agencies to include information security as part of each agency's strategic information technology plan, (2) includes computer security issues as a material weakness in agencies' reports required under the Federal Managers' Financial Integrity Act, (3) requires employees and contractors to complete awareness training, (4) improves planning for contingencies, and (5) establishes and employs formal emergency response capabilities.

Several efforts are under way to help train and provide assistance in information technology to federal employees. For example, GSA and the Treasury cosponsor a workshop to explore alternatives to classroom education with a focus on network-based training. The impetus for this workshop came from efforts to create an interagency group at the assistant secretary level to sponsor and develop a broad program covering differing aspects of information technology training. In addition, OPM's *Guide to Senior Executive Service Qualifications* includes a competency requirement for information technology management.

Rethinking Program Design

NPR Recommendations

DES01	Activate Program Design as a Formal Discipline
DES02	Establish Pilot Program Design Capabilities in One or Two Agencies
DES03	Encourage the Strengthening of Program Design in the Legislative Branch
DES04	Commission Program Design Courses

Progress to Date

While these specific recommendations have not been implemented, the principles involved provided the framework for the implementation of the recent agency reviews that were undertaken by the Vice President at the President's direction.

Strengthening the Partnership in Intergovernmental Service Delivery

NPR Recommendations

FSL01	Improve the Delivery of Federal Domestic Grant Programs
FSL02	Reduce Red Tape Through Regulatory and Mandate Relief
FSL03	Simplify Reimbursement Procedures for Administrative Costs of Federal Grant Disbursement
FSL04	Eliminate Needless Paperwork by Simplifying the Compliance Certification Process
FSL05	Simplify Administration by Modifying the Common Grant Rules on Small Purchases
FSL06	Strengthen the Intergovernmental Partnership

Progress to Date

To improve dramatically the delivery of federal domestic grants, the Administration has encouraged agencies to use their existing waiver authority—and seek new waiver authority—to allow bottom-up innovation in the intergovernmental service delivery system. From January 1993 through June 1996, President Clinton approved more than 67 welfare demonstration projects in more than 40 states. He has also approved 13 comprehensive Medicaid reform demonstrations permitting states to increase greatly their use of managed care, to subsidize health insurance for employed but uninsured workers, and to expand Medicaid eligibility by increasing income limits. The President has also granted 19 states Medicaid waivers as part of larger welfare reform demonstrations.

Congress has granted agencies additional waiver authorities. The Secretary of Education was authorized to waive statutory requirements in the Goals 2000: Educate America Act (Public Law 103-227), the School to Work Opportunities Act (Public Law 103-239), and the Improving America's Schools Act (Public Law 103-382) to clear the way for better teaching and learning. He has approved more than 100 waivers under these authorities. The Department of Education also may devolve its waiver authority to 12 states under the Ed-Flex program which provides flexibility to state education agencies. In exchange for agreeing to greater accountability for results (e.g., academic performance of their students), Ed-Flex states are given the authority to waive federal statutes for themselves and their school districts, rather than submit waiver requests to the Secretary of Education. Eight Ed-Flex states have been designated so far. Similarly, the Secretary of Labor has new authority to waive certain regulations of the Job Training Partnership Act to help states and communities achieve workforce goals. And pending before Congress is a bill, the

Local Empowerment and Flexibility Act (S. 88, H.R. 2086), that would give broader waiver authority to most federal agency heads to provide flexibility to states and communities in achieving results.

To restrict unfunded mandates by federal agencies, President Clinton signed Executive Order 12875 in 1993. Congress later passed the Unfunded Mandate Reform Act of 1995 (Public Law 104-4) to limit its ability to impose new mandates on state and local governments without providing funds. It also requires greater intergovernmental consultations in the administrative rulemaking process, and allowance for the least costly and most effective means of complying with federal regulations.

In April 1995, OMB revised Circular A-87 to encourage federal agencies to test fee-for-service procedures for cost reimbursement to states and localities. A fee-for-service alternative would be simpler than the existing cost allocation rules and would encourage cost containment. In addition, OMB revised the common rules for small purchases by local governments by increasing the dollar threshold from $25,000 to $100,000.

The Administration has undertaken a series of initiatives to strengthen the intergovernmental partnership. First, it created the Community Empowerment Board, chaired by the Vice President, to oversee a process whereby member agencies may grant waivers. Eleven empowerment zones and 94 empowerment communities were designated in December 1994. Each of these entities is provided with additional flexibility, funding, and tax incentives to implement their community-developed, comprehensive, strategic plans.

Second, the Administration is reforming the federal grant process into a system of performance partnerships to be more responsive to locally perceived needs and bottom-up planning strategies. In his FYs 1996 and 1997 budgets, President Clinton proposed performance partnerships that would consolidate over 200 existing programs in the areas of public health, rural development, education and training, housing and urban development, transportation, and the environment. This initiative exemplifies the replacement of a program-oriented mentality with a comprehensive approach to problem solving; it signals a shift away from the present emphasis on how to manage federal grant programs toward an emphasis on getting results. To date, Congress has authorized two of these six partnerships.

The Federal Agricultural Improvement and Reform Act of 1996 (Public Law 104-127) creates three rural development performance partnerships in which a large number of rural utility, economic development, and housing programs will be administered together in a flexible manner and focused on results. The Environmental Protection Agency's (EPA's) performance partnerships legislation (Public Law 104-134) passed in early 1996; by May, Colorado and Utah had signed performance partnership grants with the agency. They can now decide how many of their environmental grants (air, water, hazardous waste, toxic substances, etc.) they want to combine into one "multimedia" (air, water, solid waste) partnership grant to achieve better environmental results.

Other federal agencies are forging ahead without waiting for the passage of legislation still pending before Congress. The Department of Health and Human Services, for example, convened meetings with over 1,000 stakeholders around the country to develop a list of desired results in each of the performance partnership grant areas (substance abuse, mental health, immunization, chronic diseases, etc.).

Separately, NPR has facilitated a series of administratively designated partnerships with states and localities. The Oregon Option—a 1994 partnership with the state of Oregon—focuses on bringing together community, local, state, and federal agencies to agree on desired results, how to accomplish them, how to measure them, and how to break down barriers to achieving them.

NPR also facilitates the Connecticut Neighborhood Revitalization Partnership, which is based on that state's innovative law requiring the state and its municipalities to break down barriers in response to neighborhoods' comprehensive plans and measurable goals to revitalize their economies and neighborhoods. In February 1996, Vice President Gore and other federal officials joined the governor and other state officials in signing an agreement to eliminate federal, state, and local barriers to develop and revitalize Connecticut's poorest communities.

Finally, four areas—metro Atlanta, metro Denver, the District of Columbia, and the state of Nebraska—have joined with the federal government to reduce crime and violence in a project called Pulling America's Communities Together (PACT). Through Project PACT, the federal government is vigorously fostering and supporting the development of broad-based, fully coordinated local and statewide initiatives that work strategically to secure community safety. Additionally, EPA, through its brownfields initiative, is providing new flexibility to states and communities to return contaminated urban lands to productive use.

Reinventing Environmental Management

NPR Recommendations

ENV01	Improve Federal Decisionmaking Through Environmental Cost Accounting
ENV02	Develop Cross-Agency Ecosystem Planning and Management
ENV03	Increase Energy and Water Efficiency
ENV04	Increase Environmentally and Economically Beneficial Landscaping

Progress to Date

President Clinton signed Executive Order 12873 in 1993 requiring agencies to purchase goods and services that are "environmentally preferable." The order also begins to reflect environmental concerns such as life cycle costs. In addition, EPA expanded from 5 to 24 the number of items containing recovered materials that agencies must purchase.

Cross-agency ecosystem management teams were formed to conduct management and budget reviews of federal programs affecting four ecosystems: South Florida, Anacostia River Watershed, Prince William Sound, and Pacific Northwest Forests. In addition, the President signed a directive requiring federal agencies to increase energy and water efficiency.

In July 1995, an interagency workgroup published guidance in the Federal Register to implement President Clinton's April 26, 1994, Executive Memorandum on Environmentally and Economically Beneficial Landscape Practices on Federal Landscaped Grounds. An interagency working group on environmental cost analysis has begun work and will report back to the Council on Environmental Quality in late 1996.

Improving Regulatory Systems

NPR Recommendations

REG01	Create an Interagency Regulatory Coordinating Group
REG02	Encourage More Innovative Approaches to Regulation
REG03	Encourage Consensus-Based Rulemaking
REG04	Enhance Public Awareness and Participation
REG05	Streamline Agency Rulemaking Procedures
REG06	Encourage Alternative Dispute Resolution When Enforcing Regulations
REG07	Rank Risks and Engage in "Anticipatory" Regulatory Planning
REG08	Improve Regulatory Science
REG09	Improve Agency and Congressional Relationships
REG10	Provide Better Training and Incentives for Regulators

Progress to Date

In September 1993, the President signed Executive Order 12866, Regulatory Planning and Review, which articulated the Administration's regulatory principles and created an interagency Regulatory Working Group. This group helped coordinate implementation of many of NPR's regulatory recommendations and meets frequently to serve as a forum to help agencies implement various provisions of the order, including those that encourage innovative approaches to regulation. The Regulatory Working Group also prepared guidelines on agency use of risk assessment and cost/benefit analysis. It has helped lead ongoing regulatory reinvention efforts—most recently, those involving the effort to eliminate 16,000 obsolete pages of the Code of Federal Regulations.

Over the past three years, many regulatory agencies have made significant progress in streamlining rulemaking. A May 1996 survey of 60 regulatory agencies showed more than half had streamlined their internal rulemaking processes and nearly half had gotten legislative changes to speed their rulemaking processes and make them more consensus-based. One-third of these agencies have created procedures for direct final rulemaking.

In addition, half of these agencies have expanded their use of electronic communication and information retrieval as part of their efforts to enhance public awareness and participation. For example, the Nuclear Regulatory Commission has conducted a pilot of the use of the Internet in rulemaking with its RuleNet project. The multi-agency online Business Advisor provides Internet access to the statutes and regulations of all federal agencies. Regulatory agencies are also actively pursuing the President's directives to use negotiated rulemaking (reg-neg) where feasible. President Clinton announced that limits on the creation of new advisory committees will not apply to reg-neg committees. Training materials have been disseminated, and—in response—new reg-negs have been undertaken.

Federal agency use of alternative dispute resolution (ADR) techniques is increasing dramatically. One-third of the regulatory agencies have active programs, and the Attorney General announced a new Department of Justice initiative to increase that department's reliance on and support of ADR. Pending legislation would expand ADR's use.

164

Major regulatory reform initiatives supported by this Administration have been enacted, including the Paperwork Reduction Act of 1995 (Public Law 104-13), the Small Business Regulatory Enforcement Fairness Act (Public Law 104-121), and the Unfunded Mandate Reform Act of 1995 (Public Law 104-4). The latter includes a small but important amendment to the Federal Advisory Committee Act that makes it easier for federal officials to meet with state, local, and tribal officials.

BLANK   PAGE

APPENDIX C:
SUMMARY OF SAVINGS TO DATE

Over the past three years, the National Performance Review (NPR) has made a series of recommendations that, when implemented, would save approximately $177.4 billion. To date, savings of about $97.4 billion have been ensured through legislative or administrative action. Another $5.2 billion in savings is contained in legislation pending before Congress.

- NPR's original September 7, 1993, report estimated that approximately $108 billion would be saved over the five-year period, fiscal years (FYs) 1995-1999, if its recommendations all were implemented. As of September 1, 1996, about $73.4 billion of these projected savings have been realized, either through administrative actions or enactments by Congress. An additional $1.3 billion in savings are currently pending before Congress, awaiting approval.

- NPR offered additional recommendations in September 1995 that, if implemented, would yield additional savings of $69.4 billion over the five-year period, FYs 1996-2000.[1] To date, $24.0 billion of these savings have been locked into place and an additional $3.9 billion are pending in Congress. The remainder are still in process.

Besides acting on recommendations made by NPR, agencies have achieved more than $21.5 billion in additional savings based on reinvention principles; these savings are beyond those proposed in NPR's reports.

Table C-1 compares NPR's September 1993 savings estimates to the savings that have accrued to date as a result of changes made and those that will occur in the future if these changes remain in place. It also identifies those savings that may occur in the near future as a result of legislative actions now well under way.

Table C-2 compares NPR's September 1995 savings estimates to the savings that have accrued to date as a result of changes made as well as those that may occur in the near future as a result of current legislative actions.

Following is a brief explanation of these savings estimates and how they were derived:

---

[1] Savings are calculated using the current services baseline approach. They include mandatory as well as discretionary savings and revenue increases.

167

NPR Phase I Savings

1. Streamlining the Bureaucracy Through Reengineering

The Administration is well ahead of schedule in reducing the size of the federal civilian workforce by 272,900 full-time equivalent (FTE) positions between the beginning of the Clinton Administration in January 1993 and the end of FY 1999. Specifically, the Federal Workforce Restructuring Act of 1994 (Public Law 103-226) mandated a civilian workforce reduction of 111,900 FTE positions by fiscal year 1995. The Administration, however, has reduced the civilian workforce by 185,000 FTE positions—73,100 positions more than required under the act. The Administration estimates that by FY 1997, nearly 90 percent of the workforce reduction goal will have been achieved.[2]

As a result of the fast pace in FTE cuts, total five-year savings are projected to be $46.4 billion at the end of FY 1999—an increase of $6 billion over NPR's 1993 estimate of $40.4 billion. Savings were derived by multiplying the total number of reductions by the average cost to the government for a federal employee for the year(s) following departure from federal service.[3] The Administration calculated the FY 1995 average cost to the government of each federal employee at $42,950.

2. Reinventing Federal Procurement

The Federal Acquisition Streamlining Act of 1994 (Public Law 103-355), signed into law in October 1994, incorporates many of NPR's recommendations. The Congressional Budget Office did not estimate savings from this legislation, but the Administration estimated a five-year savings of $12.3 billion. For example, the Defense Department identified savings of $4.7 billion in just three programs that it attributes to the passage of this law.[4] In early 1996, a second procurement bill, the Federal Acquisition Reform Act of 1996 (contained in Public Law 104–106), was signed into law. These additional reforms will help ensure that these savings will be met—if not exceeded.

---

[2]See Executive Office of the President, "Analytical Perspectives," *Budget of the United States, Fiscal Year 1997* (Washington, DC: U.S. Government Printing Office), p.180.

[3]This methodology does not account for severance pay, increases in annuity expenses, or the point in the year at which a person leaves federal service (obviously, savings are greater if a person leaves earlier rather than later in a year). This is why savings are not claimed until the following year. Note that the average employee cost may be lower than the actual salaries of the departing personnel, since many of the people leaving are older and more highly paid than the average employee. A report by the Congressional Budget Office (CBO) estimates higher savings—$61 billion—from personnel reductions between FYs 1994–1999. See CBO Memorandum, *Changes in Federal Civilian Employment*, July 1996, p.9

[4]Department of Defense, "Defense Acquisition Pilot Programs Forecast Cost/Schedule Savings of Up to 50 Percent From Acquisition Reform," News Release No. 138-96, March 14, 1996.

3.   Reengineering Through Information Technology

NPR's 1993 estimated savings included decreases in federal employment due to an increased use of information technology. Because these savings are not easily separable from total savings related to overall agency streamlining, they are reflected above in item 1, Streamlining the Bureaucracy Through Reengineering. Besides these FTE savings, the additional savings due to information technology include those from the implementation of electronic benefits transfer. The Federal Electronic Benefits Task Force estimated savings of about $200 million per year once the system was operational nationwide beginning in 1999. To date, 35 states have selected vendors, and the average bid prices were lower than expected, thus generating higher than estimated savings. If this trend continues, savings will likely be as much as $230 million per year. Other information technology-related savings include the closure of several large government data processing centers, beginning with $200 million in FY 1999.

4.   Reducing Intergovernmental Administrative Costs

NPR originally recommended modifying the Office of Management and Budget (OMB) Circular A-87, "Cost Principles for State, Local, and Indian Tribal Governments," to provide a fixed fee-for-service option in lieu of costly reimbursement procedures used to calculate the actual administrative costs of disbursing grants. It was originally estimated that half of the states and localities would adopt this approach, and that savings of up to $700 million a year could be realized. OMB revised Circular A-87 on April 19, 1995, to allow this approach. It is unclear, however, whether the projected cost savings will be realized. Estimates will be recalculated in the future based on actual experiences with this approach.

5.   Changes in Individual Agencies

During the past three years, President Clinton signed 54 laws containing NPR-related actions affecting individual agencies. About half of these included savings, such as the Department of Agriculture's reorganization bill, the Customs Modernization Act, and a wide range of appropriations bills (see Appendix E for details). In addition, agencies have realized billions of dollars in savings through administrative actions they have taken, such as recommended reengineering internal operations.

Additional savings related to reinvention are also being achieved by agencies beyond those savings claimed in NPR's original report. For example, the Federal Communications Commission began auctioning wireless licenses and has raised $20.3 billion since 1993, and the General Services Administration's time out and review of federal construction projects has resulted in savings of more than $1.2 billion. These savings, while included in the President's balanced budget proposal, are not included in the following tables, which only cover savings specifically recommended in NPR's 1993 and 1995 reports.

Table C-1. 1993 Estimates of Savings From NPR Recommendations Compared With Savings Estimates From Actions to Date

(in billions of dollars)

	FY95	FY96	FY97	FY98	FY99	Total
1. Streamlining the Bureaucracy Through Reengineering						
Savings estimated in September 1993 report	5.0	5.8	7.4	9.5	12.7	40.4
Savings based on actions to date	4.4*	8.2	9.8	11.5	12.5	46.4
2. Reinventing Federal Procurement						
Savings estimated in September 1993 report	0	5.6	5.6	5.6	5.7	22.5
Savings based on actions to date	0.7	2.8	2.8	2.9	3.1	12.3
3. Reengineering Through Information Technology						
Savings estimated in September 1993 report	0.1	0.5	1.2	1.6	2.0	5.4
Savings based on actions to date	0	0	0	0	0.4	0.4
4. Reducing Intergovernmental Administrative Costs						
Savings estimated in September 1993 report	0.5	0.7	0.7	0.7	0.7	3.3
Savings based on actions to date	0	CBE	CBE	CBE	CBE	CBE
5. Changes in Individual Agencies						
Savings estimated in September 1993 report	7.0*	6.2	7.0	7.3	8.9	36.4
Savings based on actions to date	4.3*	3.9	2.0	2.1	2.1	14.4
Savings pending in legislation	0	0	0.4	0.4	0.5	1.3
Total Savings for NPR Phase 1						
Savings estimated in September 1993 report	12.6*	18.8	21.9	24.7	30.0	108.0
Savings based on actions to date	9.4*	14.9	14.5	16.4	18.2	73.4
Savings pending in legislation	0	0	0.4	0.4	0.5	1.3

CBE=Cannot be estimated at this time; estimates will be developed later.
*Figures include some FY 1994 savings.
Note: Details may not equal totals due to rounding.

NPR Phase II Savings

In December 1994, President Clinton asked Vice President Gore to conduct a second review of federal agencies, focusing on whether existing functions could be terminated, privatized, or restructured. These recommendations resulted in cost savings totaling $69.4 billion over the five-year period, FYs 1996-2000. The following table summarizes savings for each major agency. A number of these savings were incorporated in the President's 1997 budget proposal.

Table C-2. Estimates of Five-Year Savings From New NPR Recommendations: FY 1996-2000

(budget authority, in millions of dollars)

	FY96	FY97	FY98	FY99	FY00	Total
Savings estimated in September 1995 report	4.9	12.4	16.5	15.9	19.8	69.4
Savings based on actions to date	3.0	4.0	4.8	5.7	6.5	24.0
Savings pending in legislation	0.0	0.3	0.7	1.4	1.6	3.9

Note: Savings are calculated from the current services baseline approach. They include mandatory as well as discretionary savings and revenue increases. Details may not equal totals due to rounding.

BLANK   PAGE

APPENDIX D:
STATUS OF REGULATORY REFORM INITIATIVES

Agency Efforts

The Clinton Administration has made reinventing the federal government's regulatory system a top priority. Consistent with this commitment, the President and the Vice President charged agencies and departments with making the regulatory process open and results-oriented. Specifically, in early 1995, the President directed agencies to:

1. Conduct a page-by-page review of all their regulations in the Code of Federal Regulations (CFR), eliminating or revising those that are outdated or otherwise in need of reinvention.

2. Reward results, not red tape, by changing performance measurement systems to focus on ultimate goals (e.g., cleaner air and safer workplaces) rather than on the number of citations written and fines assessed.

3. "Get out of Washington" and create grassroots partnerships between the frontline regulators and the people affected by their regulations.

4. Negotiate, rather than dictate, by expanding opportunities for consensual rulemaking wherever possible.

5. Waive fines or allow them to be used to fix the problem when a small business is a first-time violator and has been acting in good faith.

6. Double the amount of time that passes before a report is required to be filed (e.g., a semiannual report should now be required annually) and accept reports filed electronically whenever possible.

In response, agencies have taken a number of concrete steps to change the way the federal government regulates and interacts with the public. Here are some of their achievements.

Cutting Obsolete Regulations

After the President asked agencies to eliminate obsolete rules and simplify those that remained, agencies did a page-by-page review of their contribution to the CFR. On June 11, 1995, President Clinton announced that agencies had identified 16,000 pages of the CFR that had outlived their usefulness and another 31,000 pages that needed reinventing. Eliminating rules—just like making them—requires sufficient time for public input. But agencies are well on their way toward reform. As of June 30, 1996, 70 percent of the rules to be eliminated were gone, and almost half of the rules to be reinvented had been fixed. The rest of the work to be done is well under way.

Part of the fix for those regulations being rewritten is adopting a "plain English" approach. One of the most important ways the government interacts with the general public is through the written word. Regulations should be written so that they make sense to the reader and address the reader's concerns. This plain-English approach has to start with those who write the regulations in the first place. The National Performance Review (NPR) and the Office of Information and Regulatory Affairs (OIRA) are working with agency representatives and the Office of the Federal Register (which publishes rulemaking documents) to develop plain English guidance for regulations writers. Workshops and an Internet reference site are part of the plan to produce federal regulations that are more easily understood by the American public. The Plain English Team is building on the success of the Department of the Interior and the Small Business Administration. These agencies have replaced entire sections of their previous regulations with one or two simple sentences that anyone can understand.

Rewarding Results, Not Red Tape

Equally as important as the content of the rules that regulatory agencies enforce is the way in which they enforce them—that is, the way in which federal government inspectors and employees do their business. President Clinton, on March 4, 1995, directed federal regulatory agencies to change the way they measure the performance of their frontline regulators by shifting their focus from punishment to results. Almost half of the regulatory agencies report that they have completed this shift. The other half are continuing to make progress. While maintaining its commitment to safety, the federal government is developing new ways to meet goals that result in less red tape and more flexibility for the private sector. These changes are occurring on a number of fronts, as the following examples demonstrate.

Compliance Achievement Reporting System (CARS). Food and Drug Administration (FDA) field investigators and inspectors traditionally have been rewarded for detecting violations. Their goal was to collect evidence that resulted in enforcement. In fiscal year 1995, FDA's Office of Regulatory Affairs changed investigator/inspector performance plans to emphasize safety over disciplinary action. In addition, FDA's reporting system was modified and renamed (as CARS) to encourage actions resulting in immediate compliance. This reorientation enhances, supports, and encourages more open communication between FDA and industry. For example, FDA recently inspected a low-acid canned food canning operation and identified a malfunction in the sealing equipment. The canned food was not receiving a proper seal, a serious problem that could have led to a botulism outbreak. Rather than taking disciplinary action that would have required seizing the goods and initiating litigation, the FDA inspector recommended that the canning operation destroy all cans in the lot and repair the sealing equipment. The problem was resolved immediately; the FDA inspector achieved on-the-spot compliance for which he would get credit. This type of teamwork saved the agency and industry thousands of dollars and immediately protected consumers from dangerous products.

Strong, Targeted Enforcement Program (STEP-UP). In mid-1994, the Environmental Protection Agency (EPA) Region I, New England, undertook a comprehensive assessment of the resources it historically devoted to enforcement. The analysis indicated that these resources addressed so many different program priorities, no overall direction for enforcement was apparent. Therefore, Region I decided to target enforcement resources to situations where human health and the environment face the highest risk. The region is now devoting 80 percent of its inspection resources to these targeted areas to ensure that the resulting enforcement is comprehensive in sector coverage, thorough in case preparation, and aggressive in results. Enforcement

174

success will not be measured just by numbers of inspections or cases initiated, but by the total reduction in pollutants or environmental threats faced by the public.

Joint Training on Hazard Analysis Critical Control Points (HACCP) Based Systems. Recognizing that safe food is more important to consumers than bureaucratic checkpoints, FDA is teaming up with restaurant operators to improve restaurant food safety. FDA and the National Restaurant Association have joined forces to design and deliver workshops to regulators and industry operatives. These workshops aim to bring FDA inspectors, state and local health officials, and restaurant personnel together to discuss ways all can use the cutting-edge scientific principles embodied in HACCP systems to improve food safety. As a result of this new training partnership, regulators and industry participants have begun to realize that both have expertise to share with each other that will help make foods safer. Communication, understanding, and cooperation are enhanced as government and industry work together toward a common goal.

Creating Grassroots Partnerships

Partnerships with the private sector that have produced good results are outlined in "Secret Three: Government Is in Partnership With Business." But many other opportunities for partnership exist as well. Those that have the most immediate interest in local decisions are the people that are affected by them. Consequently, states, tribes, and communities are anxious for greater autonomy and responsibility for results. Agencies, in response, are moving regulatory decision-making and accountability to the level closest to the problem. A major part of achieving a shift in authority is building the capacity at the state and local levels to solve local problems.

The stories highlighted below demonstrate the importance of federal-state-local partnerships. To solve problems effectively, different levels of government must understand and integrate the needs of culturally, geographically, and economically diverse communities into the decision making process.

North Boulder Project. When EPA became involved at a potential Superfund cleanup site in North Boulder, Colorado, several parties were entrenched in litigation over groundwater contamination. EPA informed the parties of the potential risks involved in taking a status quo approach to the groundwater problem and provided an opportunity for the community to develop a solution before the agency took any steps toward creating a Superfund listing. EPA then invited all parties—including citizens—to accept some responsibility for resolving the situation. It assumed the role of facilitator in hearing the various disputes that had arisen among the parties. Six months later, a technically sound solution to the groundwater problem in North Boulder was developed and paid for by residents; industry; and state, city, and county governments. This approach saved millions of private and federal dollars—and saved the community from being immersed in the Superfund program for the next decade.

Interstate Technology Regulatory Cooperation (ITRC) Workgroup. The Department of Energy (DOE), the Department of Defense, and EPA, along with 22 state environmental agencies, have pioneered a successful partnering effort to improve the cleanup process for contaminated toxic sites. Together, these groups break down the barriers to using innovative environmental technologies for remediation and treatment of hazardous and radioactive wastes. "The success of these partnerships proves that the President's reinventing government initiatives reduce costs and expedite cleanup at DOE sites. Progress made by the ITRC will allow DOE to move forward toward becoming a performance organization," says Alvin Alm, Assistant Secretary for Environmental Management. Partnering has streamlined the regulatory process for environmental technologies and moved states and federal agencies toward results-oriented cleanup.

Resource Advisory Councils. In 1995, the Bureau of Land Management created 27 resource advisory councils in the Western states to advise the Bureau on issues concerning management of public rangelands. These councils are made up of 12-to-15 members appointed by the Secretary of the Interior from among individuals nominated by the public and state governors. Three groups are represented on these councils: commodity interest, such as ranchers, oil and gas developers, and miners; groups interested in natural and cultural preservation; and local citizens, including representatives of local government and Indian tribes in the area covered by the councils.

The councils have been very successful at bringing diverse—and often competing—interests to the table to deal with each other on issues of mutual concern. The approach shows great promise in successfully solving long-standing problems of public land management. Many individuals who were initially skeptical of the councils are now quite supportive of their work and are optimistic that they will be a strong force in resolving disputes about the uses of public land in the West.

Negotiating, Rather Than Dictating

Partnerships can lead to a lot more than just improved relationships. Including partners in the development of rules can educate federal agencies about specific concerns and needs and, ultimately, can lead to a better, more flexible, regulatory framework. The President is encouraging consensual rulemaking, both through partnerships and the formal process of negotiated rulemaking. In addition, federal agencies are encouraging communication in a wide range of areas. Some highlights of these negotiation and communication efforts follow.

Federal Railroad Administration (FRA). Rail workers performing routine maintenance on railroad tracks were sometimes hit and killed by trains running on adjacent tracks. There was no federal safety rule to address this issue. FRA's initial inclination was to rely on the traditional rulemaking process—the agency would write a rule, affected parties would comment, FRA would revise the proposed rule, and the cycle would continue until the final rule was issued. This is a time-consuming process that minimizes real and meaningful communication. So this time, FRA decided to do it differently: It brought interested parties into roundtable discussions from day one. Out of those conversations grew a powerful negotiated rulemaking process—and a proposed rule that is satisfactory to all. The final rule should be issued in early fall of 1996, well ahead of the traditional rulemaking timeframe.

The Access Board. The Americans With Disabilities Act (ADA) was passed to give all Americans greater access to facilities and opportunities. The U.S. Architectural and Transportation Barriers Compliance Board, commonly known as the Access Board, wrote guidelines for accessibility required in the construction or alteration of any building covered by ADA. When the guidelines were issued, they often were met with confusion, anger, and uncertainty. Those who had to comply with the guidelines found them to be unclear and, in some cases, in conflict with existing building codes. Disability advocates grew concerned that if people were confused by Access Board guidelines, they might refuse to comply with ADA.

To address these concerns, the Access Board set up an advisory group that included representatives from all sides of the issue and committed itself to working through the problems the guidelines had created. As a result, groups that always seemed to meet on the battleground to resolve issues are now working together to find common ground. The rules are being rewritten, and ADA will now be implemented in a more inclusive and effective way.

The Orange County Central and Coastal Natural Communities Conservation Plan (NCCP). In Orange County, California, biologists cited 42 species they believe are in danger of extinction, six of which are already on the endangered species list. At the same time, the area is grappling with suburban development and land values as high as $1 million per acre. To preserve the quality of life in Orange County and allow developers to build free of red tape, local citizens, businesses, and state and local governments developed a landmark conservation plan that will protect the wildlife-rich coastal sagebrush landscape in the area while permitting development. By shifting its emphasis from species protection to a multi-species habitat conservation approach, the Department of the Interior is able to offer participating landowners long-range certainty about the future development of their land.

NCCP is a first of its kind partnership among federal, state, and county governments; municipalities; land developers; and other property owners sharing a common interest in protecting open space. The plan will serve as a model for the nation, pointing the way to protect wildlife and conserve open space in areas of increasing urban pressure. It creates a win-win situation for both economic security and species conservation.

Putting Fines to Good Use

Even companies that are trying to comply with laws and regulations can make mistakes. Many of these mistakes can be prevented with a little education—another reason that partnering is so important. President Clinton asked agencies to give companies a break when they have a first-time offender who has been acting in good faith. As a result, over 50 percent of regulatory agencies have taken steps to introduce waivers into their enforcement strategy. By being flexible where appropriate, agencies are finding that industry becomes better educated and better able to comply. For example:

- The National Oceanic and Atmospheric Administration has developed a new regulatory enforcement regime, called the "fix-it" ticket, in which first-time good-faith offenders receive a warning instead of a fine.
- The Research and Special Projects Administration is implementing a program to waive penalties for violations that are corrected within a stated timeframe.
- The Nuclear Regulatory Commission currently waives civil penalties for first-time offenders who take prompt and comprehensive corrective action.

Making Reporting Easier

While the federal government needs certain information to compile national statistics, allocate resources, etc., the need to reduce reporting burdens is just as important. Much of the information currently gathered by the federal government is required by statute. Agencies do, however, have some discretion in their collection efforts. Notably, they can collect data less frequently, thereby imposing less burden on reporting entities. As a result of the President's April 24, 1995, memorandum permitting agencies to double reporting periods, over eight million work hours will be eliminated by having agencies extend the time that passes between report filings. The Paperwork Reduction Act (Public Law 104-13), which the President signed in May 1995, will also lead agencies to reduce the amount of required reporting.

Regulatory Sector Report Updates

In addition to their work in the areas highlighted above, selected federal regulatory agencies have also prepared 10 reports that contain recommendations for reinventing entire regulatory systems. Following are brief descriptions of these reports and agency progress in meeting report recommendations organized chronologically by publication date. Also included are agency contact points for obtaining additional information about sector-specific regulatory reform.

Reinventing Environmental Regulations

Released March 17, 1995. For plan copies or additional information, contact Jay Benforado at (202) 260-4255.

Principles for Regulatory Reform. EPA protects the public health and safeguards and improves the natural environment. It is focusing its regulatory review around preventing pollution rather than simply controlling pollutants and cleaning them up. Further, the agency is designing regulations to achieve environmental goals that minimize costs to individuals, businesses, and other levels of government; to use market incentives to achieve environmental goals whenever appropriate; and to revise government regulations so they can be understood by those affected by them. EPA is basing environmental regulations on the best scientific and economic analysis and fostering collaborative—not adversarial—decisionmaking in devising environmental standards. Additionally, EPA is committed to protecting minority and low-income populations from disproportionately high and adverse health or environmental impacts. The agency is determined to protect national goals for public health and the environment as it compels individuals, businesses, and government to take responsibility for the impacts of their actions.

Agency Progress. Of the 39 recommendations laid out in EPA's initial report, the agency has completed 11 and is making significant progress on 16 others. Here are some highlights:

- To help businesses comply with environmental laws faster and more efficiently, EPA is making changes to more than 70 percent of its regulations and eliminating 1,400 pages of obsolete rules.
- To achieve environmental policy goals, EPA is piloting innovative approaches to focus on problems that pose the highest risks to public health.
- To increase community participation and intergovernmental partnerships, EPA expanded public access to agency information through the Internet, strengthened community right-to-know projects, and established performance partnerships that give states and tribes funding flexibility to meet their environmental needs.
- To make it easier for businesses to comply with environmental laws, EPA waives or reduces penalties for first-time violators if the business corrects the problem or comes into compliance with the law.
- Through Project XL, EPA challenges industry to exceed environmental performance standards. If a business can meet standards higher than those set by the agency, EPA will cut red tape and be flexible to help find the cheapest, most efficient way to do so. EPA is applying the XL concept to communities, federal facilities (such as army bases) and other regulated parties to encourage these groups to work together to identify environmental problems and

develop innovative solutions. Today, there are 14 government and industrial facilities working with EPA to formulate XL performance agreements.

Reinventing Drug and Medical Device Regulations

Released April 5, 1995. For plan copies or additional information, contact Brad Stone at (301) 443-3285.

Principles for Regulatory Reform. FDA is the agency within the Department of Health and Human Services charged with ensuring that drugs, vaccines, and medical devices are safe and effective, and that foods meet basic safety standards. In carrying out its regulatory review, FDA carefully considered the financial burdens that its requirements impose on industry and consumers. It looked for ways to lessen these burdens so that its regulatory systems would not stand in the way of bringing beneficial new products to market. As a result, FDA is now implementing performance standards, rather than command-and-control regulations, whenever possible. FDA expedites product review without sacrificing the public health and safety. The agency also is eliminating unnecessary requirements that may once have been appropriate but that are now no longer necessary for public health.

Agency Progress. Of the 14 recommendations laid out in FDA's initial report, the agency has completed 10; it is making significant progress on the remaining four. Here are some highlights:

- To help businesses comply with drug and medical device regulations quicker and more efficiently, FDA clarified how it determines the effectiveness of new drugs and devices. Also, FDA ensures that market clearances of devices will not be withheld unless it finds a reasonable relationship between current violations and applications under review.
- To expedite product review, FDA now permits greater flexibility in the appearance of distributors' names in labeling, exempts categories of low-risk medical devices from premarket review, and speeds marketing of medical devices.
- By working in partnership with the medical device community, FDA has developed a pilot program for preannounced inspections for "good players."

Reinventing Worker Safety and Health Regulations: The New OSHA

Released May 16, 1995. For plan copies or additional information, contact Frank Frodyma at (202) 219-8021.

Principles for Regulatory Reform. The Occupational Safety and Health Administration (OSHA) within the Department of Labor ensures safe and healthy working conditions for America's workers. OSHA's approach to regulatory reform dramatically increases safety and eases the adversarial relationship between regulators and industry by placing primary responsibility for ensuring safety in the hands of managers and workers at worksites across the country. In its report, OSHA changed its approach to regulation by focusing on key building block rules such as training programs, maintenance of records, monitoring of risk exposure, and medical surveillance. In addition, OSHA is identifying clear and sensible priorities, eliminating or fixing out-of-date or confusing standards, and emphasizing interaction with business and labor in rule development. Also, to save lives and protect against workplace injuries and illnesses, OSHA is developing performance measures so that programs will be evaluated based on results achieved rather than procedural checkpoints.

Agency Progress. Of the 15 recommendations laid out in OSHA's initial report, the agency has completed five and is making significant progress on the remaining 10.

- To help businesses comply with worker safety and health regulations quicker and more efficiently, OSHA eliminated 920 pages of outdated or confusing regulations.

- OSHA is working with stakeholders to identify the 20 leading causes of workplace injury, illness, and death and is developing a national campaign to reduce exposure to these hazards. The agency announced an initial set of 18 priority workplace safety and health issues in December 1995.

- To encourage worksite partnerships, OSHA is providing incentives to employers to work with their employees to develop worksite-specific safety and health programs that can reduce job-related injury, illness, and death. OSHA is working with states to implement cooperative compliance programs (like Maine 200) across the country. To date, 21 states are participating in such programs, and 11 states are slated to sign performance agreements soon.

- To make it easier for businesses to comply with worker safety and health regulations, OSHA's Quick Fix initiative provides a 15–percent penalty reduction for violations that an employer corrects on the spot.

Reinventing Pension Regulations

Released June 11, 1995. For copies of the report or additional information, contact Vicki Judson at (202) 622-1357.

Principles for Regulatory Reform. Among their many tasks, the U.S. Departments of the Treasury and Labor, including the Pension Benefit Guaranty Corporation, regulate pensions to ensure that pension tax benefits are used to increase retirement savings for a broad cross-section of workers and that all participants in pension plans get the benefits they have earned. The two departments, working in coordination with the National Economic Council, have developed recommendations that would eliminate complex pension rules that were outmoded, redundant, or no longer necessary to achieve policy goals. The basic aim here is to reduce the administrative and paperwork burden on employers.

Agency Progress. Of the 32 recommendations laid out in the initial report, 21 have been implemented, although some have been modified in the legislative process. Many of these were included in the recently enacted Small Business Job Protection Act of 1996 (Public Law 104-188), which, among other things:

- creates a new 401(k)-type plan for small businesses with no red tape and no complicated forms or calculations,

- repeals the family aggregation rule which prevented family-owned businesses from providing meaningful benefits to all family members,
- encourages expansion of 401(k) plans by simplifying rules and eliminating the need for complicated and expensive testing,
- reduces the vesting period from 10 to five years for multi-employer plans,
- repeals the complex combined limit on benefits and contributions for employees covered by both defined benefit and defined contribution plans of the same employer, and
- permits tax-exempt organizations to maintain 401(k) plans.

The Administration will continue to pursue implementation of the remaining recommendations both legislatively and administratively. For example, steps will be taken in further simplifying the rules applicable to multi-employer plans, further promoting portability, and better ensuring that moderate and lower wage workers receive a fair share of the benefits.

Reinventing Service Regulations to Small Business: The New Small Business Administration

Released June 11, 1995. For plan copies or additional information, contact Ronald Matzner at (202) 205-6882.

Principles for Regulatory Reform. SBA champions the entrepreneurial spirit of America's small business community to create the jobs and opportunities necessary for this country to remain competitive in the global marketplace. SBA works with the private sector to expand access to credit and capital, provide needed training and assistance, and serve as an advocate and watchdog for small business owners. In line with this reinvention enterprise, SBA is reducing paperwork burdens on small business and streamlining regulations as much as possible. Most significantly, SBA ensures that affected small businesses are included at every important step in the regulatory development process.

Agency Progress. Of the 18 recommendations laid out in SBA's initial report, the agency has implemented 10; it is making significant progress on six others.

- To help businesses comply with regulations quicker and more efficiently, SBA eliminated all of its duplicate, outdated, inconsistent, and confusing regulatory provisions. SBA thus eliminated 54 percent of the pages in its section of the CFR. In addition, SBA streamlined its cosponsorship training program to reduce the private sector paperwork burden for SBA's partners from 76 to 26 pages.
- To promote better access to capital, SBA revised small business investment company regulations; strengthened oversight, screening, and credit review; and created a class of larger, better-capitalized small business investment companies. Consequently, more new private venture capital has been injected into small business investment company programs since January 1995 than in the previous 10 years combined.
- To foster public-private partnerships, SBA is expanding business information centers to provide better access for small businesses to state-of-the-art technologies and information sources. SBA, in cooperation with other agencies, also developed the U.S. Business Advisor, a one-stop electronic center for small businesses to access business, economic, and regulatory information.

- To create jobs and opportunities, SBA implemented a pilot program to increase the number of loans made to women business owners. To date, SBA has piloted the program at 16 offices nationwide. Through the program's prequalification process, over 500 women have been able to obtain funding. SBA also simplified the disaster loan assistance program by reducing filing requirements.

Reinventing Health Care Regulations

Released July 11, 1995. For plan copies or additional information, contact Mary Ann Troanovitch at (202) 690-7890.

Principles for Regulatory Reform. The primary mission of the Health Care Financing Administration (HCFA) is to ensure health care security for nearly 37 million Medicare beneficiaries and—in partnership with state governments—for another 36 million Medicaid beneficiaries. HCFA's approach to regulatory reform is defined by three principles underlying the agency's new, improved approach to customer service:

- HCFA communicates through listening and consulting to ascertain how best to serve its customers.
- HCFA educates customers about agency programs and policies instead of inundating them with information that does not speak to their needs.
- HCFA is relying more on innovation in program operations and administration than on regulation.

At HCFA, communication, cooperation, and partnership are the guiding principles for the regulatory process, replacing the adversarial environment that often existed in the past.

Agency Progress. Of the 13 regulatory reform initiatives in HCFA's initial report, the agency has completed five and is making significant progress on the remaining eight. Here are some highlights:

- To help reduce the paperwork burden and decrease administrative costs for hospitals, HCFA eliminated the physician attestation form. Additionally, HCFA clarified and expanded clinical laboratory improvement waiver criteria and streamlined the waiver process to give more flexibility to laboratories and create incentives for manufacturers.
- To foster public-private partnerships, HCFA is conducting a pilot project to identify, recognize, and reward End Stage Renal Disease (ESRD) facilities that have successfully demonstrated their commitment to ongoing patient care. HCFA also is involving patients and health care providers in revising home health agency conditions of participation, hospital conditions of participation, and ESRD conditions of coverage.
- To make it easier for businesses to comply with health care regulations, HCFA has reduced oversight of excellent performers, allows third-party accreditation where appropriate, rewards good performance with fewer inspections, and exempts labs whose state requirements meet or exceed clinical laboratory improvement amendments requirements.
- HCFA is actively pursuing legislative opportunities to reduce the burden on long-term care facilities to eliminate duplicate annual assessments of the mentally ill and mentally retarded

and to make it easier for nurse aides to obtain the training they need to provide quality services to nursing home patients.

Reinventing the Regulation of Drugs Made From Biotechnology

Released November 9, 1995. For plan copies or additional information, contact Lisa Helmanis at (301) 443-3480.

Principles for Regulatory Reform. FDA houses two product centers responsible for helping to regulate biotech drugs: the Center for Biologics Evaluation and Research and the Center for Drug Evaluation and Research. In accordance with FDA's efforts to reform the regulation of biotech drugs used for therapy, these centers are undertaking initiatives that will greatly streamline the regulation of biotech drugs, harmonize manufacturing requirements, and facilitate the development and marketing of biotech drugs while not diminishing the safety and effectiveness of these drugs. According to the biotechnology industry, these changes will save companies millions of dollars, reduce required paperwork by thousands of pages, and cut months off drug development time.

Agency Progress. FDA committed to six specific reforms in the regulation of biotech products. To date, the agency has completed three of these commitments.

- FDA has eliminated lot-by-lot evaluations on biotechnology for which the marketing and manufacturing process has been validated. This is resulting in significant savings in time and resources for both the agency and industry.
- FDA will use a single form to replace 21 different approval application forms for biotech drugs, blood, vaccines, and other drugs. This will prevent companies from having to file multiple applications with FDA for product approvals.
- To streamline regulation of biotech drugs, FDA eliminated the current requirement that promotional labeling be approved prior to the launch of a biotech drug and for 120 days following its approval.

Reinventing Food Safety Regulations

Released January 1996. For plan copies or additional information, contact Judith Riggins at (202) 720-7025.

Principles for Regulatory Reform. FDA is charged with ensuring that foods are safe, wholesome, and properly labeled. The agency also protects consumers from economic fraud and promotes sound nutrition. The Food Safety and Inspection Service (FSIS) is a consumer protection safety agency of the U.S. Department of Agriculture that regulates meat and poultry products. FDA and FSIS are working together to adopt a common approach to food safety. The agencies agree that the regulatory efforts that successfully protected the public over the past century must be reassessed as new food safety inspection techniques are developed. As they design new food safety regulations, both agencies are shifting away from command-and-control requirements to performance standards. They are eliminating unnecessary requirements in regulation and incorporating science-based systems of preventive controls for food safety. FDA and FSIS are reinventing food safety regulations to provide consumers with safe foods and the knowledge to make informed choices in the marketplace.

Agency Progress. These initiatives require that FDA and FSIS work both independently with their respective constituencies and closely with each other. As a result of that work, the Administration recently announced a new regulatory framework to ensure safe food for Americans which uses modern science and performance standards. Here are some highlights:

- To help businesses comply with food safety regulations quicker and more efficiently, FDA and FSIS proposed regulations to eliminate duplicate premarket approval of substances used in preparation of meat and poultry products.
- To make FDA and FSIS meat and poultry inspection systems consistent with cutting- edge scientific techniques, the agencies are implementing systems based on Hazard Analysis and Critical Control Points.
- FDA and FSIS are harmonizing international standards related to food safety and expanding the use of the private sector in monitoring imported foods.
- FDA and FSIS are working toward reforming the Food-Additive and Petition Review process.
- To make it easier for businesses to comply with food safety regulations, FDA and FSIS have proposed alternatives to the present food "standards of identity." These standards define a food's composition and prescribe minimum levels of valuable ingredients, such as milkfat in dairy products and meat in meat food products, or maximum levels for cheaper ingredients, such as fillers or water. The agencies also increased the number of categorical exclusions from the Environmental Assessment and Environmental Impact Statements for animal drugs, animal feed additives, food additives, and color additives.

Reinventing the Regulations of Cancer Drugs

Released March 29, 1996. For plan copies or additional information, contact Randy Wykoff at (301) 827-3320.

Principles for Regulatory Reform. As the agency charged with ensuring that drugs and vaccines are safe and effective, FDA has demonstrated a long-standing commitment to the prompt consideration and—when appropriate—early approval of new therapies for cancer patients. FDA is providing greater patient access to potentially effective cancer treatments and accelerating the entire cancer drug approval process for drugs that show evidence of tumor shrinkage. In addition, FDA now provides patient representation on its cancer-related advisory committees. The agency is undertaking these initiatives after careful consideration of suggestions and advice offered by patients and their advocates, pharmaceutical industry representatives, and physicians and researchers.

Agency Progress. As this report is quite recent, no formal assessment of progress has been undertaken. FDA is moving forward to implement all initiatives. For example:

- FDA will expand access to investigational cancer therapies that have been approved in other countries.

- To foster clinical research and reduce paperwork burdens, FDA will clarify its requirements for filing Investigational New Drug Applications so that physicians and manufacturers will submit them only when necessary.

Reinventing the Regulation of Animal Drugs

Released May 10, 1996. For plan copies or additional information, contact Lisa Helmanis at (301) 443-3480.

Principles for Regulatory Reform. FDA is charged with ensuring that drugs used to treat animals are safe and effective. In reinventing its regulation of animal drugs, the agency is working on a series of regulatory and procedural initiatives designed to speed the development and review of new therapies to treat animals. The central concept behind these reforms is to encourage greater direct interaction between animal drug sponsors and FDA at every stage of the drug development process. This close interaction provides manufacturers with greater guidance in study design and data submission, and grants FDA reviewers quicker access to the pivotal data on which drug approval decisions can be based. These reforms promise to cut FDA's review time significantly for a new animal drug application—and thereby shorten products' overall development time.

Agency Progress. As this report is quite recent, no formal assessment of progress has been undertaken. FDA is moving forward to implement all initiatives. For example:

- FDA continues to make progress toward full implementation of a streamlined procedure for the approval of animal drugs. Several recent New Animal Drug Applications (NADA) have required fewer than 45 days for approval.
- The agency is also working on updating guidance and regulations. FDA has completed a Clinical Investigator Guideline that describes the agency's best thinking on how clinical trials for new animal drugs should be conducted. This guideline is in final clearance within the agency.
- FDA has also produced two concept papers, one for the NADA regulations and one for the Investigational New Animal Drug (INAD) exemption. These concept papers discuss the changes made to the animal drug process and recommend changes to the NADA and INAD regulations.

185

BLANK   PAGE

APPENDIX E:
PRESIDENTIAL AND CONGRESSIONAL
ACTIONS TAKEN TO DATE

Between September 1993 and August 1996, President Clinton signed 40 presidential directives to implement National Performance Review (NPR) recommendations. He also signed 54 laws implementing NPR-related recommended actions in whole or in part—one-third of all NPR actions requiring legislative action. In addition, there are at least 94 bills with NPR-related provisions that have been introduced in the 104th Congress.

Following are lists of these NPR-related presidential directives, signed legislation, and pending bills in Congress. The NPR recommendations related to these actions, along with the specific identifier codes listed in previous NPR reports, are also provided.

Presidential Directives

The President's Community Enterprise Board, Presidential Memorandum, September 9, 1993
FSL01   Improve the Delivery of Federal Domestic Grant Programs

Streamlining the Bureaucracy, Presidential Memorandum, September 11, 1993
ORG01   Reduce the Costs and Numbers of Positions Associated With Management
              Control Structures by Half

Setting Customer Service Standards, Executive Order 12862, September 11, 1993
ICS01   Create Customer-Driven Programs in All Departments and Agencies
              That Provide Services Directly to the Public

Elimination of One-Half of Executive Branch Internal Regulations,
Executive Order 12861, September 11, 1993
SMC07   Reduce Internal Regulations by More Than 50 Percent

President's Foreign Intelligence Advisory Board, Executive Order 12863, September 13, 1993
INTEL06   Merge the President's Intelligence Oversight Board With the President's
              Foreign Intelligence Advisory Board

Regulatory Planning Review, Executive Order 12866, September 30, 1993
FSL02   Reduce Red Tape Through Regulatory and Mandate Relief
REG01   Create an Interagency Regulatory Coordinating Group

Agency Rulemaking Procedures, Presidential Memorandum, September 30, 1993
REG05   Streamline Agency Rulemaking Procedures

Negotiated Rulemaking, Presidential Memorandum, September 30, 1993
REG03   Encourage Consensus-Based Rulemaking

Report of Regulations Reviewed, Presidential Memorandum, September 30, 1993
FSL02   Reduce Red Tape Through Regulatory and Mandate Relief
REG01   Create an Interagency Regulatory Coordinating Group

Trade Promotion Coordinating Committee, Executive Order 12870, September 30, 1993
DOC02   Provide Better Coordination to Refocus and Leverage Federal Export Promotion

Implementing Management Reform in the Executive Branch, Presidential Memorandum, October 1, 1993
QUAL01   Provide Improved Leadership and Management of the Executive Branch

Labor-Management Partnerships, Executive Order 12871, October 1, 1993
HRM13   Form Labor-Management Partnerships for Success

Enhancing the Intergovernmental Partnership, Executive Order 12875, October 26, 1993
FSL02   Reduce Red Tape Through Regulatory and Mandate Relief

Streamlining Procurement Through Electronic Commerce, Presidential Memorandum, October 26, 1993
PROC14   Expand Electronic Commerce for Federal Acquisition

U.S. Policy on International Counter-Narcotics in the Western Hemisphere, Presidential Decision Directive No. 14, November 2, 1993
DOJ03/   Redirect and Better Coordinate Resources Dedicated to the Interdiction
TRE03   of Drugs
           • Make the Director of Law Enforcement Responsible for Drug Interdiction
             Operations Appropriations (partial)

Establishment of the National Science and Technology Council, Executive Order 12881, November 23, 1993
NSF01   Strengthen Coordination of Science Policy

President's Committee of Advisors on Science and Technology, Executive Order 12882, November 23, 1993
NSF01   Strengthen Coordination of Science Policy

Federal Actions to Address Environmental Justice in Minority Populations and Low-Income Populations, Executive Order 12898, February 11, 1994
EPA09   Establish a Blueprint for Environmental Justice Throughout EPA's Operations

Environmental Justice, Presidential Memorandum, February 11, 1994
EPA09   Establish a Blueprint for Environmental Justice Throughout EPA's Operations

Energy Efficiency and Water Conservation at Federal Facilities, Executive Order 12902, March 8, 1994
ENV03   Increase Energy and Water Efficiency

Coordinating Geographic Data Acquisition and Access: The National Spatial Data Infrastructure, Executive Order 12906, April 11, 1994
DOI03   Establish a National Spatial Data Infrastructure

Environmentally and Economically Beneficial Practices on Federal Landscaped Grounds, Presidential Memorandum, April 26, 1994
ENV04   Increase Environmentally and Economically Beneficial Landscaping

Environmental Polar Satellite Program, Presidential Decision Directive NSTC-2, May 5, 1994
DOC12   Establish a Single Civilian Operational Environmental Polar Satellite Program
          • Establish a Single Environmental Polar Satellite Program Under
            the Direction of NOAA

Expanding Family-Friendly Work Arrangements in the Executive Branch, Presidential Memorandum, July 11, 1994
HRM07   Enhance Programs to Provide Family-Friendly Workplaces

Promoting Procurement With Small Businesses Owned and Controlled by Socially and Economically Disadvantaged Individuals, Historically Black Colleges, Universities and Minority Institutions, Executive Order 12928, September 29, 1994
HRM07   Enhance Programs to Provide Family-Friendly Workplaces

Continued Commitment to Small, Small Disadvantaged, and Small Women-Owned Businesses in Federal Procurement, Presidential Memorandum, October 13, 1994
PROC07   Enhance Programs for Small Business and Small Disadvantaged
          Business Concerns

Federal Procurement Reform, Executive Order 12931, October 13, 1994
PROC12   Allow for Expanded Choice and Cooperation in the Use of Supply Schedules

Expansion of Federal Executive Boards, Executive Order 12862, December 8, 1994
ICS01   Create Customer-Driven Programs in All Departments and Agencies
          That Provide Services Directly to the Public

Governmentwide Reform of Regulatory System, Further Reform of Executive Order 12866, February 21, 1995
FSL02   Reduce Red Tape Through Regulatory and Mandate Relief
REG01   Create an Interagency Regulatory Coordinating Group

Regulatory Reinvention Initiative, Presidential Memorandum, March 4, 1995
REG03   Encourage Consensus-Based Rulemaking
REG04   Enhance Public Awareness and Participation
REG10   Provide Better Training and Incentives for Regulators

Improving Customer Service, Presidential Memorandum, March 22, 1995
ICS01   Create Customer-Driven Programs in All Departments and Agencies
           That Provide Services Directly to the Public
ICS05   Streamline Ways to Collect Customer Satisfaction and Other Information
           From the Public

Classified National Security Information, Executive Order 12958, April 17, 1995
INTEL03   Reassess Information Collection to Meet New Analytical Challenges

Waiver of Penalties and Reduction of Reports, Presidential Memorandum, April 24, 1995
SmBus16   Use Discretionary Enforcement Authority to Modify or Waive Penalties
           in Specific Instances
SmBus17   Reduce the Paperwork Burden on Small Businesses

Democracy Funding Programs, Presidential Letter, May 11, 1995
AID01   Redefine and Focus AID's Mission and Priorities

Supporting the Role of Fathers in Families, Presidential Memorandum, June 16, 1995
HRM07   Enhance Programs to Provide Family-Friendly Workplaces

Career Transition Assistance for Federal Employees, Presidential Memorandum, September 12, 1995
HRM14   Provide Incentives to Encourage Voluntary Separations

Export Licensing Procedures, Executive Order 12981, February 5, 1996
DOC03   Reform the Federal Export Control System for Commercial Goods
           • The President Should Direct Basic Overhaul of Export Licensing Procedures

Civil Justice Reform, Executive Order 12988, February 5, 1996
REG06   Encourage Alternative Dispute Resolution When Enforcing Regulations

Implementing Federal Family Friendly Work Arrangements, Presidential Memorandum, June 21, 1996
HRM07   Enhance Programs to Provide Family-Friendly Workplaces

Federal Information Technology, Executive Order 13011, July 17, 1996
IT01   Provide Clear, Strong Leadership to Integrate Information Technology
           Into the Business of Government
IT09   Improve Government's Information Infrastructure
IT11   Improve Methods of Information Technology Acquisition

Public Laws

Public Law 103-66, The Omnibus Budget Reconciliation Act of 1993
FSL01   Improve the Delivery of Federal Domestic Grant Programs

Public Law 103-87, The Foreign Operations Export Financing and Related Programs
Appropriations Act of 1994
AID02   Reduce Funding, Spending, and Reporting Micromanagement

Public Law 103-103, The Federal Employees Leave Sharing Act of 1993
HRM07   Enhance Programs to Provide Family-Friendly Workplaces

Public Law 103-111, Agriculture, Rural Development, Food and Drug Administration
and Related Agencies Appropriations Act, FY 1994
USDA02   Eliminate Federal Support for Honey

Public Law 103-112, The Labor, HHS, and Education Appropriations Act, FY 1994
DOL20   Reduce Federal Employees' Compensation Act Fraud

Public Law 103-121, The Commerce, Justice and State Appropriations Act, FY 1994
DOJ04   Improve Department of Justice Debt Collection Efforts
DOJ10   Improve White Collar Fraud Civil Enforcement
            • Improve White Collar Crime Enforcement

Public Law 103-123, The Treasury, Postal Service, and General Government
Appropriations Act, 1994
BGT05   Provide Line Managers With Greater Flexibility to Achieve Results

Public Law 103-130, Amendments to the National Wool Act of 1954
USDA01   End the Wool and Mohair Subsidy

Public Law 103-160, The National Defense Authorization Act for Fiscal Year 1994
ENV03   Increase Energy and Water Efficiency

Public Law 103-182, The North American Free Trade Agreement
TRE10   Modernize the U.S. Customs Service

Public Law 103-208, The Higher Education Technical Amendments of 1993
ED07   Simplify and Strengthen Institutional Eligibility and Certification
            for Participation in Federal Student Aid

Public Law 103-211, Emergency Supplemental Appropriations Act of 1994
DOT19   Rescind Unobligated Earmarks for the FTA New Starts and Bus Program
DOT21   Terminate Grant Funding for Federal Aviation Administration Higher
            Education Programs

Public Law 103-226, The Federal Workforce Restructuring Act of 1994

HRM06   Clearly Define the Objective of Training as the Improvement of Individual
          and Organizational Performance; Make Training More Market-Driven

HRM14   Provide Incentives to Encourage Voluntary Separations

Public Law 103-227, Goals 2000: Educate America Act

ED11   Build a Professional, Mission-Driven Structure for Research

FSL01   Improve the Delivery of Federal Domestic Grant Programs

FSL02   Reduce Red Tape Through Regulatory and Mandate Relief

Public Law 103-233, Multifamily Housing Property Disposition Reform Act of 1994

HUD02   Improve Multifamily Asset Management and Disposition

Public Law 103-236, Foreign Relations Authorization Act, FY 1994-95

DOS06   Consolidate U.S. Nonmilitary International Broadcasting

Public Law 103-239, School to Work Opportunities Act

FSL01   Improve the Delivery of Federal Domestic Grant Programs

Public Law 103-271, Board of Veterans' Appeals Administrative Procedures Act of 1994

DVA04   Streamline Benefits Claims Processing

Public Law 103-305, Federal Aviation Administration Authorization Act of 1994

DOT10   Establish Aeronautical Telecommunications Network to Develop
          a Public-Private Consortium

Public Law 103-306, Agency for International Development Appropriations of 1995

AID02   Reduce Funding, Spending, and Reporting Micromanagement

          • Congress Should Appropriate Funding for AID Development Assistance
            Programs on a Two-Year or Multi-Year Basis Depending on Specific
            Assistance Needs

Public Law 103-316, Energy and Water Development Appropriations Act, FY 1995

DOE06   Redirect Energy Laboratories to Post-Cold War Priorities

Public Law 103-317, Department of Commerce and Related Agencies Appropriations Act, FY 1995

DOC10   Amend the Omnibus Trade and Competitiveness Act to Increase the Data
          Quality of the National Trade Data Bank

DOJ04   Improve Department of Justice Debt Collection Efforts

DOJ10   Improve White Collar Fraud Civil Enforcement

Public Law 103-327, VA, HUD and Independent Agencies Appropriations Act of 1995

HUD08   Reduce Section 8 Contract Rent Payments

Public Law 103-333, Department of Labor, HHS, Education Appropriations Act of 1995
DOL20   Reduce Federal Employees' Compensation Act Fraud

Public Law 103-354, Department of Agriculture Reorganization Act
USDA03   Reorganize the Department of Agriculture to Better Accomplish Its Mission, Streamline Its Field Structure and Improve Service to Its Customers

Public Law 103-355, Federal Acquisition Streamlining Act of 1994
PROC01   Reframe Acquisition Policy
- Provide New Legislation Authority to Test Innovative Procurement Methods

PROC02   Build an Innovative Procurement Workforce
- Provide Civilian Agencies With Authority Similar to DOD's for Improving the Acquisition Workforce

PROC03   Encourage More Procurement Innovation
- Maintain the $500,000 Threshold for Cost and Pricing Data Requirements for Civilian Agencies

PROC04   Establish New Simplified Acquisition Threshold and Procedures
- Enact Legislation Simplifying Procurement

PROC06   Amend Protest Rules
- Allow Penalties for Frivolous Protests

PROC07   Enhance Programs for Small Business and Small Disadvantaged Business Concerns
- Amend Small Business Act to Authorize Civilian Agencies to Conduct Small/ Disadvantaged Business Set-Asides

PROC12   Allow for Expanded Choice and Cooperation in the Use of Supply Schedules
- Allow State and Local Government, Grantees, and Certain Nonprofit Agencies to Use Federal Contracts as Sources of Supply or Services

PROC13   Foster Reliance on the Commercial Marketplace
- Make It Easier to Buy Commercial Items

PROC18   Authorize Multi-Year Contracts
- Amend Federal Property and Administrative Services Act to Authorize Multi-Year Contracts
- Amend the Federal Property and Administrative Services Act to Allow Contracts for Severable Services to Cross Fiscal Years

PROC19   Conform Certain Statutory Requirements for Civilian Agencies to Those of Defense Agencies
- Repeal the Requirement for Commercial Pricing Certificates and Authorize Contract Awards Without Discussions
- Maintain the $500,000 Threshold for Cost and Pricing Data Requirements for DOD

DOD04   Outsource Non-Core Department of Defense Functions
- DOD Should Work With Congress to Implement Recommendations of the Acquisition Law Advisory Panel's Section 800 Report

DOD10   Give Department of Defense Installation Commanders More Authority and Responsibility over Installation Management

193

- DOD and Congress Should Work to Empower Installation Commanders to Make Best Value Purchases
- Legislation Should Be Enacted to Permit Use of Simplified Acquisition Procedures for Contracts Between $25,000 and $100,000
- DOD Should Amend the Federal Acquisitions Regulations to Permit Purchasing From Large Businesses Based on Cost and Quality of Items Required
- DOD Should Reform Contract Protest Procedures

SUP03   Improve Distribution Systems to Reduce Costly Inventories
SUP09   Simplify Procedures for Acquiring Small Blocks of Space to House Federal Agencies
SBA02   Improve Assistance to Minority Small Businesses
- Give Civilian Agencies the Same Authority That DOD Has in Its Small Disadvantaged Business Set-Aside Program

Public Law 103-356, Government Management Reform Act of 1994
FM03   Fully Integrate Budget Financial and Program Information
FM04   Increase the Use of Technology to Streamline Financial Services
FM06   "Franchise" Internal Services
FM09   Simplify the Financial Reporting Process

Public Law 103-382, Improving America's Schools Act
ED01   Redesign Chapter 1 of Elementary and Secondary Education Act
ED02   Reduce the Number of Programs the Department of Education Administers
- Consolidate the Drug-Free Schools and Communities Act and Safe School Act Programs
ED05   Streamline and Improve the Department of Education's Grant Process

Public Law 103-403, Small Business Act Reauthorization
SBA05   Manage the Microloan Program to Increase Loans for Small Business
- Congress Should Amend the Small Business Act so that SBA Can Guarantee 100 Percent of Loans to SBA Selected Intermediaries

Public Law 104-4, Unfunded Mandate Reform Act of 1995
FSL02   Reduce Red Tape Through Regulatory and Mandate Relief

Public Law 104-19, FY 1995 Rescissions/Disaster Assistance
ED02   Reduce the Number of Programs the Department of Education Administers
HUD01   Reinvent Public Housing
DOT17   Eliminate Funding for Highway Demonstration Projects
DVA03   Eliminate Legislative Budget Constraints to Promote Management Effectiveness
OTH2-02   Terminate the Chemical Safety and Hazard Investigation Board

Public Law 104-23, Fish Hatchery to the State of Arkansas
DOI2-07   Divest Fish and Wildlife Service Activities

Public Law 104-24, Fish Hatchery to the State of Iowa
DOI2-07   Divest Fish and Wildlife Service Activities

Public Law 104-25, Fish Hatchery to the State of Minnesota
DOI2-07   Divest Fish and Wildlife Service Activities

Public Law 104-28, Federal Tea Tasters Repeal Act of 1996
            Eliminate What We Don't Need

Public Law 104-36, Small Business Lending Enhancement Act of 1995
SBA2-01   Reduce the Government's Cost of Financing Small Business While Serving
            More Customers

Public Law 104-46, Energy and Water Appropriations Act of 1996
DOD12   Streamline and Reorganize the U.S. Army Corps of Engineers
DOE02   Incorporate Land Use Planning in Cleanup
DOE06   Redirect Energy Laboratories to Post-Cold War Priorities

Public Law 104-50, Department of Transportation Appropriations Act of 1996
DOT04   Establish a Corporation to Provide Air Traffic Control Services
            (partial—flexibilities granted in procurement and personnel authority)
DOT17   Eliminate Funding for Highway Demonstration Projects
DOT20   Reduce Annual Essential Air Service Subsidies (partial)
DOT2-03   Streamline DOT's Organizational Structure

*Public Law 104-52, Treasury, Postal Service and General Government Appropriations
Act of 1996*
BGT05   Provide Line Managers With Greater Flexibility to Achieve Results
            • Permit Agencies to Roll Over 50 Percent of Their Unobligated Year-End
              Balances in Annual Operating Costs to the Next Year
HRM01   Create a Flexible and Responsive Hiring System
HRM07   Enhance Programs to Provide Family-Friendly Workplaces

Public Law 104-58, Alaska Power Administration Asset Sale and Termination Act of 1995
DOE08   Support the Sale of the Alaska Power Administration

Public Law 104-59, National Highway System Designation Act of 1995
DOT05   Permit States to Use Federal Aid as a Capital Reserve
DOT2-02   Capitalize State Infrastructure Banks

Public Law 104-66, Federal Reports Elimination and Sunset Act of 1995
AID02   Reduce Funding, Spending, and Reporting Micromanagement
            • Statutory Reporting and Notification Requirements Should Be Reduced
SMC06   Reduce the Burden of Congressionally Mandated Reports
            • Eliminate at Least Half of All Congressionally Mandated Reports

Public Law 104-88, Interstate Commerce Commission Termination Act of 1995
OTH2-01   Terminate the Interstate Commerce Commission

Public Law 104-91, Fish Hatchery to the Commonwealth of Massachusetts
DOI2-07   Divest Fish and Wildlife Service Activities

Public Law 104-106, National Defense Authorization Act for FY 1996
DOE2-02   Privatize the Naval Petroleum Reserves in Elk Hills, California
DOE2-03   Sell Uranium No Larger Needed for National Defense Purposes After
           Rendering It Suitable for Commercial Power Reactors
PROC05   Reform Labor Laws and Transform the Labor Department Into an Efficient
           Partner for Meeting Public Policy Goals
PROC06   Amend Protest Rules
PROC11   Improve Procurement Ethics Laws
PROC17   Authorize a Two-Phase Competitive Source Selection Process
IT01   Provide Clear, Strong Leadership to Integrate Information Technology
           Into the Business of Government
IT09   Improve Government's Information Infrastructure
IT11   Improve Methods of Information Technology Acquisition
ORG01   Reduce the Costs and Numbers of Positions Associated With Management
           Control Structures by Half (would cut DOD headquarters by 25 percent)

Public Law 104-107, Foreign Operations Appropriations of FY 1996
AID02   Reduce Funding, Spending, and Reporting Micromanagement
           • Congress Should Appropriate Funding for AID Development Assistance
             Programs on a Two-Year or Multi-Year Basis Depending on Specific
             Assistance Needs
           • The Administration and Congress Should Work to Appropriate
             Development Assistance Funds as Part of a Single Account

Public Law 104-121, Contract with America Advancement Act of 1996
SBA01   Allow Judicial Review of the Regulatory Flexibility Act

Public Law 104-127, Federal Agriculture Improvement and Reform Act of 1996
USDA2-06   Shift USDA's Peanut Program to No-Net-Cost Basis
USDA2-09   Streamline USDA Rural Development Programs

Public Law 104-130, Line Item Veto Act of 1995
BGT08   Seek Enactment of Expedited Rescission Procedures

Public Law 104-134, Omnibus Appropriations of 1996
ED2-04   Terminate Low-Priority Education Programs
DOE03   Make Field Facility Contracts Outcome-Oriented
DOE04   Increase Electrical Power Revenues and Study Rates (partially enacted)
EPA03   Shift EPA's Emphasis Toward Pollution Prevention and Away From
           Pollution Control
EPA2-07   Create Performance Partnership Grants
HUD04   Create an Assisted-Housing/Rent Subsidy Demonstration Project

- HUD Should Conduct Negotiated Restructuring of Assisted Housing Projects on a Demonstration Basis

HUD2-01	Consolidate 60 Programs Into Three
HUD2-02	Transform Public Housing
HUD2-03	Reinvigorate the Federal Housing Administration
SSA2-03	Allow Electronic Fund Transfers for Beneficiary Payment
TRE2-05	Improve Collection of Delinquent Debt Owed the Federal Government
FM11	Strengthen Debt Collection Programs

Public Law 104-182, Safe Drinking Water Act Amendments of 1996

EPA2-01	Consolidate State Revolving Funds Into a Performance Partnership

Public Law 104-188, Small Business Job Protection Act of 1996

PENS01	Create a Simple Retirement Savings Plan for Small Employers
PENS02	Eliminate the Family Aggregation Rule Requiring Certain Highly Compensated Employees and Their Families to Be Treated as Single Employees
PENS03	Eliminate the Special Restrictions on Plans Maintained by Self-Employed Individuals
PENS05	Provide Design-Based Nondiscrimination Safe Harbors That Would Give Employers the Option of Avoiding Testing Contributions
PENS06	Facilitate Testing by Using Prior Year Data Rather Than Ongoing Testing or Post-Year-End Corrections
PENS07	Improve Fairness in Correcting Distribution Rules
PENS08	Permit Tax-Exempt Organizations to Maintain 401(k) Pension Plans
PENS09	Standardize Distribution Rules for All Rural Cooperatives
PENS10	Eliminate Excessive Testing by Simplifying the Definition of a Highly Compensated Employee
PENS11	Exempt Defined Contribution Plans From the Requirement That at Least 50 Employees, or 40 Percent of All Employees in Smaller Companies, Be Covered
PENS12	Eliminate the Special Vesting Schedule for Multi-Employer Plans
PENS15	Eliminate the Combined Plan Limit on Contributions and Benefits (Section 415(e))
PENS16	Exempt Government and Multi-Employer Plans From Certain Benefit and Contribution Limits
PENS17	Allow Tax-Exempt Organizations to Provide Excess Benefit Plans
PENS19	Eliminate the Rule Requiring Employer Plans to Begin Minimum Distribution Before Retirement
PENS20	Simplify Taxation of Annuity Distributions
PENS24	Establish Uniform Penalties for Failure to Provide Information Reports

Public Law 104-191, The Health Insurance Accountability and Portability Act of 1996

HHS2-01	Strengthen Medicare Program Integrity

Public Law 104-193, Personal Responsibility and Work Opportunity Act of 1996

USDA2-02	Change Family Day Care and Child Care Rates
USDA2-03	Allow States Greater Flexibility in Food Stamp Program
USDA2-04	Include Food Stamp Anti-fraud Provisions for Retailers and Recipients

Pending Legislation

Although the Administration supports some of these bills, others are objectionable to varying degrees as currently drafted. The Administration will work with Congress to address these objections satisfactorily and to conform some of the NPR-related items more closely to NPR policy.

Agency Recommendations Requiring Legislation

Department of Agriculture (USDA)

USDA07   Deliver Food Stamp Benefits Via Electronic Benefits Transfer to Improve Service to Customers While Remaining Cost-Effective

      H.R. 3697, Encouragement of Electronic Benefits Transfer Systems Act

USDA2-08   Consolidate Nutrition Program for the Elderly With the Administration on Aging Congregate Feeding Programs

      H.R. 2570, Older Americans Act Amendments of 1996

      H.R. 3603, Agriculture and Rural Development Appropriations Act of 1997

Department of Commerce (DOC)

DOC06   Improve Marine Fisheries Management

      H.R. 39, Fishery Conservation and Management Amendments of 1995

      S. 39, Sustainable Fisheries Act

DOC13   Use Sampling to Minimize Cost of the Decennial Census

      H.R. 919, Poverty Data Improvement Act

DOC2-01   Transform the Patent and Trademark Office Into a Performance-Driven, Customer-Oriented Agency

      H.R. 2533, U.S. Intellectual Property Organization Act of 1995

      H.R. 3460, Moorehead–Schroeder Patent Reform Act

      S. 1961, Omnibus Patent Act of 1996

DOC2-06   Expedite Closure of National Weather Service Field Offices

      H.R. 1450, Eliminate Certain Activities From the Functions Performed by the National Weather Service

Department of Defense (DOD)

DOD02   Establish a Unified Budget for the Department of Defense

      H.R. 3610, Defense Department Appropriations Act of 1997

      S. 1894, Defense Department Appropriations Act of 1997

DOD09   Maximize the Efficiency of DOD's Health Care Operations

      S. 42, Uniformed Services University of the Health Sciences Termination and Deficit Reduction Act of 1995

Department of Energy (DOE)

DOE08   Support the Sale of the Alaska Power Administration

      H.R. 1122, Alaska Power Administration Sale Act of 1995

Environmental Protection Agency (EPA)
EPA2-03   Broaden State Participation in Superfund Program
           H.R. 228, Superfund Reform Act of 1995
EPA2-06   Create Sustainable Development Challenge Grants
           H.R. 3666, VA, HUD and Independent Agencies Appropriations Act of FY97

Federal Emergency Management Agency (FEMA)
FEMA03   Create Results-Oriented Incentives to Reduce the Costs of a Disaster
           H.R. 1731, Earthquake, Volcanic Eruption and Hurricane Hazard Insurance Act
           H.R. 1856, Natural Disaster Protection Act of 1995
           S. 1043, Natural Disaster Protection and Insurance Act of 1995

Department of Health and Human Services (HHS)
HHS02   Reengineer the HHS Process for Issuing Regulations
           S. 555, Health Professions Education Consolidation and Reauthorization Act
           of 1995
           S. 1447, Older Americans Act Amendments of 1995
HHS2-02   Create Performance Partnerships
           H.R. 2206, Health Centers Consolidation Act of 1995
           H.R. 2207, Substance Abuse and Mental Health Performance Partnership Act
           of 1995
           S. 555, Health Professions Education Consolidation and Reauthorization
           Act of 1995
           S. 1044, Health Centers Consolidation Act of 1995
           S. 1180, SAMHSA Reauthorization, Flexibility Enhancement,
           and Consolidation Act of 1995
           H.R. 2056, Older American Act Amendments of 1995
HHS2-05   Improve Coordination of Programs for Older Americans
           • Improve Coordination of Programs for Special Population Groups
           H.R. 2056, Older Americans Act of 1995
           H.R. 2570, Older Americans Act Amendments 1995
           S. 1447, Older Americans Act Amendments of 1995
           S. 1643, Older Americans Act Amendments 1996

Department of Housing and Urban Development (HUD)
HUD01   Reinvent Public Housing
           H.R. 2406, United States Housing Act of 1996
           S. 1260, Public Housing Reform and Empowerment Act of 1996
HUD2-01   Consolidate 60 Programs Into Three
           H.R. 2406, United States Housing Act of 1996
           S. 1260, Public Housing Reform and Empowerment Act of 1996
HUD2-02   Transform Public Housing
           H.R. 2406, United States Housing Act of 1996
           S. 1260, Public Housing Reform and Empowerment Act of 1996
Department of the Interior (DOI)
DOI01   Establish a Hard Rock Mine Reclamation Fund to Restore the Environment
           H.R. 357, Mineral Exploration and Development Act of 1995

H.R. 1580, Mining Law Reform Act of 1995

S. 639, Locatable Mineral Mining Reform Act of 1995

DOI04   Promote Entrepreneurial Management of the National Park Service

H.R. 773, National Park Service Concessions Policy and Reform Act of 1995

H.R. 2028, Federal Land Management Agency Concessions Reform Act of 1995

H.R. 2107, National Park Service Fee Management Act of 1995

S. 309, National Park Service Concessions Policy and Reform Act of 1995

• The Secretary of the Interior Should Submit Legislation Giving NPS the Authority to Set Fees at All Parks

H.R. 2025, Park Renewal Fund Act

H.R. 2107, National Park Service Fee Management Act of 1995

S. 964, Park Renewal Fund Act

S. 1144, National Park Service Enhancement Act

• The National Park Service Should Work With Congress to Accelerate Its Concession Reform and Renewal Program

H.R. 773, National Park Service Concessions Policy and Reform Act of 1995

H.R. 2028, Federal Land Management Agency Concessions Reform Act of 1995

H.R. 2181, Common Sense National Park System Reform Act

S. 309, National Park Service Concessions Policy and Reform Act of 1995

S. 1144, National Park Service Enhancement Act

• Legislation Should Be Enacted to Enhance the Legal and Financial Flexibility of National Park Service Fundraising

H.R. 773, National Park Service Concessions Policy and Reform Act

H.R. 2181, Common Sense National Park System Reform Act

H.R. 3819, Amendments to the Act Establishing the National Park Foundation

S. 309, National Park Service Concessions Policy and Reform Act of 1995

S. 1148, National Park Service Enhancement Act

S. 1703, Amendments to the Act Establishing the National Park Foundation

DOI05   Obtain a Fair Return for Federal Resources

• The Administration Should Support Hard Rock Mining Reform Legislation

H.R. 1580, Mining Law Reform Act of 1995

S. 506, Mining Law Reform Act of 1995

DOI13   Improve the Federal Helium Program

H.R. 846, Helium Act of 1995

S. 45, Helium Reform and Deficit Reduction Act of 1995

S. 898, Helium Disposal Act of 1995

DOI2-06   Reinvent Bureau of Land Management Energy and Road Maintenance Programs

H.R. 2372, Surface Mining Control and Reclamation Amendment of 1995

DOI2-13   Privatize the Helium Program

H.R. 846, Helium Act of 1995

H.R. 873, Helium Privatization Act of 1995

H.R. 2906, Helium Privatization Act of 1996

H.R. 3008, Helium Privatization Act

S. 45, Helium Reform and Deficit Reduction Act of 1995

S. 898, Helium Disposal Act of 1995

200

DOI2-14   Expand Lease Authority to the National Park Service

H.R. 2067, Facilitate Improved Management of NPS Lands

   H.R. 2941, Housing Improvement Act for Land Management Agencies

Department of Justice (DOJ)

DOJ05   Improve the Bureau of Prisons Education, Job Training,

and Financial Responsibilities Programs

- Enact Legislation to Authorize BOP to Develop Additional Markets for UNICOR Products

H.R. 2553, Prison Inmate Training and Rehabilitation Act of 1995

DOJ15   Improve the Professionalism of the U.S. Marshals Service

H.R. 2641, U.S. Marshals Service Improvement Act of 1996

S. 1338, U.S. Marshals Service Improvement Act of 1995

Department of Labor (DOL)

DOL02   Develop a Single Comprehensive Worker Adjustment Strategy

- DOL Should Work With Congress to Develop a Single, Integrated Worker Adjustment Assistance Program for Workers Who Are Jobless or Face the Potential to Permanently Lose Their Jobs

H.R. 1617, Consolidated and Reformed Education, Employment, and Rehabilitation Systems Act of 1995

S. 143, Workforce Development Act

DOL05   Automate the Processing of ERISA Annual Financial Reports (Forms 5500) to Cut Costs and Delays in Obtaining Employee Benefit Plan Data

- DOL and IRS Should Develop an Automated Processing System for Form 5500-Series Data

H.R. 3520, Retirement Savings and Security Act

S. 1818, Retirement Savings and Security Act

DOL06/   Amend the ERISA Requirement for Summary Plan Descriptions

DOL2-17   • Congress Should Amend ERISA to Eliminate the Requirement for Filing All Summary Plan Descriptions With DOL

H.R. 3520, Retirement Savings and Security Act

S. 1818, Retirement Savings and Security Act

DOL08   Create One-Stop Centers for Career Management

H.R. 1617, Consolidated and Reformed Education, Employment, and Rehabilitation Systems Act of 1995

S. 143, Workforce Development Act of 1995

- DOL Should Lead the Establishment of Comprehensive, Integrated Program of One-Stop Shopping Centers for Career Management

H.R. 1617, Consolidated and Reformed Education, Employment, and Rehabilitation Systems Act of 1995

S. 180, Workforce Development Act

DOL10   Refocus the Responsibility for Ensuring Workplace Safety and Health

- DOL Should Require Employers to Develop Worksite Safety and Health Programs and to Conduct Inspections for Worksite Safety and Health

S. 592, Occupational Safety and Health Reform Act

S. 1423, Occupational Safety and Health Reform Act

- DOL Should Establish a Sliding Scale for Incentives and Penalties for Ensuring Workplace Safety and Health

S. 592, Occupational Safety and Health Reform Act

S. 1423, Occupational Safety and Health Reform Act

DOL11   Open the Civilian Conservation Centers to Private and Public Competition

- Congress Should Amend Title IV of the Job Training Partnership Act to Authorize Public and Private Competition for Operation of the 30 Job Corps Civilian Conservation Centers

H.R. 1617, Consolidated and Reformed Education, Employment, and Rehabilitation Systems Act of 1995

S. 143, Workforce Development Act

DOL2-02   Transfer the Community Service Employment for Older Americans Program to the HHS Administration on Aging

H.R. 2570, Amend the Older Americans Act of 1965

S. 1643, Amend the Older Americans Act of 1965

Office of Personnel Management (OPM)

OPM01   Strengthen OPM's Leadership Role in Transforming Federal Human Resource Management Systems

H.R. 3756, Treasury, Postal Service and General Government Appropriations of 1997

Small Business Administration (SBA)

SBA06   Establish User Fees for Small Business Development Center Services

H.R. 3719, Small Business Programs Improvement Act of 1996

Department of Transportation (DOT)

DOT04   Establish a Corporation to Provide Air Traffic Control Services

H.R. 1441, U.S. Air Traffic Service Corporation Act of 1995

S. 1239, U.S. Air Traffic Service Corporation Act

DOT15   Provide Reemployment Rights for Merchant Mariners

- Legislation Should Be Enacted to Provide Reemployment Rights for Merchant Mariners Who Are Called to Active Duty During a War or National Emergency

H.R. 1350, Mariners Security Act

S. 1139, Maritime Reform and Security Act

DOT2-02   Capitalize State Infrastructure Banks

H.R. 2439, State Infrastructure Banks Act of 1995

Department of Treasury (TRE)

TRE09   Modernize the IRS

H.R. 3756, Treasury, Postal Service and General Government Appropriations Act of FY 1997

TRE15   Increase IRS Collections Through Better Compliance Efforts

H.R. 3756, Treasury, Postal Service and General Government Appropriations Act of FY 1997

Transform the U.S. Mint Into a Performance-Driven, Customer-Oriented Agency

Department of Veterans Affairs (DVA)

DVA01   Develop the Master Veteran Record and Modernize the Department's Information Infrastructure

          S. 1345, VA Improvement and Reinvention Act of 1995

DVA06   Enhance VA Cost Recovery Capabilities

          H.R. 1482, Veterans Programs Amendments of 1995

          H.R. 2234, Debt Collection Improvement Act of 1995

DVA07   Establish a Working Capital Fund

          H.R. 3666, VA, HUD and Independent Agencies Appropriations Act of 1997

DVA14   Raise the Fees for Veterans Affairs' Guaranteed Home Loans

          H.R. 2530, Common Sense Balanced Budget Act of 1995

DVA2-01   Reform VA Health Care Eligibility and Treatment

          H.R. 3118, Veterans Health Care Eligibility Reform Act of 1996

          S. 1345, VA Improvement and Reinvention Act of 1995

DVA2-03   Allow VA to Retain a Greater Portion of Collections From Third-Party Insurers for Treating Veterans' Nonservice-Connected Conditions

          S. 1345, DVA Improvement and Reinvention Act of 1995

DVA2-10   Terminate the Manufactured (Mobile) Home Loan Guaranty Program

          S. 1345, DVA Improvement and Reinvention Act of 1995

Systems Recommendations Requiring Legislation

Mission-Driven, Results-Oriented Budgeting (BGT)

BGT07   Institute Biennial Budgets and Appropriations

          H.R. 252, Legislative Reorganization Act of 1995

          H.R. 766, Biennial Budgeting Act of 1995

          H.R. 2599, Budget Enforcement Simplification Trust Act

          S. 1434, Biennial Budgeting Act of 1995

Improving Financial Management (FM)

FM04   Increase the Use of Technology to Streamline Financial Services

          H.R. 1698, Mandatory Electronic Funds Transfer Expansion Act of 1995

Strengthening the Partnership in Intergovernmental Service Delivery (FSL)

FSL01   Improve the Delivery of Federal Domestic Grant Programs

          H.R. 2086, Local Empowerment and Flexibility Act

          S. 88, Local Empowerment and Flexibility Act

Reinventing Human Resource Management (HRM)

HRM07   Enhance Programs to Provide Family-Friendly Workplaces

H.R. 3756, Treasury, Postal Service and General Government Appropriations Act of 1997

H.R. 3841, Omnibus Civil Service Reform Act of 1996

Reinventing Federal Procurement (PROC)

PROC02   Build an Innovative Procurement Workforce

H.R. 1770, Civilian Agency Acquisition Workforce Improvement Act

Improving Regulatory Systems (REG)

REG06   Encourage Alternative Dispute Resolution When Enforcing Regulations

H.R. 2977, Administrative Dispute Resolution Act of 1996

H.R. 3841, Omnibus Civil Service Reform Act of 1996

Reinventing Support Services (SUP)

SUP03   Improve Distribution Systems to Reduce Costly Inventories

• Eliminate Federal Prison Industries as a Mandatory Source

H.R. 3745, Federal Prison Industries Competition in Contracting Corrections Act of 1996

S. 1797, Federal Prison Industries Procurement Reform

SUP07   Simplify Travel and Increase Competition

H.R. 3230, National Defense Authorization

SUP08   Give Customers Choices and Create Real Property Enterprises That Promote Sound Real Property Asset Management

S. 1005, Public Buildings Reform Act of 1995

Reengineering Through Information Technology (IT)

IT09   Improve Government's Information Infrastructure

H.R. 3756, Treasury, Postal Service, and General Government Appropriations Act of 1997

IT10   Develop Systems and Mechanisms to Ensure Privacy and Security

H.R. 184, Individual Privacy Protection Act of 1995

Reinventing Environmental Management (ENV)

ENV02   Develop Cross-Agency Ecosystem Planning and Management

S. 93, Ecosystem Management Act of 1995

Regulatory Reform Efforts
Requiring Legislation

Reinventing Pension Regulations

PENS04 Simplify Substantial Owner Rules Relating to Plan Terminations
        H.R. 3520, Retirement Savings and Security Act
        S.1818, Retirement Savings and Security Act.

PENS13 Allow Multi-Employer Plans to Return to Triennial, Rather Than Annual,
        Actuarial Evaluations
        H.R. 3520, Retirement Savings and Security Act
        S. 1818, Retirement Savings and Security Act

PENS14 Eliminate Partial Termination Rules for Multi-Employer Plans
        H.R. 3520, Retirement Savings and Security Act
        S. 1818, Retirement Savings and Security Act

PENS17 Allow Tax-Exempt Organizations to Provide Excess Benefit Plans
        H.R. 3520, Retirement Savings and Security Act
        S. 1818, Retirement Savings and Security Act

PENS18 Repeal the 150-Percent Limitation on Deductible Contributions
        for Multi-Employer Plans
        H.R. 3520, Retirement Savings and Security Act

PENS26 Eliminate Mandatory Filing of Summary Plan Descriptions
        With the Department of Labor and Authorize DOL to Obtain
        Descriptions From Plan Administrators
        H.R. 3520, Retirement Savings and Security Act
        S. 1818, Retirement Savings and Security Act

BLANK   PAGE

APPENDIX F:
PROGRESS IN DOWNSIZING THE FEDERAL GOVERNMENT

In January 1996, the Clinton Administration reported that the count in the number of civilian executive branch federal employees—excluding employees of the independent Postal Service—had been reduced by almost 240,000 since the Administration took office in January 1993.[1] This is the smallest federal workforce in 30 years (see Table F-1). A variety of mechanisms

Table F-1. Trend in Federal Employment, January 1980—January 1996

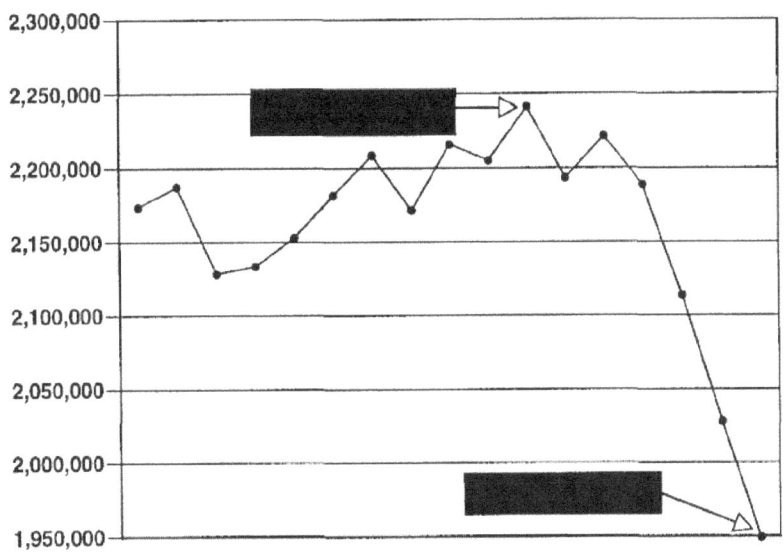

<hr />

[1] This appendix is based on the monthly head count of federal employees compiled by the Office of Personnel Management. This measure counts part-time, full-time, and seasonal employees employed on the last day of each month. An alternative count of the federal employment is also used, called "full-time equivalent" (FTE). An FTE is equal to one work year, or 2,080 non-overtime hours. This number is normally calculated at the end of each fiscal year. A special estimate was calculated in January 1993 that serves as a baseline used by the Clinton Administration to measure its progress in reducing the size of the federal workforce. Between this baseline and September 30, 1995, about 185,000 FTEs have been cut from the executive branch agencies. In the President's fiscal year 1997 budget, the Office of Management and Budget estimates that the number of FTEs will have been cut by 214,400 by September 30, 1996.

have been used to accomplish this, thereby keeping the use of involuntary terminations to a minimum. In fact, of the 239,286 person reduction, only 20,702 have been involuntarily separated. Most of the reductions were in three categories: administrative staff (44 percent); blue collar staff (33 percent); and engineers, scientists, or medical personnel (22 percent).

Major Trends in Staff Reductions

Thirteen of the 14 executive branch departments have reduced their employee count since President Clinton took office in January 1993. The exception is the Department of Justice, which is hiring additional law enforcement employees. Six cabinet agencies have had reductions of 10 percent or more. Other major agencies have experienced relatively large cuts in percentage terms; for example, the Office of Personnel Management had reduced its staff by 38 percent, as of January 1996 (see Table F-2).

Defense civilians comprised 154,000, or 64 percent, of the reductions. To put this figure in context, note that Defense civilians accounted for 43.2 percent of the executive branch workforce in January 1993 and 41.7 percent in January 1996. Note too that the scale of the Defense Department is enormous compared to civilian agencies. For example:

- The Defense Logistics Agency has four times the number of employees as the entire Department of Housing and Urban Development.

- The staff at the Defense Contract Audit Agency is larger than that of the Department of Education; the Defense Department's civilian school system has three times the number of employees as does the Department of Education.

- The Defense Finance and Accounting Service has as many employees as the State Department.

- The Defense Commissary Agency has a larger staff than the Environmental Protection Agency.

Defense employment is decreasing primarily because of the end of the Cold War; however, a large number of positions are also being eliminated through reinvention initiatives. The civilian Defense cuts are being driven by budgetary necessity, but the proposed reengineering efforts of the National Performance Review (NPR) have enabled the Defense Department to downsize without impairing readiness or service delivery. Of the 110,100 positions that Defense eliminated in fiscal years 1994 and 1995, over 12,000 were in occupational areas targeted specifically by NPR for reduction:

- Nearly 5,800 Defense procurement positions have been eliminated.

- Over 2,500 personnel specialist positions and nearly 3,700 financial management positions have been eliminated.

- Another 5,000 positions in these occupational areas are expected to be eliminated in the next two years.

Staff Reductions
Based on Doing Things Better With Less

Thousands of positions on the civilian side of the government have been eliminated because of reinvention's new ways of doing things better with less:

- Overall, agencies have reduced the number of supervisors by 20 percent—54,000.

- The Department of Agriculture has eliminated 14,954 positions by reducing its agencies from 43 to 30 and consolidating or eliminating 1,200 obsolete county-level field offices.

- The Department of the Interior has decreased its staff by 9,400 positions by reducing its support staff and eliminating entire organizations such as the Office of Territorial and International Affairs and the Bureau of Mines.

- The Department of Health and Human Services, including the Social Security Administration, has reduced its staff by 7,259 positions by eliminating an entire layer of management, by consolidating personnel and support functions, and through other streamlining measures.

- The General Services Administration has eliminated 4,839 positions by streamlining its real estate and procurement functions.

- The National Aeronautics and Space Administration has reduced its staff by 3,795 positions.

- The Office of Personnel Management reduced its staff by nearly 45 percent—2,616 employees—in part by privatizing its training and investigations functions.

Federal Employment

Table F-1. Executive Branch Employment January 1965—January 1996

(excludes U.S. Postal Service)

	Employment		
	Total	Defense	Non-Defense
1965	1,857,958	1,016,967	840,991
1966	1,917,888	1,063,005	854,883
1967	2,137,148	1,246,345	890,803
1968	2,190,618	1,267,152	923,466
1969	2,227,583	1,315,260	912,323
1970	2,165,642	1,251,982	913,660
1971	2,095,532	1,149,802	945,730
1972	2,105,708	1,126,301	979,407
1973	2,087,984	1,080,747	1,007,237
1974	2,052,268	1,034,180	1,018,088
1975	2,103,387	1,038,071	1,065,316
1976	2,128,006	1,023,255	1,104,751
1977	2,119,037	993,516	1,125,521
1978	2,138,374	982,198	1,156,176
1979	2,150,696	971,968	1,178,728
1980	2,173,917	963,598	1,210,319
1981	2,187,373	972,990	1,214,383
1982	2,128,336	1,008,366	1,119,970
1983	2,133,432	1,023,776	1,109,656
1984	2,153,005	1,041,586	1,111,419
1985	2,181,624	1,065,119	1,116,505
1986	2,208,577	1,094,743	1,113,834
1987	2,171,716	1,070,435	1,101,281
1988	2,216,059	1,081,659	1,134,400
1989	2,205,165	1,058,198	1,146,967
1990	2,241,361	1,070,529	1,170,832
1991	2,193,358	1,014,212	1,179,146
1992	2,221,483	1,006,003	1,215,480
1993	2,188,647	966,087	1,222,560
1994	2,113,645	905,167	1,208,478
1995	2,028,022	859,598	1,168,424
1996	1,949,366	812,323	1,137,043

Source: Office of Personnel Management, Monthly Report of Federal Civilian Employment (SF 113-A).

Table F-2. Changes in Federal Civilian Employment, by Major Agency, January 1993–January 1996

Department or Agency	Civilian Employees			
	Jan 93	Jan 96	Change	Percent Change
Agriculture	113,687	98,733	-14,954	-13.2%
Commerce	37,608	35,497	-2,111	-5.6
Defense (civilian)	966,087	812,923	-153,164	-15.9
Education	4,995	4,795	-200	-4.0
Energy	20,706	18,983	- 1,723	-8.3
Environmental Protection Agency	18,351	17,476	-875	-4.8
Federal Emergency Management Agency	4,554	3,853	-701	-15.4
General Services Administration	20,690	15,851	-4,839	-23.4
Health and Human Services	131,066	123,807	-7,259	-5.5
Housing and Urban Development	13,292	11,575	-1,717	-12.9
Interior	77,313	67,913	-9,400	-12.2
Justice	97,652	104,244	6,592	6.8
Labor	17,719	15,722	-1,997	-11.3
National Aeronautics and Space Administration	25,191	21,396	-3,795	-15.1
National Science Foundation	1,270	1,269	1	0.1
Office of Personnel Management	6,861	4,245	-2,616	-38.1
Small Business Administration	5,768	4,827	-941	-16.3
State	25,982	24,538	-1,444	-5.6
Transportation	70,086	62,782	-7,304	-10.4
Treasury	165,904	154,920	-10,984	-6.6
United States Agency for International Development	4,218	3,484	738	-17.4
U.S. Information Agency	8,283	7,280	-1,003	-12.1
Veterans Affairs	260,349	258,275	-2,074	-0.8
Subtotal	2,097,631	1,874,389	-223,242	-10.6%
All Other Agencies	91,216	74,945	-16,241	-17.8%
Total	2,188,847	1,949,364	-239,483	- 10.9%

Source: Office of Personnel Management, Monthly Report of Federal Civilian Employment (Form SF 113-A).

BLANK   PAGE

Appendix G:
Contractors Are Not Replacing
Departing Federal Workers

Some observers of the Administration's downsizing initiative have concluded that because the federal workforce is decreasing, agencies must be replacing lost employees with contract workers. Careful assessment of trends in federal service contracting shows that this is not generally the case. Governmentwide, there has been no statistically significant increase in real dollars spent on service contracts over the past three years. Moreover, between fiscal years (FYs) 1993 and 1995, the majority of large agencies with significant service contract spending decreased both their number of employees and dollars spent on service contracts.

Several federal policies affect the use of contractors in providing services to the government:

- Public Law 103-226, the Federal Workforce Restructuring Act of 1994, states in sec. 5(g): "The President shall take appropriate action to ensure that there is no increase in the procurement of service contracts by reason of the enactment of this Act, except in cases in which a cost comparison demonstrates such contracts would be to the financial advantage of the Federal Government."

- Office of Management and Budget (OMB) Policy Letter 92-1, dated September 23, 1992, prohibits federal agencies from contracting out "inherently governmental functions."

- OMB Circular A-76 defines various service functions and encourages contracting out these functions, but only if they can be done more cost effectively than inside the government.

To determine if contractors were replacing departing federal workers, we compared the trends in personnel reductions and federal spending on service contracts. We measured the change in staffing in terms of full-time equivalent (FTE) employees at each major agency between FYs 1993 and 1995. We measured the change in spending on service contracts by comparing the dollars spent on these contracts by each major federal agency between FYs 1993 and 1995. We deflated the service contract dollars to account for inflation.

The overall dollars spent on federal service contracts, when adjusted for inflation, have been basically flat for the past three years. In FY 1993, the federal government spent $106.1 billion on service contracts; in FY 1995, it spent $106.5 billion—a change of less than one-tenth of a percent. However, not all service contracts are for services that federal employees might perform. For example, the federal government rarely performs its own architectural or engineering services. Therefore, we identified those functions that might be performed by either a federal employee or a contractor. These commercial-type services we refer to as "A-76-type" services (see the technical note for details). The federal government's spending for A-76-type services through service contracts totaled $29.4 billion in FY 1993 and decreased to $28.9 billion in FY 1995—a drop of 1.6 percent in inflation-adjusted terms.

We then broke down the overall trends by agency to see the agency-by-agency patterns. We found that 13 of the 21 largest agencies with significant service contract spending decreased both the number of employees and the dollars spent on A-76-type service contracts between FYs 1993 and 1995 (see Table G-1). At the remaining eight agencies, service contracting increased, but the number of employees was decreased. The service contracting increases at seven of the eight agencies were unrelated to agency personnel cuts; the eighth agency's increase reflected a decision to contract out certain service functions.

- The Agency for International Development shifted funds away from direct grants to foreign governments into contracts that provide the same assistance. This was unrelated to staffing reductions.
- The Army Corps of Engineers' increase in service contracts reflects new assigned responsibilities—logistics pre-positions and base closures—and the decision to use contracts rather than hire new federal employees to perform these functions.
- The Department of Commerce increased contract spending on modernization efforts at the National Weather Service.
- The Department of Energy increased contracts as a result of policy decisions to expand its hazardous waste cleanup efforts.
- The Department of Justice contracting increase is proportional with its general budget increase.
- Increases in the Office of Personnel Management's service contracting represent training funds passed through from other agencies; the department now contracts for training on behalf of these agencies and no longer delivers training directly.
- The Tennessee Valley Authority increased contract spending because of one-time costs related to the start-up of the Watts Bar Nuclear Plant.

The one agency that increased contracting to substitute for former federal employees is the Department of Veterans Affairs (VA), which made a policy decision to outsource some service functions, such as janitorial services. It also closed some supply depots and shifted to the use of prime vendor contracts (these deliver supplies directly to VA hospitals instead of to centrally located warehouses).

Table G-1: Comparison of Personnel Reduction and Service Contract Level

	Jan. 1993–Sept. 1995 FTE Employees		FYs 1993-95 A-76-Type Services Contract Levels	
	Numeric Change	Percentage Change	Dollar Change (in thousands)	Percentage Change
Reductions in FTEs and Contract Dollars				
Agriculture	-11,800	-10.2	-38,912	-13.6
Defense	-109,600	-11.8	-1,009,787	-5.6
Education	-200	-4.0	-29,496	-15.6
Environmental Protection Agency	-100	-5.9	-34,951	-5.3
General Services Administration	-3,600	-17.5	-39,515	-9.0
Health & Human Services/Social Security Administration	-6,500	-5.0	-856	-0.1
Housing & Urban Development	-1,500	-11.0	-20,011	-24.1
Interior	-7,300	-9.2	-8,032	-4.1
Labor	-1,500	-8.2	-8,525	-6.6
National Aeronautics and Space Administration	-3,300	-12.8	-55,066	-2.0
State	-2,100	-8.1	-328	-0.1
Transportation	-7,100	-10.1	-175,683	-15.7
Treasury	-8,600	-5.2	-2,533	-0.8
Reductions in FTEs and Increases in Contract Dollars				
Agency for International Development	-800	-18.2	164,616	17.5
Army Corps of Engineers	-1,500	-5.1	216,514	36.0
Commerce	-1,400	-3.8	36,966	31.2
Energy	-900	-4.4	128,845	12.0
Justice	-1,500	-1.5	176,460	58.5
Office Of Personnel Management	-2,000	-32.3	3,841	8.7
Tennessee Valley Authority	-2,400	-12.6	55,337	19.7
Veterans Affairs	-3,900	-1.7	94,644	25.2
All Other Agencies	-6,400	-7.4	74,948	33.1
Total	-185,000*	-8.6	-471,578	-1.6

*Total not exact due to rounding.

Technical Note:

In calculating its figures, the National Performance Review identified certain categories of service contracts as including commercial or industrial functions that might be performed by either federal employees or contractor employees. We refer to these as commercial-type or "A-76-type" services; these include such activities as maintenance; repair and rebuilding of equipment; technical representation services; medical services; professional, administrative, and management support services; training services; and housekeeping services. They do not include such activities as construction or architect and engineering services, which the government almost always contracts out.

The personnel data in Table G-1 are from Executive Office of the President, "Analytical Perspectives," *Budget of the United States, Fiscal Year 1997* (Washington, DC: Government Printing Office), p. 180. The procurement data are from the General Services Administration's Federal Procurement Data System, Form SF-279, for FYs 1993 and 1995.

BLANK   PAGE

APPENDIX H:
PROGRESS IN STREAMLINING
MANAGEMENT CONTROL POSITIONS

One of the key recommendations in the 1993 report of the National Performance Review (NPR) was to pare down the systems of overcontrol and micromanagement—oversized headquarters; multiple layers of supervisors and; offices specializing in budgeting, personnel, audit, procurement, and finance.

NPR found that nearly one in three federal workers worked in these systems and that their salaries consumed about $35 billion a year. NPR recommended reducing these costs in half by eliminating 252,000 positions (which was later raised to 272,900 positions by law) over a six-year period ending in 1999. NPR also recommended reducing the number of management positions by setting a challenging governmentwide goal of roughly doubling the span of control. The governmentwide ratio of supervisors to employees in 1993 was 1:7, and NPR recommended halving the ratio to 1:15.

These goals are important because employees cannot be empowered to serve their customers unless the red tape that binds them is removed. So the goal of reduction in the workforce—especially the reduction of management control positions—is not only to save money but to improve the working conditions for frontline federal workers—particularly those who serve the public—and expedite the flow of information between top administrators and frontline workers by reducing decisionmaking bottlenecks.

Within days of the release of the 1993 report, President Clinton issued a memorandum to department and agency heads directing the downsizing and asking that the existing ratio of employees to supervisors be doubled. In late 1994, the Office of Management and Budget (OMB) followed up this memorandum with additional guidance directing agencies to develop streamlining plans and submit them to OMB for approval.

The downsizing initiative is now at its halfway point, and progress is being made. Some agencies have met many of the goals already—even though they have six years to do so. Most agencies, however, do not plan to meet the goal of cutting management control positions in half. Many believe the goal is not appropriate for their agency and maintain that meeting it would disrupt existing operations.

Table H-1 shows the progress of departments and major agencies in meeting the NPR goals over the 1993-96 period. Table H-2 shows planned efforts in meeting the goals over the full six-year period 1993-99. Finally, Table H-3 shows agency efforts to increase the ratio of employees to supervisors. Overall agency progress toward NPR's management control streamlining goals is summarized below:

---

[1]Presidential Memorandum to Department and Agency Heads, "Streamlining the Bureaucracy," September 11, 1993.

[2]Director, Office of Management and Budget, Memorandum to Department and Agency Heads, "Streamlining Plans," August 19, 1994.

- **Reducing the Number of Supervisors by Half.** Halfway through the six-year streamlining initiative, 11 of the 27 largest departments and agencies have reduced their number of supervisors by 25 percent or better, thereby indicating they are making visible progress in reducing the number of supervisors by half. By 1999, 20 plan either nearly to meet or to exceed this goal. As a result, on a governmentwide basis, the number of supervisors should be reduced by nearly 50 percent.

- **Reducing the Number of Headquarters Staff by Half.** Eight of 27 agencies are making progress in reducing headquarters staff at the halfway point. In addition, eight plan to come close to or exceed the goal by 1999. As a result, on a governmentwide basis, the number of headquarters staff should be reduced by about 25 percent.

- **Reducing the Number of Management Control Positions by Half.** Three of 27 agencies are making progress in reducing the number of management control positions. In all, only two plan to come close to that goal by 1999. As a result, on a governmentwide basis, the number of management control positions should be reduced by about 21 percent.

- **Doubling the Ratio of Employees to Supervisors.** Three of 27 agencies say they have already met the goal of doubling the ratio of employees to supervisors. Eight additional agencies plan to do so by 1999.

Table H-1. Streamlining Changes to Date: FYs 1993–1996 (in percentages)

Agency	Percentage Change in the Number of:		
	Supervisors	Headquarters Staff	Management Control Positions
Agency for International Development	-3	-14	+5
Agriculture	-21	-15	-11
Commerce	-18	-20	-16
Defense (total)	-16	-10	-8
Air Force	-13	-8	-8
Army	-14	-17	-8
Navy	-19	-7	-8
Defense Agencies	-19	-3	-8
Education	-24	-12	-11
Energy	-53	-27	-16
Environmental Protection Agency	-38	-10	+4
Federal Emergency Management Agency	-20	-22	+l7
General Services Administration	-28	-21	-l8
Health and Human Services	-29	-15	-11
Housing and Urban Development	-37	-36	-17
Interior	-29	-27	-32
Justice	+4	-5	+9
Labor	-19	-25	-17
National Aeronautics and Space Administration	-40	-34	-16
National Science Foundation	-24	-18	+8
Office of Personnel Management	-53	-65	-4l
Small Business Administration	-28	-28	-30
Social Security Administration	-25	-23	-14
State	-8	-7	-1
Transportation	-22	-25	-17
Treasury	-10	+4	+4
United States Information Agency	-22	-15	-17
Veterans Affairs	-28	-19	-6
Average	-20	-14	-9

Note: OMB Circular No. A-11 (1995), sec. 15.4, pp. 47-48, contains the definitions of the job series included in each of these three categories.

Table H-2. Planned Changes in Streamlining: FYs 1993–1999 (in percentages)

| Agency | Percentage Change in the Number: | | |
	Supervisors	Staff Headquarters	Management Control Positions
Agency for International Development	-23	-23	-6
Agriculture	-36	-26	- 17
Commerce	-45	-26	- 19
Defense (total)	-58	-15	-22
Air Force	-55	-10	-22
Army	-55	-19	-22
Navy	-62	-17	-22
Defense Agencies	-60	-10	-22
Education	-45	- 16	-23
Energy	-67	-43	-21
Environmental Protection Agency	-48	-28	-8
Federal Emergency Management Agency	-20	-20	-20
General Services Administration	-58	-25	-24
Health and Human Services	-51	-37	-20
Housing and Urban Development	-49	-44	-24
Interior	-59	-49	-35
Justice	-7	-7	+ l
Labor	-42	-53	-21
National Aeronautics and Space Administration	-62	-49	-32
National Science Foundation	-37	-22	+2
Office of Personnel Management	-53	-67	-42
Small Business Administration	-55	-35	-39
Social Security Administration	-51	-50	-26
State	-21	- 18	-4
Transportation	50	-50	-50
Treasury	-24	-13	-1
United States Information Agency	-32	-19	-27
Veterans Affairs	-43	-30	-9
Average	-49	-25	-21

Note: OMB Circular No. A-11 (1995), sec. 15.4, pp. 47-48, contains the definitions of the job series included in each of these three categories.

Table H-3. Ratio of Supervisors to Other Employees: FYs 1993, 1996, and 1999

Agency	Ratio of Supervisors to Other Employees		
	1993	1996 (est)	1999 (planned)
Agency for International Development	1:10	1:8	1:8
Agriculture	1:8	1:10	1:11
Commerce	1:7	1:8	1:12
Defense (total)	1:7	1:8	1:14
Air Force	1.7	1:8	1:14
Army	1:7	1:8	1:14
Navy	1:8	1:9	1:16
Defense Agencies	1:7	1:8	1:14
Education	1:6	1:8	1:10
Energy	1:5	1:11	1:15
Environmental Protection Agency	1:5	1:11	1:11
Federal Emergency Management Agency	1:6	1:13	1:15
General Services Administration	1:5	1:5	1:9
Health and Human Services	1:6	1:8	1:11
Housing and Urban Development	1:6	1:8	1:12
Interior	1:6	1:9	1:14
Justice	1:6	1:6	1:8
Labor	1:5	1:5	1:9
National Aeronautics and Space Administration	1:5	1:8	1:11
National Science Foundation	1.5	1.8	1.9
Office of Personnel Management	1:8	1:12	1:11
Small Business Administration	1:4	1:5	1:7
Social Security Administration	1:7	1:10	1:15
State	1:11	1:10	1:12
Transportation	1:6	1:7	1:11
Treasury	1:8	1:9	1:10
United States Information Agency	1:5	1:6	1:6
Veterans Affairs	1:8	1:11	1:15

BLANK   PAGE

APPENDIX I:
LIST OF HAMMER AWARDS AS OF
AUGUST 1, 1996

The Hammer Award is Vice President Gore's special recognition to teams of frontline federal workers who have made significant contributions to the National Performance Review (NPR) principles of putting customers first, cutting red tape, empowering frontline employees, and getting back to basics. The $6.00 hammer—with a little red, white, and blue ribbon—is the Vice President's symbolic answer to the $400.00 hammer of yesterday's government.

As of August 1, 1996, almost 500 teams of federal employees across the country have been recognized for their heroic contributions to reinventing their part of the federal government. Awardees are selected from among teams nominated through agency programs, Federal Executive Board/Federal Executive Association programs, and others. Following is a list of these teams. More information about each of these awards is available on NPR's World Wide Web home page (http://www.npr.gov).

Team Name	Location
Agencies	
Agency for International Development	
AID Reengineering Team	Worldwide
Department of Agriculture	
5th Floor Combined Services Support Staff - Forest Service	Juneau, AK
America's Outdoors	Milwaukee, WI
The Animal and Plant Health Inspection Service Reinvention Advocates–International Agreements Team	Riverdale, MD
Animal Damage Control Reimbursable Agreements Group	Minneapolis, MN
Automated Records Management System	Kansas City, MO
Automation Training Branch	St. Louis, MO
Business and Industry Guaranteed Loan Regulation and Streamlining Accelerated Support of Agency Programs Group	Nationwide
California Emergency Watershed Protection Team	Davis, CA
Eastern Pennsylvania Veterinary Services Field Team	Harrisburg, PA
Field Servicing Office - Animal and Plant Health Inspection Service	Minneapolis, MN
Forest Service and State of Oregon One Stop Shop	Portland, OR

Fremont Information Resource Services Team	Portland, OR
Georgia Emergency Watershed Protection Team	Atlanta, GA
International Bird Importation and Quarantine Processes Team	Minneapolis, MN
National Veterinary Services Laboratories	IA
Seed Visibility and Storage Research Team	Fort Collins, CO
Simplifying Rulemaking Lab - Animal and Plant Health Inspection Service	Nationwide
Termite Report Team	Toiyabe National Forest, NV

Department of Commerce

Census Bureau Internet Team	Nationwide
Computer-Assisted Survey Information Collection	Washington, DC
Export Enforcement Customer Service Team	Nationwide
National Telecommunications and Information Administration	Washington, DC
Office of Domestic Operations	Nationwide
One-Stop Import-Export Bank[1]	Nationwide
STAT-USA	Washington, DC

Consumer Product Safety Commission

Consumer Information Hotline Team	Bethesda, MD
Field Office Telecommuting Pilot Team	Philadelphia, PA

Department of Defense

Administrative Support Center - Defense Logistics Agency	Nationwide
Aircraft Carrier Anti-Submarine Warfare Module Team	Keyport, WA
Air Force 497th Intelligence Group	Nationwide
Air Force Air Reserve Personnel Center	Denver, CO
Air Force Beryllium Machine Shop Self–Directed Work	Columbus, OH
Air Force Civilian Personnel Division – Kelly Air Force Base	San Antonio, TX
Air Force Design Section	Mobile, AL
Air Force Recruiting Squadron Process Action Team	Middle TN
Air Force Small Computer Maintenance Process Team	Oklahoma City, OK
Air Force Weapons and Tactics Center	Las Vegas, NV
Alternate Technologies and Home Care Services	Charleston, SC
Army Armament and Chemical Acquisition and Logistics Agency Team Paladin	Rock Island, IL
Army Publication Distribution Center	Baltimore, MD
Army Simplified Nonstandard Item Acquisition Program Team	Detroit, MI
Columbus Regional Control Center	Columbus, OH

---

[1]Hammers were awarded to the Baltimore, Chicago, and Long Beach import–export centers.

Corps of Engineers Algiers Lock Dewatering Team	New Orleans, LA
Corps of Engineers Chief Counsel Alternative Dispute Resolution	Nationwide
Corps of Engineers Process Action Team, Harry S Truman Power Plant and Dam	Kansas City, MO
Defense Contract Audit Agency	Nationwide
Defense Contract Audit Agency Team	Ft. Belvoir, VA
Defense Contract Management Area Operations	Hartford, CT
Defense Distribution Depot	Columbus, OH
Defense Distribution Depot	Atlanta, GA
Defense Finance and Accounting Service – Finance Operations	Cleveland OH
Defense Finance and Accounting Service – Columbus Center	Columbus, OH
Defense Finance and Accounting Service – Defense Retiree and Annuitant Pay	Cleveland, OH
Defense Finance and Accounting Service – Directorate of Annuity Pay	Nationwide
Defense Finance and Accounting Service – Office of Retired Pay, Casualty Branch	Cleveland, OH
Defense Finance and Accounting Service, Phase IV – Army Carryover	Cleveland, OH
Defense Finance and Accounting Service Whiteworks Project Team	Kansas City, MO
Defense Personnel Support Center Electronic Commerce	Nationwide
Defense Priority Service Detachment Office Plant Consolidation Team	Great Lakes, IL
Defense Supply Center – Columbus/Defense Logistics Agency Wood Products Team	Columbus, OH
Depot–Level Quality Management Board	Corpus Christi, TX
Destruction Process Action Team	Newport, RI
Dewitt Army Community Hospital Primary Care Reinvention Team	Ft. Belvoir, VA
Directorate of Information Operations and Reports – Internet Implementation Team	Washington, DC
Directorate of Information Operations and Reports/Systems and Services/Technical Services Division/Inventory Team	Nationwide
Directorate of Military Pay	Indianapolis, IN
Document Automation Center – Defense Printing Service	Washington, DC
Document Automation Center Team – Defense Printing Service	St. Louis, MO
Fairchild Air Force Base Hospital Pharmacy	Spokane, WA
Fleet and Industrial Supply Center, Pearl Harbor (SERVMART)	Honolulu, HI
Health Care Systems Support Activity	San Antonio, TX
Hydrographic Survey and Physical Support Section	Savannah, GA
Lockheed Sanders Pricing Team	Manchester, NH

Marine Corps Logistics Base, Ace–in–the–Hole Gang	Nationwide
Marine Corps Support Activity	Kansas City, MO
MegaCenter Migration Team – Defense Logistics Agency	Columbus, OH
Michigan National Guard	Lansing, MI
Modeling Effort for Space Availability Quality Team	Albuquerque, NM
Mortar Shared Management Team	Rock Island, IL
National Defense Real Food Team	Nationwide
National Operation and Maintenance Program Plan of Improvement	Washington, DC
National Recreation and Parks Association Partnership (AFRS)	Nationwide
Naval Air Technical Training Center Curriculum Review Team	Memphis, TN
Naval Air Warfare Center Weapons Division	China Lake, CA
Naval Undersea Warfare Center Detachment	Hawthorne, NV
Naval Weapons Station (Base–wide reinvention)	Seal Beach, CA
Naval Weapons Station (customer service)	Seal Beach, CA
Navy AN/SQS–53A Engineering Change 16 Development Team	Nationwide
Navy Asset Visibility Team	Central PA
Navy Fleet – Labor Management Partnership Council	Mechanicsburg, PA
Office of Civilian Personnel – Defense Logistics Agency	New Cumberland, PA
Operational Process Improvement Office Team	Falls Church, VA
Operations Support Center, Provisional	Fort Lee, VA
Portsmouth Navy Shipyard Pollution Prevention Team	Portsmouth, NH
Productivity Enhancement Group V	Newark, NJ
Provider Workstation	Scott AFB, IL
Quick Response/Prime Vendor – Defense Personnel Support Center	Philadelphia, PA
Real Estate and Facilities Director, Washington Headquarters Services	Washington, DC
Red River Army Depot Super Crew	Texarkana, TX
Reinvention Task Force	Fairfax, VA
Silo Based ICBM Maintenance Corporate Board	Ogden, UT
Transportation Management Office	Camp Pendleton, CA
Travel Process Action Team	Newport, RI
Travel Team	Nationwide
Vance Air Force Base Education Team	Oklahoma City, OK

Department of Education

Cleveland/Bradley 2000	Cleveland, TN
Cooperative Audit Resolution and Oversight Initiative	Washington, DC
Georgia Partnership for Excellence in Education	Atlanta, GA
Goals 2000 Application and Review Team	Nationwide

Goals 2000 Teacher Forum   Washington, DC
Government Performance Appraisal System   Washington, DC
Kansas City Enforcement Office – Region VI   Kansas City, MO
Office for Civil Rights   New York, NY
Payment Management Team   Washington, DC
Rehabilitation Services Administration   Nationwide
Rocky Mount Business–Education Partnership   Raleigh, NC

Department of Energy
Columbus Initiative – Oak Ridge National Laboratories   Oakridge, TN
The Competitiveness Project – Bonneville Power Administration   Nationwide
Directives Reengineering Group   Oak Ridge, TN
Environmental Management Change Gang   Washington, DC
Life Cycle Asset Management Process Improvement Team   Washington, DC
Office of Chief Financial Officer   Nationwide
Office of Science Technology, Office of Environmental   Washington, DC
    Management
Performance Agreement Team   Washington, DC
Plantex Plant Facility   Amarillo, TX
Uranium Mine Tailings Reclamation Administration   Albuquerque, NM

Environmental Protection Administration
33/50 Program Team   Washington, DC
33/50 Program   St. Paul, MN
Community Environmental Compliance Flexibility Team   Seattle, WA
North Boulder Project Team   Boulder, CO
Safety, Health, and Environmental Management Team   Nationwide

Equal Employment Opportunity Council
National Labor–Management Council   Washington, DC
Teamwork—Making It Happen   Milwaukee, WI

Executive Office of the President
White House Visitors Office Team   Washington, DC
White House Presidential Correspondence Quality   Washington, DC
    Assurance Team

Federal Emergency Management Agency
Agency–Wide Reinvention Team   Nationwide
Hazard Mitigation Team – Region VII   Kansas City, MO
Regional Interagency Steering Committee – Region IV   Atlanta, GA

General Service Administration

100 Percent Satisfaction Team	Nationwide
Aggregated Switch Procurement – Region 3	Philadelphia, PA
Architect/Engineer Procurement Business Process Redesign Service	Nationwide
Chicago Customer Supply Team	Chicago, IL
Contract Management Division – Region 5	Chicago, IL
Heartland Region Business Development Team	Washington, DC
Lease Acquisition Business Process Redesign Team	New York, NY
No Hassle Customer Supply Team	Nationwide
Office Automation Team	Nationwide
Philadelphia Information Resources Management Service Office	Philadelphia, PA
The Public Building Service Rocky Mountain Property Team	Denver, CO
Space Acquisition Team	Seattle, WA

Department of Health and Human Services

International Cancer Information Center	Nationwide
Miami Import Group – FDA	Miami, FL
Respirator Certification Program Team – National Institute of Occupational Safety and Health/ Centers for Disease Control and Prevention	North Central, WV
Shelf Life Team – FDA	Detroit, MI
Task Force for Streamlining Documentation – Indian Health Service	Phoenix, AZ

Department of Housing and Urban Development

Acquisition/Rehabilitation Loan Program	Detroit, MI
Community Assistance Coordination Teams	Buffalo, NY
Harris County Housing and Community Development Agency	Houston, TX
Multifamily Insurance Applications Fast Track Processing Team	Seattle, WA
Office of Housing Neighborhood Networks Team	Nationwide
Office of Housing Reorganization Single Family Processing Center	Denver, CO
Reinvention of the Fair Housing Initiatives Program	Washington, DC
Single Family – Ft. Worth and Denver	Ft. Worth, TX Denver, CO
Streamline 203K Team	Detroit, MI
Streamline Certification Team	Washington, DC
Voucher Processing Task Force	Kansas City, KS

Intelligence Community

CIA Logistics Operations Center	McLean, VA
CIA Retirement and Investments Group	McLean, VA

Central Imagery Office Project ExPReS — McLean, VA
Defense Intelligence Agency Bottom–up Reinvention Team — Washington, DC
Intelligence Community Foreign Language Committee Reinvention Laboratory — McLean, VA
Intelligence Community (INTELINK) — McLean, VA
Intelligence Community Tipster Text Program — McLean, VA
National Photographic Interpretation Center Operations Vision Team — Washington, DC
National Security Agency Multifunction Technician Team — Ft. Meade, MD
National Security Agency Support to the Combat Operator Team — Ft. Meade, MD
National Security Agency Support to State Team — Ft. Meade, MD

Department of the Interior

America's Outdoors — Milwaukee, WI
Bureau of Mines, Albany Research Center & Partnership Council — Salem, OR
Bureau of Reclamation — Nationwide
Change in Organizational Design – Bureau of Indian Affairs — Portland, OR
Customer Service/Visitor Services Project – National Park Service — Washington, DC
Department of Interior Streamlining Effort — Nationwide
Idaho Ecosystem Management Strategy Team — Boise, ID
Regional Community Economic Revitalization Team — Portland, OR
Reinventing Regulations Using Plain English Team — Denver, CO
Reservoir Management and Solid Materials Team – Bureau of Land Management — Tulsa, OK
Review of Planning/Design/Construction Reengineering Lab — Denver, CO
USGS Information Dissemination System Reinvention Lab Team — Nationwide

Department of Justice

Border Crossing Card Reengineering Team — Nationwide
Citizenship USA, El Monte Office — Los Angeles, CA
Drug Enforcement Agency Mobile Enforcement Team — Atlanta, GA
El Centro Service Processing Center — Imperial Valley, CA
El Paso Immigration and Naturalization Service Process Action Team — El Paso, TX
FBI Semi–Automated Mailer Team — Nationwide
Immigration and Naturalization Service Operation Jobs — Dallas, TX
Immigration and Naturalization Service Team BISON — Buffalo, NY
Immigration and Naturalization Service Team Easi — St. Albans, VT
Partnerships Against Violence Network Online — Washington, DC
Vehicle–Equipment Reutilization Program — Salem, OR

Department of Labor

Administrative Efficiency Task Groups –   Washington, DC
    Office of the Assistant Secretary
    for Administration and Management

America's Job Bank on the Internet Team   Washington, DC

Concept 9   San Francisco, CA

Design Team – OSHA   Parsippany, NJ

Design Team – OSHA   Atlanta, GA

Design Team—Getting Results, Improving Performance – OSHA   Washington, DC

Dislocated Worker Team –   Seattle, WA
    Employment and Training Administration Region X

Electronic Data Interchange – Bureau of Labor Statistics   Nationwide

The Enterprise Council – Employment and Training   Nationwide
    Administration

Eradicating Sweatshops Initiative   Los Angeles, CA

Fax on Demand   Washington, DC

Federal Employees' Compensation Reengineering Project Team   Washington, DC

LABSTAT   Washington, DC

Maine Top 200 – OSHA   Bangor, ME

The New Nonformal Complaint Process   Chicago, IL

Pension and Welfare Benefits Administration   Washington, DC

Pension and Welfare Benefits Field Focus Group   Washington, DC

Re–engineering Establishment Survey Data Collection   Washington, DC

Residential Construction and Acute and Long Term Health Care   Buffalo, NY

Statistics Price Publications Improvement Team –   Washington, DC
    Bureau of Labor Statistics

Timely Service to Complainants   Chicago, IL

Voluntary Protection Programs Participants Association – OSHA   Chicago, IL

Voluntary Protection Programs Participants Association – OSHA2   Nationwide

Working Women Count Honor Roll   Washington, DC

National Aeronautics and Space Administration

Mission Control Design Pirate Team   Houston, TX

Mission to Planet Earth – Earth Observing System   Greenbelt, MD
    and Data Information System Version O Team

WSTF AlliedSignal ISO 9001   Las Cruces, NM
    Implementation Team

---

[2]Ten separate Hammers were awarded to the regional offices in California, Colorado, Georgia, Illinois, Massachusettes, Missouri, New York, Pennsylvania, Texas, and Washington.

National Archives and Records Administration
Nontextual Archives Division   College Park, MD
Waltham Federal Record Center Team   Boston, MA

Office of Management and Budget
Office of Federal Procurement Policy Reform
and Innovation Team   Nationwide

Office of Personnel Management
Automatic Staffing Team   Nationwide
Buy–Out Team   Washington, DC
The Electronic Highway: New Partnerships in Communications   Nationwide
Federal Personnel Manual Sunset Team   Nationwide
National Partnership Council   Washington, DC
SF–171 Elimination Team   Nationwide

Pension Benefit Guaranty Corporation
Customer Service Initiatives Team   Nationwide
Early Warning Program   Washington, DC
Missing Participants Program   Nationwide

Peace Corps
Property and Supply Division   Nationwide

Railroad Retirement Board
Bureau of Taxation   Chicago, IL

Small Business Administration
SBA Low–Doc Team   San Antonio, TX

Social Security Administration
800–Number Benchmarking   Baltimore, MD
Automated Clearinghouse Development Team   Nationwide
Chicago Near Southwest Hospital   Chicago, IL
Classification and Organizational Management Team   Baltimore, MD
Cooperative Disability Project   Miami, FL
Disability Reengineering/Design Training Team   Baltimore, MD
Disability Reengineering Team   Nationwide
Houston Metro Managers Network   Houston, TX
Iowa Video–Conferencing Workgroup   Des Moines, IA
Microfilm Reengineering Team   Baltimore, MD
Paperless Pilot Team   Baltimore, MD

Region V Manual Adjustment Credit and Award Data Entry System	Chicago, IL
Regional Office Decision Writing Unit	New York, NY
Relocation Management Team	Nationwide
SSA Teleservice Center3	Nationwide
Team Internet	Nationwide
World Class Service Team	Nationwide

Department of State

Children's Issues Team	Nationwide

Department of Transportation

Acquisition Reform Team	Washington, DC
Coast Guard Group and Reserve Unit Group	San Diego, CA
Coast Guard Industrial Support Activity	Governors Island, NY
Coast Guard Notice of Violation Team	Washington, DC
Data User Services Division—Information Technology	Washington, DC
FAA Administrative Support Services Center	Des Plaines, IL
FAA Casper Automated Flight Service Station	Casper, WY
FAA Litigation Tracking and Document Generation System	New York, NY
FAA Personnel System Reform Team	Washington, DC
FAA System Management Branch, ASW–530	Dallas, TX
Federal Highway Administration Electronic Billing	Montpelier, VT
Federal Railroad Administration Office of Safety Field Liaison Staff	Washington, DC
Federal Transit Administration Electronic Grant Making and Management Team4	Washington, DC
Federal Transit Administration	Nationwide
First Coast Guard District Marine Safety Division	Boston, MA
Grand Forks Automated Flight Service Station	Grand Forks, ND
Grants Process Improvement Quality Action Team	Atlantic City, NJ
Houston Civil Aviation Security Field Office	Houston, TX
Maritime Administration Office of Acquisition	Nationwide
Office of Hazardous Materials Initiatives and Training	Washington, DC
Santa Monica I–10 Freeway Team	Santa Monica, CA
St. Louis Airport Service Improvement Team	St. Louis, MO

3Thirty Teleservice Centers were awarded Hammers in the following cities: Birmingham, AL; Phoenix, AZ; Los Angeles, CA; Richmond, CA; Salinas, CA; San Diego, CA; Golden, CO; Fort Lauderdale, FL; Tampa, FL; Chicago, IL; Indianapolis, IN; New Orleans, LA; Boston, MA; Baltimore, MD; Detroit, MI; St.Paul, MN; Kansas City, MO; Albuquerque, NM; Cincinnati, OH; Portland, OR; Philadelphia, PA; Pittsburg, PA; Upper Derby, PA; San Juan, PR; Grand Prairie, TX; Houston, TX; Manassas, VA; Auburn, WA; and Milwaukee, WI.

4This team received 11 plaques.

Department of the Treasury

Community Bank Procedures – Office of the Comptroller of the Currency	Washington, DC
Compliance 2000 Fishing Industry Team	Augusta, ME
Customs Airport Operations Branch	Houston, TX
Customs Cargo Examination Task Force	Newark, NJ
Customs Carrier Initiative Program Anti–Smuggling Division	Washington, DC
Customs Commercial Air Passenger Operations	Washington, DC
Customs National Initiative Committee for Entry	Nationwide
Customs Service, Miami District	Miami, FL
Customs Service Team, Charlotte District	Charlotte, VA
Detroit Computing Center – GSA, IRS (Chicago team initiated)	Chicago, IL
Electronic Tax Form Dissemination Team	Nationwide
Financial Crimes Management Program, Secret Service Risk Analysis	Nationwide
FMS Center for Applied Financial Management	Nationwide
FMS Check Claims	Nationwide
IRS Business Assistance Center	Buffalo, NY
IRS Cooperative Projects Staff	Nationwide
IRS Customer Processing Section, Operations Branch	Philadelphia, PA
IRS/DPS Development Center Work Systems Design Team	Austin, TX
IRS Headquarters Operations Customer Service Center	Nationwide
IRS Integrated Customer Service Desk Development Team	San Francisco, CA
IRS Listens Days	Charlotte, NC
IRS Maine Recreation Industry Federal/State Team	Bangor, ME
IRS Multimedia Production Division	Nationwide
IRS Ogden	Ogden, UT
IRS Philadelphia Service Center	Philadelphia, PA
IRS St. Paul District Federal/State Team	Minneapolis, MN
Magnetic Media Project Team	Philadelphia, PA
Mint Customer Service	Nationwide
Procurement Team	Nationwide
Regulation Review Group – Office of the Comptroller of the Currency	Washington, DC
Volunteer Income Tax Assistance Program	Northridge, CA

Tennessee Valley Authority

Accounts Payable Team	Knoxville, TN
Browns Ferry Outage High Impact Teams	Decatur, AL
Clean Water Initiative	Knoxville, TN
Cumberland Acid Cleaning Team	Cumberland City, TN
Cumberland Tube Menders Team	Cumberland City, TN

Employee Accounting Travel and Benefit Team   Knoxville, TN
Inspection Services Organization   Chattanooga, TN
Maintenance Controlled Inventory Team   Cumberland City, TN
Safety Eyewear Process Improvement Team   Knoxville, TN

United States Information Agency
Bureau of Information   Washington, DC

Department of Veterans Affairs
Acquisition and Material Management Service Team   Pittsburgh, PA
Asbestos Management Team   Lebanon, PA
Black Hills VA Alliance (two teams received Hammers   Fort Meade, MD
   at two locations)   Hot Springs, SD
Civilian Health and Medical Program of the Department Denver, CO
   of Veterans Affairs Center
Clinic Clerk Team   Des Moines, IA
Colmery–O'Neal VA Medical Center   Topeka, KS
Consolidated Contracting Activity Team   Denver, CO
Contract Service Center   Milwaukee, WI
Customer Service Team   St. Paul, MN
Drugs 'R' Us – Pharmacy Acquisition and Material   Dayton, OH
   Management Services
Electronic Paperless Travel Management Team   Louisville, KY
Facilities Management Office   Washington, DC
Financial Operations Team   Nationwide
Food Concept Development Team – San Diego Leadership Nationwide
   Conference
Geriatrics Health Care Center   Richmond, VA
Greater New York City VA Consortium on Homeless Veterans New York, NY
Guest Relations Team of the Prescott VA Medical Center   Phoenix, AZ
Home Oxygen Continuous Quality Improvement Team   Milwaukee, WI
Houston Enhanced Use Project   Houston, TX
Interim Compensation Committee   New York, NY
Loan Guaranty Division (two teams received Hammers   Los Angeles, CA
   at two locations)   Manchester, NH
Managed Care System Development Group   Chicago, IL
Manchester VA Medical Center Surgical Service   Manchester, NH
Medical Administration – Ann Arbor Medical Center   Detroit, MI
Medical Care Cost Recovery Fiscal Service   Omaha–Lincoln, NE
Medical Care Cost Recovery Team   Columbus, OH
National Acquisition Center   Hines, IL
New York Benefits Office   New York, NY

On–The–Spot Customer Service Team	Pittsburgh, PA
Original Claims Team	Little Rock, AR
Parking Veterans First Team	Pittsburgh, PA
Partnership Council	Detroit, MI
Policy and Procedure Re–Engineering Team	White City, OR
Rochester Outpatient Clinic Relocation Redesign Team	Buffalo, NY
Service and Distribution Center	Hines, IL
Sharing Agreement Team – Audie Murphy VA Medical Center	San Antonio, TX
Systems Integration Center, National Cemetery System	Nationwide
Telepathology Team	Iron Mountain, MI
Telepathology Team – Zablocki VA Medical Center	Milwaukee, WI
Telephone Linked Care Team	Tucson, AZ
Total Hip Replacement – Clinical Pathway Development Team	Northeastern NY
VA Medical and Regional Office Center	Sioux Falls, SD
Valencia Telecommuting Center	Los Angeles, CA
VA-ONLINE	Martinsburg, WV
Veterans Assistance Inquiry Team	Buffalo, NY
Veterans Benefits Administration – Central Area Human Resources Management Office	Detroit, MI
Veterans Health Administration – Office of Quality Management	Nationwide
Veterans Service Center	Portland, OR
Veterans Service Division Nu Team	Oakland, CA

Federal Executive Boards/Federal Executive Associations

The Atlanta Diversity Council	Atlanta, GA
Beckley FEB	Beckley, WV
Denver FEB Board of Directors	Denver, CO
FEB/FEMA Disaster Assistance Centers Project	Long Beach, CA
Human Relations and Diversity Committee	Milwaukee, WI
Oklahoma City FEB	Oklahoma City, OK
Production Team, Philadelphia FEB/Greater Philadelphia Radio	Philadelphia, PA
Project SATISFY	San Antonio, TX
Regional Community Economic Revitalization Team	Portland, OR

Interagency

Alaska Joint Pipeline Office	Anchorage, AK
Black Hills National Forest Shared Services and Facilities Team	Custer, SD
Clothing for Homeless Veterans – DOD, GSA, VA	Washington, DC
Electronic Benefits Transfer Team	Washington, DC
Fort Collins Natural Resource Research Center	Fort Collins, CO
FTS 2000 Year 7 Price Redetermination Service Reallocation	Falls Church, VA
Georgia Common Access Team	Atlanta, GA

Government and Industry Quality Liaison Panel	Nationwide
Government Owned Real Estate Team	Atlanta, GA
International Entry Subcommittee	Atlanta, GA
Mojave Desert and California Desert Initiative	Ft. Irwin, CA
Mojave Desert and California Desert Initiative Teams	Ft. Irwin, CA
Operation Enhanced Clearance	Los Angeles, CA
Property Management and Warehouse Team	Billings, MT
Retiree Gratuity Payment Team	Cleveland, OH
Risk Management for Housing Loans, Portfolio Analysis Database	Nationwide
Snake River Activity Operations Plan Team	Idaho Falls, ID
Tri–Agency Ad–Hoc Convergence Transition	Silver Spring, MD
TRICARE Project Office II	Hampton, VA
Tri–State Education Initiative – Education, NASA	Nationwide
U.S. General Store for Small Business	Houston, TX
VA Medical Center	Hampton, VA
Y–12 Interagency Calibration Team	Nationwide

Partnerships
Federal–State

Customer Service/Visitor Services Project – National Park Service	Washington, DC
Council of State Administrators of Vocational Rehabilitation	Washington, DC
Department of Education, Rehabilitation Services Administration	Washington, DC
Santa Monica I–10 Freeway Team	Santa Monica, CA

Federal–Local

Boston Empowerment Center	Boston, MA
Chicago Near Southwest Hospital	Chicago, IL
Partnership Minnesota	Twin Cities, MN
NASA–Mississippi Band of Choctaw Indians Education Partnership	Philadelphia, MS

Public–Private Sector

DOD–Motorola	Nationwide
DOD–Texas Instruments	Nationwide
Performance Measurement Action Team5	Washington, DC
Review Advisory Committee–U.S. Access Board	Washington, DC

---

[5]Individual Hammers were awarded to each of the 14 teams in this participation.

ADDITIONAL RESOURCES

The following National Performance Review (NPR) resources and reports are available in hard copy from the Government Printing Office (202-512-1800) or National Technical Information Service (703-487-4650). Materials can also be accessed electronically; see below for further ordering and access information.

Video

"Reinventing the Government . . . By the People" .... S/N 040-000-00649-4

Reports

Creating a Government That Works Better & Costs Less:
Report of the National Performance Review .... S/N 040-000-00592-7

Creating a Government That Works Better & Costs Less:
Status Report, September 1994.................................... S/N 040-000-00646-0

Putting Customers First: Standards for Serving the
American People.. S/N 040-000-00647-0

Common Sense Government: Works Better & Costs Less....... S/N 040-000-00662-1

Putting Customers First '95: Standards for Serving the
American People.. S/N 040-000-00663-0

Reinvention's Next Steps: Governing in a Balanced
Budget World.. S/N 040-000-00671-1

NPR On-Line Library

NPR's extensive, 800-document library can be accessed through the World Wide Web. The library contains a wide range of information (http://www.npr.gov).

BLANK   PAGE

INDEX